European Job

Jonathan Booth

Published by
TravellersEye Ltd
London

The European Job
1st Edition
Published by TravellersEye Ltd 2002

Head Office:
TravellersEye Ltd
Colemore Farm, Colemore Green
Bridgnorth, Shropshire
WV16 4ST, United Kingdom

Tel: (0044) 1746 766447 fax: (0044) 1746 766665
Email: books@travellerseye.com
Website: www.travellerseye.com
Website for this title also at: www.theeuropeanjob.com

Set in Adobe Garamond & Meta

ISBN: 1 903070 252
Copyright © 2002 Jonathan Booth
British Library Cataloguing in Publication Data
A catalogue record for this book is available from the British Library.

The events and opinions in this book originate from the author.
The publisher accepts no responsibility for their accuracy.

The moral right of Jonathan Booth to be identified as author of this work has been
asserted by him in accordance with the Copyright, Designs and Patents Act 1988.

All rights reserved. No part of this publication may be reproduced, stored in a
retrieval system or transmitted in any form or by any means, electronic,
mechanical, photocopying, recording or otherwise, except brief extracts for the
purpose of review, without the prior permission of the publisher and copyright
owner.

Printed and bound in Great Britain by Cox & Wyman, Reading, Berks

Edited by Caroline Sylge
Design by Henry Iles

for Ali
for then, and for them

and

for Dad
who had his first line,
but never got the chance to write it down

ACKNOWLEDGEMENTS

It was a long road we travelled in this book, but a longer road to put it in your hands. Many people helped and encouraged, whether they believed or not, and I'd like to thank them all, but in particular: from first to last, my darling Ali, staunchest friend and sternest critic, who gave up countless days and nights of my time (gosh, this writing lark is tough on your family); Gail, Lynne and the team at Quality Travel for enthusiasm and hidden gems; Dan Hiscocks and Toby Steed at TravellersEye for bringing it all together; Paul Kent and the team at Oneword for the break; Jessica Bowles for contacts and confidence; Steve Parks for the final nudge; Anthony Weldon for selfless advice and encouragement; Matt Hopper for audio excellence; Mark Titmus for minding the shop and being a great audience; Frank the Mechanic for rueful optimism and practical help in the face of rose-tinted stupidity; all the interesting, exuberant, strange, garrulous, enigmatic, drunk and delightful Europeans we met, and Caroline and Tim for a warm bath of approval.

AND LISTEN...

You can hear me reading the whole of The European Job on Oneword Radio, the international speech station, on a regular basis. You can receive Oneword on a digital radio set (if you can find one to buy!) on the Digital One radio platform; across Europe on Sky TV Channel 877; across the UK on digital terrestrial channel Freeview; and streaming live on the worldwide web on www.oneword.co.uk

AND LOOK...

There's a special website for this book, where you'll find some extra information and photographs we've not had room for here. I'll be adding to it over the course of time. You can also e-mail me direct from the site and I'll do my best to reply to your comments and questions. There's an easy one-product shopping cart for you to buy more copies, and you can even request personalised signed copies, which I'll be happy to do.

The site is usefully called **www.theeuropeanjob.com**

THE AUTHOR

Jonathan Booth has won buckets of awards for writing, but all for pieces that have taken exactly thirty seconds to read – radio commercials. Nowadays he writes and produces programmes and ads for radio and video, narrates lots of TV documentaries, and created and produced the only exhibit in the Millennium Dome devoted to Radio.

Never having had a proper job, Jonathan's career could hardly even be described as chequered. Among a list of oddments he has: compéred the Royal Philharmonic Orchestra live in concert; commentated Princess Anne round a cross-country course; hung out of a Cessna fifty feet above the Jamaican surf; presented a TV series on antiques for the Discovery Channel; written a song that charted in Greece (yah boo, Tony); and voiced the world's first live radio ad from inside a carwash.

For a while now he has dreamed of writing something that could hold the reader or listener's attention for more than half a minute, and be remembered for more than ten seconds after that. So following his three-month sabbatical Grand Tour, with his fiancée Ali, he wrote their experiences down as The European Job.

Despite nearly killing her in a fireball outside Valencia (see inside), Ali actually married Jonathan, and even gave him a daughter, Lucy and a son, Sam. They all live in Hampshire, where Ali writes books for children.

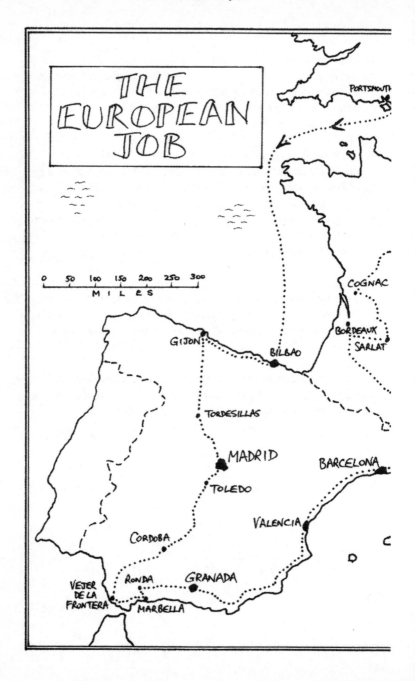

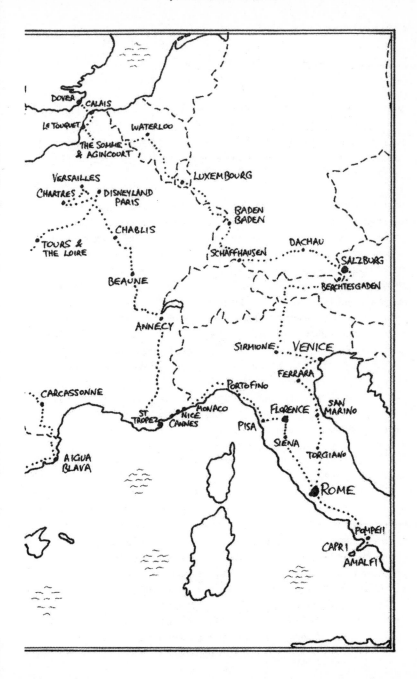

AUTHOR'S NOTE

I didn't set out to write a book about this journey. I'm not a journalist or author; I've just always wanted to do this trip. So nobody knew we were coming, we carried no special laminated cards marked 'PRESS – Fat Discount Required', and we paid full price (in some cases much more) for everything. This meant we could be entirely objective about places, hotels, people, food and so on, and tell you what we really thought. If we thought a hotel was crap during our stay at it, I'll name it, and tell you why. Similarly if we thought it was fabulous and we'd heartily recommend it to you.

And that's part of the point of this book. Yes, it's supposed to be a travel book that might divert you for a few hours with some amusing anecdotes and interesting trivia, but I hope it will also be of some use. I've always found word of mouth to be the best weathervane when planning travel. If somebody I know has been to a certain place or hotel, and can recommend it or warn me off it, then I'm almost guaranteed to take their advice. We stayed at forty-one hotels in seven countries, from no-star village inns to the Gritti, and apart from the descriptions in the text, you'll find a full list of them with comprehensive word-of-mouth ratings at the back. It's only fair to point out that we did this journey in 1998, which might seem a long time ago in media terms, but isn't really in travel terms – some of the hotels may be under new management or had a refurb, but most will be the same. Where prices are mentioned they're in francs or pesetas or lire, not euros, but they won't have changed a great deal, and are only for illustrative purposes; what's important is that you're getting an honest opinion by an ordinary casual traveller – like you. I would be delighted to hear about your experiences or impressions of the places mentioned – you can e-mail me direct at author@theeuropeanjob.com, and I'll do my best to reply.

Although we used dozens of different guidebooks in our ten country trip, my main sources of bare facts about places were the Michelin Green Guides – always accurate, always upright and correct, never judgemental or emotional. Other facts, factoids, conjecture, gossip, opinions, fantasy or emotional rant I've added to any description must be considered only probably accurate. Trust Michelin, not me – any mistakes are mine, not theirs.

If you travel to any of the places we went to, and you find any part of this book useful or interesting, then, for me, that's what it's all about.

CONTENTS

ALL MAPS, DRAWINGS AND PHOTOGRAPHS BY THE AUTHOR

Introduction

"No song unsung, no wine untasted"

"Round Europe? In *that*?"

Since Frank the Mechanic looked like a London cabbie and did actually know what he was talking about, I began to feel the clammy hand of apprehension tighten around my lower intestine.

"When you say 'Round Europe'," he went on, "you mean, what...? South of France an' back?"

"Er, no. All the way round. About 10,000 miles, we reckon."

At this point Frank's eyes closed and he began to rock with silent laughter. Leaning against the car for support, he dabbed a tear of mirth away, and when he could speak, said, "Sorry mate, but just so's I'm clear; you want to take this 1974 Jensen Interceptor III – this *particular* one, out of which you *might* get nine to the gallon – put yourself, your fiancée and all your stuff in it, and drive round Europe for three months?"

"Well, er, yeah."

He held my gaze for a moment longer, as if searching for inner demons, then said briskly, "Right!", and turned away to pop the bonnet and start shaking his head and sucking his teeth.

I swore I could hear him say, under his breath, "And I hope you brought your chequebook, squire."

I can't remember what first made me want to do the Grand Tour. I suspect a combination of Forster's *A Room With A View*; Sebastian Flyte (Venice, not Tangiers); the wonderful Michael Kitchen in *Enchanted April*; and Bertie Wooster cavorting at Cannes in that white mess jacket that Jeeves disapproved of so much.

Surely I too could stroll along La Croisette in a linen jacket; mix effortlessly with royalty in Monte; take the waters at Baden Baden, and get pleasantly pissed on Puligny Montrachet in Beaune. All I would need would be more money than I could spare, a reckless abandonment of a precarious career for three months, some sort of flash open-top jalopy to pootle around in – oh, and a gorgeous woman to share it all with.

Ah.

That was ten years ago, and of course it got shelved – alongside the dusty dreams of being able to write like Stephen Fry, play piano like Bruce Hornsby and place vision on celluloid like Steven Spielberg.

Then a glorious triple alignment of the fates happened. The small flat I owned in Balham, South London, which had been in negative equity for four years, suddenly became Property of the Quarter; work was healthy enough for me not to actually starve if I took a sabbatical; and I met her.

Now any sensible person would have thought, 'Ooh, here's a nice girl, take chunk of dosh from flat for deposit on love nest; then marriage, kids, old age, blah blah'. Luckily, Ali didn't respond too badly when I said we should blow the property windfall on a Grand Tour, early honeymoon and a whizbang reception. Of course, it might mean no holidays ever again, but what the hey!

Europe is like an onion, with many layers of micro-cultures. On the outside, we are all Europeans – we all breathe air; we all put clothes on in the morning; we all feel a little uneasy about the Austrians – but then the concentric layers of differences start. This is the very stuff of life, from far-reaching differences to subtle shifts in emphasis, from nation to region to village to house; from language to style to village fiesta, to mama's secret ragout recipe... to the last man in the valley who knows how to thatch a hut or shoe a *burro* or make a clay roof tile in the old-fashioned way.

The French say a lot of silly things, but 'vive la difference' isn't one of them.

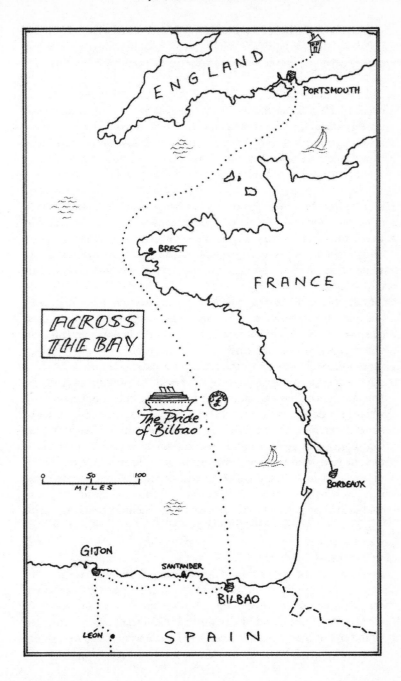

ENGLAND

PORTSMOUTH

BREST

FRANCE

ACROSS
THE BAY

'The Pride
of Bilbao'

BORDEAUX

0   50   100
MILES

GIJON

SANTANDER

BILBAO

LEON

S P A I N

DAY ONE | TUESDAY 31ST MARCH

At Sea

The stern of the great ship rises and falls with each rolling Atlantic swell, which is either therapeutic or emetic, depending on how your sea-legs are. The white aft rail cuts across the receding night water – foaming, churning, milky-white blue at the base, and deep black above, where England lies.

Our journey has begun.

We'd chosen Northern Spain as our starting point, and were to take thirty five hours on P&O's *The Pride of Bilbao* to get there. The ship eased out of her Portsmouth berth at eight p.m. – or 20.00 hours, as we jacktars say – passing dozens of hunched grey monsters with big white letters on their hulls; most of the NATO fleet, in for some summit or other.

Our cabin is not large – the door of the linen cupboard next door was open as we passed, and we tried to get upgraded into that – but adequate I suppose, and at least there is a bottle of Moët perching on the three-inch melamine shelf; a pressie from Gail at Quality Travel, for not managing to get us the cabin we wanted.

Now I wouldn't be a travel agent for all the commission in the Foreign Office. Punters ask for the impossible and complain bitterly when they don't get it; tour operators squeeze you from both ends; travel operators and airlines design schedules of Machiavellian complexity, and you're stuck in the middle with a smile super-glued to your face. Well that's my impression of it, but the girls at Quality Travel seem to sail through it untrammelled. I've known them for years, and when I called Gail and said I wanted to do this trip, her eyes shone with excitement, and she immediately dashed round with a pick-up truck full of brochures, guides, maps and assorted friends who'd been to 'the most *diviiine* places, darling!'.

Our first thought had been to just go – to airily pack a knotted handkerchief and see where the dusty roads led. But we wanted to see more of Europe than Caesar, Hannibal and Baedeker put together, and we only had three months, so if we didn't have some sort of schedule, we'd be behind by day three, and only half way round Spain by the end of June. So while I closeted myself away trying to earn the money to pay for it all, Ali and Gail spent weeks planning.

Our travel agent Gail's first obstacle had been with P&O, who had reserved us a cabin with enough room to turn round in (and a window large enough to get out of), but when she rang to confirm, they'd sold it. She ranted and raved a bit, and embarrassed them into giving us 'VIP' status, whatever that meant. What it turned out to mean was a car sticker which got us on the boat near the front, a bottle of fizz in the cabin, and a visit to the bridge. So, V slightly IP then.

Here's a tip: if travelling on an overnight car ferry, having packed for three months, do not park the car and airily say to your companion, "I'll just whip the cases up to the cabin. See you in the bar!" The eight flights of iron stairs you will have to mount are barely wide enough for one suitcase, let alone a fat git with two, and are set at mountaineering pitch.

Ali has taken a box and a half of Sturgeron to combat her reputedly poor sea-legs, so we stride out confidently to explore our vessel.

I'm always rather alarmed by the cross-section guide maps you find in ships' corridors. Three or four decks of cars, topped with five or six decks of cabins, topped with two or three decks of restaurants and shops, and then funnels and masts and so on. Surely the bloody thing's going to tip over? And why is the 'YOU ARE HERE' arrow always a long way below the waterline? We head up the stairs, thinking of Kate Winslet and closed gates.

Since P&O have got you right where they want you for thirty five hours, they don't miss a trick. The place is stiff with bars, shops and restaurants, the latter mostly offering motorway service station food at London hotel prices. We decide against the *Gammon Platter 'n' Slice*, and book a table in the Cavalier Restaurant. The prices on the menu posted outside have put off many of the passengers, which is a pity for them as we have an excellent dinner for not a vast amount more than they would have paid a deck below.

I have a scallops, fennel and bacon thing for starters followed by sea bass, and Ali has a mound of smoked salmon and then monkfish. We share a decent Pouilly Fumé, and four coffees and a generous cheese board round off a not at all cheap, but superbly cooked and pleasantly served dinner. Impressed, we head for the bar, having slipped far too easily and a great deal earlier than anticipated, into 'Buggerit Mode'. This "weeelll, we're on holiday!" approach is fine if you're away for a fortnight, but on a three month journey things could quite soon get out of hand.

And indeed within two minutes Ali has spotted the casino. For a girl who is often annoyingly sensible with money, Ali has a blind spot about casinos, and roulette in particular, and her eyes sparkle like chips on baize at the mere thought of the words *faites vos jeux*. Of course, this shipboard version doesn't offer the panelled rooms and clink of martinis that I know she's dreaming about for later in the trip, and this baby casino doesn't even have roulette, but... weeelll, buggerit, we're on holiday!

We pass a pleasant twenty seconds or so at the blackjack table giving P&O another fifty quid, and decide to retire to our box-file, having blown way more than our budget for Day One.

The swell has increased during the evening, and closing my eyes seems to magnify the depths of the sea's troughs by a factor of ten in my imagination. At each dip of the bows, I'm convinced we're just going to keep going, the mighty engines powering the ship towards the sea bed, while in First Class, high above us, the band....

The slap of a green Atlantic wave against the porthole that's just too small to let us get out in an emergency brings me back to reality. Three months! No income; credit cards melting; clients forgetting; mortgage not forgetting. Butterflies? Certainly. Regrets? Not yet. What an opportunity to discover places, people, food, wines, sunshine (hopefully) and each other. Let us make the absolute most of it, and return with a bucketful of memories, a bookful of lessons learned, and a rock-like base for our lives together.

Now stop talking like a hairdresser and get some sleep. That way when this tub finally sinks you'll be blissfully unaware of it.

DAY TWO | WEDNESDAY 1ST APRIL

At Sea

This is the first full day of our Tour, and at last the sun has come out, although the sea spray is always in the air as we sit on the poop in a freshening Force 5, surrounded by an alarming number of beige car-coats. *The Pride* is just starting her summer season of runs across the Bay of Biscay, and is full of over-55s taking a short cut to their Marbella villas, and other people taking a *64-Hour Shoppers'*

Minicruise. As I understand it, this tweely-titled temptation lasts, as billed, 64 hours, but an interestingly brief 240 minutes of it will be spent shopping in Bilbao. For the 92.8% of their holiday that they won't actually spend at their destination, they are promised a variety of ship-board entertainments, food, drink and activities, and lots of fun ways to spend with P&O the money they'd put aside for the Genuine Spanish Hand-Carved Wooden Donkey With Hand-Woven Straw Hat (painstakingly hand-imported from Thailand).

I am well stuck in to the new John Grisham when I remember it's time for our 'VIP bridge visit'. Hmm.

Actually it's quite interesting. You climb up dozens of stairs, past hundreds of metal doors with 'First Chief Purser's Mate's Assistant Swabhand – WPB/9960-2' written on them, and emerge in this vast greenhouse about a mile above the steel grey sheet of the Bay of Biscay. I expected to see dozens of swarthy matelots dashing about under orders from the white-bearded captain, but there is nobody about. Nobody. Just thirty yards of knobs and levers and great green radar screens, and a small box going "beep".

"Hello?", I quail, scanning the horizon for icebergs. Gratifyingly, a voice immediately says, "Afternoon", and a jolly chap in a crisp white shirt and a beard you could have hung Christmas lights on appears from a back office. I think he is the second mate, but he seems to have enough stripes to know what he is doing, and just as I am about to ask whether he does, a group of other passengers appears, and he goes to greet them.

We wander around. The bridge is enormous, the entire width of the ship, and has a reassuringly tranquil feel about it, as if all you really have to do to drive this floating city was tap in your required co-ordinates and press GO. The radar screen looks like a drawing I did in kindergarten when I'd just got my new bright green marker pen, but the digital readouts next to it seem to understand it – every few seconds the numbers change, and the panel emits a soft "beep", as if to say to anyone that happens to be around, "I've adjusted our course by .00073° to account for currency movements on the NASDAQ, and there are no periscopes in sight. Call you in an hour, alright?"

Thanking the bearded one, we clank back down the stairs in search of entertainment. The ship's two cinemas are both half way through films we've seen, and the Games Arcade sounds like it is half way through World War Three, so Ali bags a table in the bar and I go and get the Scrabble.

Now you might think Scrabble is a pretty sad thing to take on a trip-of-a-lifetime, but my experience of travelling is that you've got to pace yourselves. Yes, there are shedloads of places to go and things to see, but if you're constantly buying foot-salts and knee supports, and you're so knackered from sightseeing you fall asleep face down in the gazpacho, then you're overdoing it.

Besides, on a soaking wet night in Tordesillas when the bar closes at 8.45, and the shutters are rattling the ironwork, you'll be jolly glad to hear the clicking of the tiles, and the chance to put down 'bugger' on a triple.

A couple of defeats at Scrabble, and a reasonable dinner later, I am drawn to the ship's main evening entertainment like a moth to a flame. Sorry – **_Entertainment!_**

All the bright young girls and boys who'd been rushing around all day in tropical whites, hosting deck quoits or aerobics or bingo, have changed hats and costumes to put on the show.

What seems like the entire passenger complement have shoehorned themselves into the Neptune Lounge, and the atmosphere is thick with lager fumes and cigarette smoke. Well, I suppose it saves on the dry ice. We manage to rugby tackle a couple of old blokes and nick their red veloured chairs, from which we can just see the stage behind a pillar.

The Cruise Director chappie, who doesn't look nearly as pretty as Julie out of *The Love Boat*, announces the title of their show – *'A Taste of the West End!'* Oh God, I think, it'll be *I Know Him So Well* warbled by two bingo callers wrapped in a curtain.

To be fair it isn't too bitter a taste – they have a reasonable go at crowd-pleasers like *Memories*, *Master Of The House*, *Phantom* and *Summer Lovin'*, but then rather spoil it all by stabbing *Joseph* in the back, right through his *Dreamcoat*. The punters seem to like it though, and the cast has obviously spent some time and money on the costumes. Even the Muppet Band are pretty tight – driven by their drummer, Phil Allgaps – and the lead thesps have good voices. On what is basically a ferry, the boys and girls have done alright.

Anyway, what do I know, I can't carry a tune in a bucket.

Back to our be-bunked cubicle to pack, as we've just realised with horror that tomorrow morning they're going to chuck us out on Spanish soil at...

DAY THREE | THURSDAY 2ND APRIL

Bilbao to Gijon

06.00! No, no, really, this is too damn early. For me, six o'clock only happens once a day.

Bleary-eyed, we grab a coffee on the main deck while we wait to be shepherded down to our cars. The whole deck is draped with hundreds of barely awake travellers absentmindedly reining in children or buttoning their beige car-coats.

Finally (I could have had another forty minutes sleep) there's a long, muted creaking bump as the ship docks, and we abseil back down the metal stairs to the car decks.

And there she is, right at the front of the ramp, gleaming blackly, just waiting to not start and hold everybody up.

Every man should have a folly, and since I couldn't run to a Vanburgh crenellated tower in rolling parkland, I bought a Jensen. I'd spotted it in *The Sunday Times* a couple of years ago, and having had a Dinky version as a boy, I naturally knew all about them, so off I trotted to have a look at it. Of course she was quite stunning, and despite having made my mind up on the spot, I had to do the humming and harring, kick the tyres, go "Mmmmm!" under the bonnet and ask searching questions about tappet ratios – all the stuff that makes the vendor mentally rub his hands with glee and stick two grand on the price.

I thought to myself, *Cons*: It's twenty-five years old, it's got a ridiculous 7.2 litre engine that I'll be lucky to get ten miles per gallon out of, the steering wheel's got alarming play in it, the air-con doesn't work, the wiring under the bonnet looks suspiciously dodgy, and the vendor is a night club owner. *Pros*: It makes the sexiest noise since Lauren Bacall, and I WANT IT!

Okay, so I know absolutely nothing about cars, but for about the same money as a new Astra it was a good investment, wasn't it? Well, alright, probably not, but think of the open road, the hunched power, the girls, as I growled past, thinking, "Sad git, where's his beige car-coat?" Bollocks to it, where's my cheque book?

I'm not saying the accelerator connected you to a powerful engine, but driving it home along the M25, I slightly shifted position in my seat to adjust the rear view mirror and found I'd shot past two junctions. This was a *beast*.

A year later, when we really started planning the trip, I began to think about whether to actually take it. Of course it was entirely impracticable; the fuel bill alone, if we were going to do 10,000 miles, would be over £3,000; the insurance would be difficult or expensive or both; there's about enough luggage space for a hamster's backpack; the European roads would probably scrape an inch or so off the already stupidly-low ride height, and if it broke down (if? Ha, ha!) I would have absolutely no idea what to do.

So that's that decision made, then.

I found Frank, the Jensen expert mechanic, in South London, and told him what I was going to do. After I helped him up and dusted him down, he said he'd be happy to take my money, and promptly disappeared under the bonnet for three weeks. Actually, he was very kind and very understanding. Apart from not understanding, of course. He even lent me a box of starter motors, alternators, fan belts, workshop manuals, bulbs and his mobile phone number; "just so's I can 'av a laugh, mate".

So here we were, 10,000 miles of Europe in front of the hunched and louvred bonnet, waiting for the man in the day-glo coat to beckon us through the bow doors onto Spanish tarmac.

Bloody hell, she started first time! Perhaps this wasn't such a bad idea after all.

It's a mild grey drizzly morning in Bilbao, and we find our way without much difficulty onto the main E70 road, heading west along the top of Spain. Since Ali's not too keen on driving the Jensen, she is designated Navigator. Of course I've been giving her lots of male gyp about not knowing which way is up, let alone west, and indeed she'd be the first to admit that sense of direction is not her greatest skill. She unfolds the Michelin 442 map of the area and does her best General Melchett impression, "God, it's a barren, featureless desert out there!" I reach over to gently turn the map over to the side that's got colours and lines on it, when I get a Look.

I turn my attention to the scenery, which once we've got out of the city becomes an undulating vista of bright green and dark green hills in sharp relief, with glimpses of the sea to the right. It would be rather pleasant to explore if it wasn't beginning to chuck it down, and we hadn't made our first mistake by having to be in Gijon by dusk.

Christopher Columbus points the way to the New World. (To discover how many mistakes there are in that last sentence, see Barcelona)

The E70 does go to Gijon, but we thought we really should try and explore Green Spain a little, so we took a side road that dipped in and out between the mountains and the sea, through small villages sheltering from the spring rain. I'd filled up the Jensen in Bilbao, but the thing barely travels its own length before demanding more jungle juice, so I began to get a bit worried about the lack of garages. Perhaps I should have taken one friend's suggestion and hired a Texaco tanker to follow us round offering in-flight refuelling. To cheer us up, Ali rummaged in the entertainment box for some music.

We'd spent a while at the offices of ACAS before we left, negotiating what music to bring with us. We'd had to be pretty ruthless on the packing front, as the Jensen's boot was designed for nothing much more than a set of golf clubs and a casually flung Panama. We'd managed to cram both our new suitcases in with the aid of a crowbar, but then there was no room for the crowbar, so it had to go in the box of spares occupying half the back seat. The other half had both our travel bags, a camera bag and the Scrabble, while every nook and cranny in the cabin was stuffed with shoes, towels, hats, sweatshirts, the jack and the entertainment box. This contained about thirty CDs, a dozen cassettes, the mini CD player and the wires for stuffing it into the stereo.

Ali is a musicals nut, so naturally the available selection was peppered with *Oliver!*, *Phantom*, *Victor/Victoria*, *The Sound of Music* and such like, leaving my Elton John and REM gathering static at home. She suggested *Les Misérables* as our first choice. I said I didn't know it very well, but I was happy to give it a go, but when Colm Wilkinson's astonishing voice rang out, I began to warm to it, and we had the whole show through twice before we stopped. Little did I know how well I was to get to know it in the months to come.

We arrived in the outskirts of Gijon in the late afternoon, and the first job was to find the hotel. Gail had told us about the Parador chain of unusual hotels across Spain, and so we'd been booked in to the Gijon one for that night. Paradors are owned and run by the state, which means they've managed to nick all the best sites and buildings. Most of them are in old castles or monasteries, and in the reasonable to fairly expensive price bracket. This one was a converted monastery in the centre of the city's park, and had looked very nice in the brochure.

We found, eventually, the Parque Isabel de Catolica and there it was – the football stadium. Behind it though, sheltering under some large trees was the Parador. Through the pouring rain it looked fine – white stucco walls, lovely old terracotta-tiled roofs, and cedar shutters. We parked up, the Jensen steaming proudly, and carried our bags into reception. Well, Ali, game girl, attempted to lift the smaller one, couldn't, and went to open the door for me. Having deposited the cases in our perfectly acceptable room, and had a quick session with the portable de-fib unit, I dragged Ali back out into the rain to explore the city.

Gijon is a surprisingly large industrial port – over a quarter of a million people live here – but it is a very long way from anywhere, which is probably the way they like it. Its name is pronounced, as far as we can deduce, 'eeehawnnn' – try holding your nose and saying 'Eeyore'. And it's spooky, because 'Pooh' is your next reaction, when you let go of your nose and get a whiff of the harbour. I've smelled that smell before, on the seafront in Rio – a mixture of carbon monoxide, seaspray, fuel oil, effluent and *abroad*.

It got better as we walked along the promenade in the fading light, passing everyone else out for their evening constitutional. And I mean everyone; large as the city is, it seemed as if the entire population walks along the prom each evening. It was only Wednesday, but couples, joggers, whole familes and their pets were out taking the ozone and enjoying what was rapidly goldening into a lovely sunset.

On the way back we walked on the town side of the road. The shops seemed to sell nothing but 1950s electrical goods, row upon row of dried pig legs, and of course, *meubles*. I don't know what it is about Spain in particular, but there seem to be a vastly disproportionate number of furniture shops and warehouses, both in towns and on the roadside. Perhaps everyone buys furniture every fortnight.

The few restaurants seemed to be either Chinese or Italian, so we walked back through the Parque to the Parador, passing a Central Park amount of joggers, and literally hundreds of swans and ducks settling down for the night.

Dinner was really excellent – a few tapas to start, then scallop soup, sea bass *a la plancha*, and crêpes suzette. I'm going to have to start lifting heavy weights every day if this sort of standard keeps up. I wonder where...?

SPAIN

Tordesillas
In which, we discover, the New World was carved up 500 years ago. And not much else.

Madrid
In which we stay in a Palace, over-expose ourselves to high art, and walk in the park to the sound of the Gypsy Kings and gulping carp.

Toledo
In which we have the best view of the city, visit El Greco's house, and come across the first of our 'scaffolding jinxes'.

Cordoba
In which we discover an amazing church inside a mosque, and celebrate Holy Week with hooded marchers.

Vejer de la Frontera
In which we stay with an old friend in this white hilltop town, and I am nearly carried off by a prawn.

Marbella
In which we have dinner in the drug capital of the western Med.

Granada
In which we discover the breathtaking Alhambra, and climb Europe's highest road to the snow-capped Sierras.

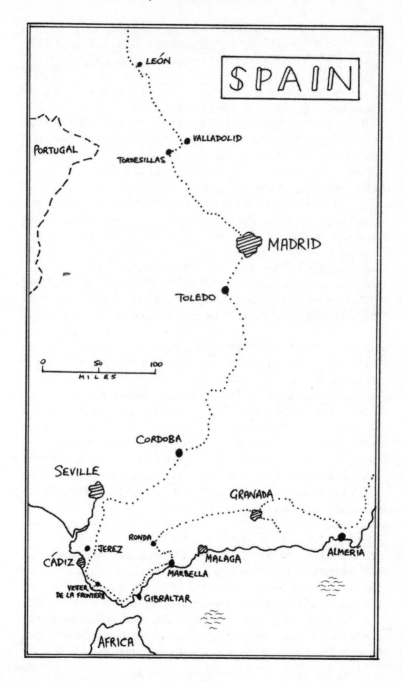

DAY FOUR | FRIDAY 3RD APRIL

Gijon to Tordesillas

I'd always imagined waking up on our first morning in a Spanish hotel and flinging open the wooden shutters to a stream of golden sunlight and the delicate scent of jasmine and wisteria. What I got was a faceful of gutter run-off and the warm sticky scent of morning rush hour.

Never mind, we were heading south today, deep into the heart of Spain – surely the weather would cheer up?

We explore a bit more of the city before we leave. We didn't want to, but the road signs, instead of saying ¡This Way Outta Town, Gringo!, seemed to say ¡No, Stay Longer And Spend Tourist Money! But we got out, and headed for the hills on the A66 towards Léon. A smooth double highway takes us up into the mountains, and through what would, we are sure, be spectacular scenery, if we could see anything beyond the hard shoulder. Through the sheets of grey rain we catch occasional glimpses of gorges and craggy peaks that speak of wilderness, but then here is a valley floor covered with mining towns and those red and white barber-pole chimney stacks. It looks like a lot of people live and work here, and I think there's some hydro plants too, presumably amply fed by the particular monsoon we're in now.

A bit worried about the Jensen. The oil pressure gauge has been dropping fast, which is strange. We eventually find a service station, and the stick says there's practically none in her at all. How can six litres of GTX just fall out over a short journey? The garage man, after some Tony Hart-like gestures and broken Spanish from me, kindly makes a suicide dash across six lanes and two barriers to his mate's garage on the other side, and comes back carrying the precious gloop. Nope, his garage hasn't run out of engine oil, he simply doesn't sell it. I fill up the car, talk nicely to it, pray to the engine gods (Castrol and Bollocks), and we're off again.

South of Léon the scenery changes dramatically. As the mountains recede in the mirror, we're on a single lane road that's arrow-straight for 120 miles across a completely flat and deserted plain. Every ten miles or so we pass through a dead town. I mean, completely dead. Derelict buildings, metal shop-signs creaking in the wind, and, dammit all, tumbleweed. I swear I saw Lee Van Cleef leaning nonchalantly in the shadows, about to fire up another evil-smelling cheroot.

A few years ago these towns must have been full of people and life, but now there's nothing and nobody. In one town we see a shambling black-clothed figure go into a house, but otherwise *nada*. I can't work out why these towns have died, until a little further on we see vast gleaming steel structures looming on the horizon – irrigation cranes. The plain had obviously turned into a dustbowl, and what little work there was for the men had disappeared when mechanisation on the edges of the plain took their jobs.

Our next stop was the small town of Tordesillas. We had hoped for something interesting here, because even though it only had 7,500 inhabitants compared to Gijon's quarter of a million, it rated a mention (although not an actual star) in the *Michelin Guide*, and Gijon simply wasn't in it at all.

We had dozens of guides and maps for our whole trip, flattened out under the back seats, and the *Michelin Green Guides* were the ones we were currently consulting. I became fond of Michelin's writing style – very upright and correct, only occasionally allowing itself to emote about a place (Versailles, for example). I longed to annotate the factual text with things it wouldn't be allowed to say.

Michelin says – "The historic town, massed upon the steep bank of the Deuro, gave its name to the famous Treaty of Tordesillas. In 1494, the kings of Spain and Portugal, under the arbitration of the Borgia Pope Alexander VI, signed the treaty dividing the New World between them."

I would add what *really* happened. 'The firelight flickered around the Great Hall. On the huge table, the map parchment crackled under Ferdinand's fat finger. "Okay Phillipe," he growled, "You take these countries *here* and subdue and kill the natives, and we'll do the same in *these* countries. Whoever kills the most people, and gets stinking rich into the bargain, wins, *si*? Alright with you, Pope? Sorted."'

We drove around the town of Tordesillas. There is really nothing to see, and we did try, honest. Our hotel for the night is another Parador, this one a converted Castillian ancestral home. Vast marbled corridors, vast black oak furniture, not much soul left. We brave the rain for a recce of the perimeter fencing, and discover charming pine-infested grounds and a pool. *Cuiso*, of course. It's still very much out of season, and there's only a dozen or so cars out front, including a couple of Brit plates. We don't find the owners.

But then we don't look very hard.

DAY FIVE | SATURDAY 4TH APRIL

Tordesillas to Madrid

Today I'm a year older. Oh well, I expect I'll do what I always do; not worry about it at all, and carry on being twenty eight for the tenth year running. Ali gave me a card she'd brought from home (bless), and a bollocking for not being awake an hour and a half earlier (07:00) like she was.

I'm going to have to get some sort of mallet.

The Beast's oil level is – what do government unemployment statistics say? – going down at a decreasing rate. So I only have to pour two litres into it this morning, and we set off to drive the easy 170 miles to Madrid – 2,000 feet up, smack in the middle of Spain.

The sun begins to come out for more than a few seconds at a time, as we negotiate the wide boulevards and urgent traffic of the capital. Ali is furiously hunched over her street map, saying through her immaculate but gritted teeth, "What do you see? ...c'mon, give me a street name for God's sake! ...left, NO! ...yes, left here... I think ...well, it *should* be...er".

And there it is, you see, right there. No trouble at all, no overshoots or go-arounds. The Palace Hotel.

At this point I'd better explain our budget strategy. We'd worked out how long the trip would be, worked out roughly what we dare spend of the flat windfall (allowing for trivial costs like getting married later in the year) and come up with £25,000. Ooof, that sounds like a lot, written out like that. Even held upside down, it's got too many zeros in it. But we thought if we're going to do this stupid thing, let's do it as properly as we can – once-in-a-lifetime; well, it is our *honeymoon*; life's not a dress rehearsal, blah, blah. Besides, I'm an old git, well I am as from today, so I can't be slumming it too much any more. Been there, done that, and so what if Ali's happy camping? She'll just have to have a marble bath occasionally and rough it.

Anyway, it works out, allowing frightening amounts for the Jensen, at around £220 a day for the two of us, all in. The Palace Hotel isn't quite the Ritz, but it's opposite it, so in we go.

Reception is a vast room full of swirly carpets, chandeliers and sweeping staircases – all a bit imposing for our standard of dress. It reminds me of the Titanic (I think they were built in the same year) but we check in anyway, and this time our leaden suitcases are carried for us from the car into the room. Luxury. The porter is half my bulk, and is struggling a bit, but I'm sorry, I don't care. By the time we get to the eighth floor, my guilt takes over and I overtip him. He's probably the Madrid Under-10 Stone Weightlifting Champion and is putting it on for the gringo punter.

We're just in time for a late lunch, and head downstairs to the Cupola Room, under the hotel's famous stained glass dome. It is magnificent, a sweeping expanse of brilliant sunlit colours over a circular cloister of classic columns, around which there are sofas and chairs and tables, and soft-footed waiters who bring you things. They bring us some sandwiches and olives, and a leather folder with a tiny scrap of paper in it, barely large enough to contain the zeros of the bill. But you don't look. If you glance once at the amount, they suss you immediately. You have to sign with a flourish and hand it back casually without looking them in the eye.

Well that doesn't work with me. However much I might wish it, I cannot be taken for anything but English. I've tried everything – Armani, Fedoras, Oakley shades, Stetsons – but it doesn't make any difference: Brit abroad, plain as day. Once in a while, a waiter thinks he sees something Teutonic in my features, and speaks to me in German, which really pisses me off – I go into the kitchen and spit in *his* food.

I feel quite sorry for Ali, having to be seen with me. With her stunning bone structure, light olive skin and long dark hair, she could be taken for Italian, French, Irish; almost anything she wanted. "She with him?", waiters whisper incredulously, "Brit then, gotta be. And, er, *why?* "

Time for the Prado, and a bit of culture. We cross the Plaza Canovas del Castillo to the imposing entrance stairs, which are littered with studenty types with sketch pads not going in. That's because, we discover, the Prado's free after 2.30 on Saturdays. So, being on a tight budget like our student friends, we go for a wander in the Botanical Gardens next door first. It's an oasis of green, pink and orange calm in a bustling metropolis, and we spend a contented half hour strolling through hectares of big spiky dark green things and small flowery light green things. Alan Titchmarsh, me.

The Prado is probably the greatest gallery of Classical paintings in the world, or so Michelin says. Certainly the galleries that weren't closed for cleaning or tea breaks that afternoon were full of stunning stuff. Acres of El Greco, Murillo, Goya, Rembrandt, Titian, and of course Velazquez – huge numbers of these huge paintings by the early 17th Century Sevillian artist. At one point I thought I'd get ten quid from *Private Eye*, as there was a big Velazquez oil of the Duc de Ortega, or some be-ruffled cove, on a socking great horse, and it *was* Robin Cook, Britain's then Foreign Secretary. How long before he does a Lord Irvine and gets us to buy it to hang over his desk at the FCO?

There was one small Rembrandt self-portrait which took my breath away; you just sink into the velvet depths of the brushstrokes, and I swear you can see his soul. The rest of it, though, is not really my sort of thing; a little too heavy and dark, and for me, receding behind the misty veil of irrelevance. I'm sure there's more to the Prado, and I'm sure it's wonderful, but at least half of the galleries were closed.

We emerged into a blue and gold sunset; perhaps spring has actually sprung after days of rain. Time for a marbled bath before my birthday supper. We'd considered several options for this (including staying in the marbled bath and ringing for civilisation's greatest invention, Room Service), but eventually we went for the Buffet under the Dome in the hotel itself. I misread the 'Eat-as-much-as-you-like' sign, thinking the last word was 'can', so a good evening was had by all, and there was even a harpist – a young chap in black tie propping up a vast golden harp, giving us selections from the collected works of Mr Harry Nilsson.

DAY SIX | SUNDAY 5TH APRIL

Madrid

This morning, after the rather stilted heaviness of the Prado, we took in the Thyssen. Spain bought the collection from Baron Hans Heinrich Thyssen-Bornemisza in 1993, and they put it in a beautifully restored 18th century palace, which, thoughtfully, is right next to our hotel. It is generally accepted to be the best private collection in the world – 800 works, from the late 13th century up to today.

You start on the top floor, with dozens of gilded icons and tryptychs – the Italian Primitives. Primitive in terms of uniformly religious content, maybe, but incredible detail and needle-fine giltwork. You then wander down through the Museo, past Murillo,

Goya, El Greco, Bernini, Caravaggio and co., and then Van Gogh, Cezanne, Monet, Manet, and two stunning Canalettos. The moderns are excellent too – Mondrian, Picasso, Miro, Kandinsky and Lichtenstein – and even a Robert Rauschenberg, whose main show we had seen in the Guggenheim the year before.

I've just realised this is dangerously close to making me sound as if I know what I'm talking about. I don't at all. I mean, I love excellence in anything – even football – but I'm equally not prepared to admit something's good simply because it's worth twenty million quid. I might not give house room to a Woolworths 'Cat in a Basket' on hessian, but nor would I to a ruddy great oppressive Velazquez. I can see that many people might appreciate greatly either of the former (although probably not both), but I have to be moved in a particular way to stand for more than a few minutes before a canvas.

Somebody must value this stuff though; there are ultra-sensitive seismic footstep-detectors everywhere, and no doubt hidden cameras and automatic lip-readers too.

Once you've negotiated and gasped your way down five floors of genius, you're rewarded with an excellent and great value lunch in the Museo's cafeteria (apparently a Madrid hot tip), surrounded by progressive black and white pics of the Baron overseeing the Collection's installation.

After lunch we go downstairs to the current visiting exhibition; works by a young German impressionist I had never heard of called August Macke. Gorgeous Lautrecian colours and shadows, and incredibly expressive and unusual blank white faces. He met and was influenced by Kandinsky and Klee, and was reaching the height of his powers when he was killed in the German trenches in 1914 at the age of twenty seven. What was particularly poignant was the vast amount of riotously-coloured paintings dated 1914, and finally, on its own, just as we were going out, a simple small sketch of his wife.

Back into the spring sunshine, and a walk up through the city centre to the Plaza Major, perhaps the main square in *viejo* Madrid. Philip III stands mutely on guard over the market stalls and milling tourists where there used to be bullfights and royal proclamations. We were, as usual, just too late for the Sunday morning market further down the street. Ali thinks I time it so that there's nothing decent left for her to buy. Anyway, we amble past the stall de-riggers and leather bag packer-uppers, and head back to enjoy one of the most delightful of European activities, Sunday in the Park.

The Parque de Madrid, or Parque del Buen Retiro, depending on which side you come in, is a vast green expanse of calm in a hot city. Formerly, and no doubt formally, Philip IV's palace gardens, they're made up of wide avenues of trees and statuary, sparkling fountains, pools and grottos and a large lake. As we approach its edge, we see that the water is dotted with evening boaters; extremely brave it seems to me, as we look down and see a seething, boiling, writhing mass of huge carp, the size of Nissan Sunnys, pushing against the balustrades demanding bread from the punters. Drop your Nikon in there and you'd be filleting for a fortnight.

Across the lake stands the vast collonnaded Monumento a Alphonso II – very similar in ego-classical style to the Vittorio Emmanuel monument in Rome – all tall thrusting marble, and winged or maned beasts in darkened bronze. We wander around the water's edge (me making sure Ali's nearer than I am) and come across Musician's Corner. Luckily the corner is fairly large or the mixed cacophony would be somewhat trying, but our first combo were churning out authentic-sounding Gypsy King stuff in spirited fashion, and with modern technology helping them along – crisp, clean PA speakers, and lip-mikes, for God's sake!

What next, Access All Areas passes?

DAY SEVEN | MONDAY 6TH APRIL

Madrid to Toledo

A morning walk to the Palacio Real, the Royal Palace, in which we were disappointed to learn Juan Carlos and Sophia don't live, and then back to check out of our Palace – which we leave with fond memories and high recommendations.

Toledo is our next map pin to aim for, about 75 clicks south west down the N401. This stunning city, raised and fortified within the lasso loop of the Tajo river, seems to have been the Iberian peninsula's capital for dozens of kings, emperors, barbarians, goths and faiths for over 2,000 years. From the Romans, via El Cid, to when Philip II moved the capital to Madrid, Toledo has seen it all; and if you know where to look, or you allow Michelin to guide you, it's all still there for the seeing.

First things first, though. Find the hotel and have lunch. We are booked into our third Parador – this one occupies its own mountain-top opposite the city walls. In fact the Parador's terrace is cited as one of the best viewing platforms in the area. Our balcony's not bad either, and I've worked out that this is the very balcony they took the brochure's main picture from – although they had the pool full of azure water, not a pile of duckboards and a cement mixer like it's got today. Yes, yes, I know the season hasn't started yet, but we're Brits – we go swimming in the Channel.

After a pleasant, though somewhat windy, lunch, we drove into the city. We parked deep underground, in a very clean and efficient multi-level car park – the first of what would turn out to be many clean and efficient multi-level underground car parks on our trip. The Sierras, Siena, Monte Carlo, Cannes, and the most pristine of all – certainly liveable in and practically eatable off – St Tropez.

Fact – continental Europeans, in general, have very nice underground car parks, where you're not likely to get mugged, ripped off or Weil's Disease. Britain, in general, has shitholes, where all the above are absolutely possible. And consider this – one of the richest fortunes in Britain was amassed by building such car parks, and yet another by giving (what am I saying? *selling*) us another invention that doesn't work very well – the cardboard milk carton.

Thanks, guys.

Emerging from our airy, bright, reasonable-smelling, *clean* car park, we wandered, along with every tourist we'd seen in Madrid plus their families (what must it be like in high season?) to the Cathedral. Built over 250 years (not ago – it took a *quarter of a millennium* to build) and moving from French to Spanish Gothic, it's impressively decorated, dripping with ornate gilded sculpture and paintings, and its crowning glory, the vast and awesome Retablo in the chancel, is... closed for repair and coyly covered with a huge photograph of itself.

Bugger.

I think it's my jinx, but Ali nobly includes herself in the spell. We appear to send out strong vibes, in advance of our arrival, which seem to move conservation leaders in cities on our itinerary to suddenly find the money to restore their city's most beloved treasure. The last scaffolding bolt is usually being tightened as we check in to our hotel.

Disappointed, but of course not in the least surprised, we finish our echoing walk around the cool cloisters of the Cathedral, and proceed to the next recommended must-see, El Greco's house. We buy our tickets, shuffle eight feet into his living room, look over the tightly-packed heads at a dark picture which they're not even sure is his, and shuffle back out through the French windows. A snip at 150 pesetas each.

A wander past ye olde shoppes selling swords – thousands of them – and back to the Plaza Major, for a *café con leche*. It felt rather strange to whip out the mobile and sit in the Spanish sun having a long and crystal-clear chat with my mate back home who's popping in every so often to check we haven't been repossessed.

Back to the Parador for a reasonable dinner in a long, dark dining room, and then Scrabble and coffee on our balcony.

This is getting tough.

DAY EIGHT | TUESDAY 7TH APRIL

Toledo to Cordoba

The morning is very grey and rainy, but we've been lucky with the walking-around weather so far, and the skies must know this is a driving day. Our longest stretch yet, 230 miles, will take us to Cordoba – ancient city of Andalucia, on the banks of the Guadalquivir, twice capital and thrice faithed.

Just after lunch we cross the romantic river, with the city ramparts banked on the other side, weave our way through the tiny streets, the Jensen only just scraping round some of the corners, and find ourselves at the Alfaros Hotel. Cool marble inside, with pretty rooms under dozens of interlocking terracotta-tiled roofs.

The weather is clearing, and for the first time the warmth of the south is beginning to put in an appearance. Ali gets her shorts out; a treat for me and the male Cordobians, of course, but perhaps ill-advised as our first stop on our city walk is a mosque. Mosque is too small a word for it really, for this is the Mezquita – a marble and stone marvel of eleven aisles, 850 pillars, cool orange groves and a towering minaret – and not a slab of it under a thousand years old.

I don't know if I've ever consciously been into a mosque before, and I dare say there aren't many thousand year old ones in Britain, but this place took my breath away. All the columns and pillars line up in any direction you look, and all the arches joining them are multi-coloured stone and marble, all reds and golds and yellows. It's like being inside a Battenberg cake. It was begun in the late 700s and added to over the next 200 years – more columns and aisles, richly gilded anterooms and niches, and the vast cobbled courtyard filled with orange trees and ornamental ponds called the Patio de Los Naranjas.

In the 13th century the Christians took over and made some changes, but somehow forgot to do what they did in lots of other places, which was raze the whole thing to the ground and start again in the name of 'their' God. What they did instead was hollow out a bit in the middle and put a socking great cathedral in it. And there they both still are – a swooping gilded high-columned Catholic cathedral with massive filigree organs and cherubim and seraphim trumpeting from every ledge, surrounded by single storey cool marble aisles and coloured stone arches.

Well, we were impressed, and the more so to discover Cordoba's third faith represented just around the corner in the Jewish quarter, where one of Spain's only two major synagogues still stands. The Jews of Cordoba had arrived with the Phoenicians, and were still here when the Arabs came in the 8th century. They got on fairly well, both being business-minded, and it wasn't until the Catholics chucked them out in the early part of the second millennium that they once again found themselves on the move.

We were enjoying an early evening glass of Gran Vina Sol in a bar, trying to get our brains round fourteen centuries of history, when the previous six struck up the band in the street outside. Of course, this is Semana Santa – Easter Week – and it's procession time. In Spain it's quicker to count the days when there isn't some sort of bunting in the streets, but this being Holy Week, the festivities are a little more sober-minded. We find a vantage point among the packed crowds, with the dirge-like sound of the first band preceding their arrival round the corner. Above us, wrought iron balconies are draped with pink geraniums and pink-faced children, straining to spot their older brothers and sisters who ("oh, Mama, when will it be *my* turn?") are actually in the parade.

Around the corner comes the first band, silver trumpets and tubas glinting in the last of the sun, playing and marching very, very slowly. It reminded me of the opening scene of *Live and Let Die*, with the New Orleans funeral cortege blues band shuffling their way past the Filet of Soul. Well, our next sight had me convinced we'd moved just a few miles up the delta from New Orleans, into the badlands of the

Deep South, where if good ol' boys don't still actually wear the bedsheets, they do keep them neatly laundered in the bottom drawer just in case. Following this first band came two or three dozen characters dressed in long flowing white robes with very tall pointed purple velvet hoods, eyeholes supplied. The vast silver crosses some of them were carrying weren't actually on fire, but the whole spectacle was rather unnerving.

The klan, sorry klang, of cymbals shook me out of that mininightmare in time to get another culture shock. Round the corner came the Romans; well, the massive standard and eagle of the Third Legion, with embroidered SPQR banner and silver emblem of she-wolf with suckling children. *Hello*?

I suppose it's not too surprising. Cordoba was a centre of the Roman occupation of Spain – four centuries of it – and Seneca *pere et fils* were born here, the son going on to become Nero's tutor. Anyway, Rome's influence is still very much in evidence here, represented this evening by a massive wooden float bedecked with silks and Senate statuary, carried on the backs of the town's young stalwarts.

After a couple of hours of slow-step parade with no respite, we repair for a pleasant dinner followed by coffee in the courtyard, the sounds of the festival, more animated and excited by now, drifting down to us over the starlit terracotta.

Now where's that copy of the *Telegraph* I've been saving?

DAY NINE | WEDNESDAY 8TH APRIL

Cordoba to Vejer de la Frontera

Today we set off on a long looping drive to the very southern coast of Spain to see an old friend. Around Seville, take a sharp left just before Cadiz, and fifty miles along the coast to the white hilltop town of Vejer de la Frontera – quintessentially Andalucian – and you can see Africa from James' balcony.

James is my brother's best friend, and has been a sort of honorary sibling for well over twenty years, so it was pretty damn good to see him, as he doesn't come home much. That's because, after nine years, this is very much home to him. While you have to have been here since the Romans left to be accepted as local, James seems to have managed to carve a unique niche for himself in this deeply Spanish community. They call him *El Rubio* (the blond one) or *Jésus*, due to his shaggy blond hair and tanned exterior, split by a perfect smile and deep laugh.

I imagine it wasn't easy to become accepted, but he opened a small business running cycling tours in the summer and skiing tours in the Sierras in the winter, learned fluent Andalucian, brought much-needed tourist pesetas into the town, and kept his gringo nose clean. I'm not sure he'll ever be allowed to be Mayor, but only because his great[20]-grandfather wasn't born within the sound of the village bells. Actually his great[20]-grandfather was King of Scotland, but that's another story.

The Jensen rumbled around the sleepy square, and Rulo, James' golden lab, shot out to greet us, followed by the boy himself. Old men sat at small tables under awnings by the side of the plaza. The sun beat down. It beat down on the awnings under which the old men sat drinking their *cervezas*. It beat down fiercely on the dust of the square, on the chickens that scratched there. The sun kept beating down. Because that's the way it was, out there.

Sorry, but there is something of the Papa Hemingway about James. He rides and surfs superbly, has a fondness for tequila, and is one of Europe's finest skiers. I don't know if he catches marlin, but I wouldn't be surprised if he just *could*, you know, naturally.

Bastard.

Several San Miguels later we examine what he's done to his house since I was last there. As with many of these 15th century hilltop towns, the older houses built into the steppes are a cobbledy mish-mash of periods and materials, so that if you knock down a wall you don't know what you might find, or what else it might have been holding up.

James' house is on six levels, from lower ground floor courtyard, to roof terrace high above the square, from which, as previously advertised, you can, on a clear day, see the coastal villages and mountains of north Africa. Between you and them is a stretch of water which to the east becomes the Straights of Gibraltar and to the west is where Nelson did his stuff for Blighty – Trafalgar.

Since last seen, James has bought the house next door and begun to do it up. He's also turned the lower two floors of his place into small but charming apartments, which he lets by the night or week to travellers and holiday-makers. He's done out the rooms in simple Andalucian style, with a wonderful sort of rhubarb colourwash on the stucco. I asked him about it and he said it was pig's blood – an old recipe which really does contain pig's blood, and which was the traditional way of colouring walls in many parts of the Med. Is that where 'pigment' comes from, I wonder?

The current occupant of these newly decorated rooms, for tonight only, was a very bubbly black French girl who was studying Arabic in Fez, over in Africa, who'd read about James' hospitality in an American guide book, hopped the ferry to Gib, hitched to Vejer, and turned up on the doorstep. What a richly fabulous world this can be!

After a late and liquid lunch, James had to go back to work at his shop, so Ali and I went down to the beach, a few miles away at El Palmar, and established ourselves at Francisco's, our favourite restaurant on the edge of the Atlantic. 'Open all hours for gringo dollars' is their motto, so we order a bottle of Barbadillo and two steaming dishes of garlic gambas. While they come I ponder on the fact that, down this end of the country, if you order what you think is correct Spanish for white wine – *vino blanco* – you'll get sherry. You have to order it by brand, because they don't really drink the stuff. Well, not like us. I suppose it's the same as going into a pub on Tyneside and ordering a scotch – you'll get a pint of dark brown beer.

As the sun dips towards the horizon we walk a mile or so along the wide sands, the last of the surfers silhouetted against the beaten copper streak of the sunset. There's nobody about, and the sky seems huge, the pink and bronze tufts of cloud above us changing hue every few seconds as the last rays underlight them. Titian and Turner combined couldn't duplicate it.

I chuck a large stone a few yards into the surf and Ali, fortified by the wine, bets me £500 I won't go in and get it. I, equally fortified, naturally charge straight in up to my waist, rummage around a bit, fish my rock out and carry it back, dripping, to an astonished companion. I don't know which of us was more stupid – her for thinking I wouldn't get a little damp for five hundred quid, or me for thinking she'd actually honour her debt.*

---

*She still hasn't paid up. Girly.

Back up the hill to Vejer (pronounced, as we true Europeans know, 'Beh-HAIR') for the real start to the day. The Andalucians don't seem to entertain at home much, so the whole town's youth turns out each night for some serious mixing and drinking. And I mean night – if you're seen out much before midnight, you're a bit of a wuss, and staggering home much before four – well, you might as well become a hairdresser.

James (pronounced, by true Andalucians, HAY-mee) seems to know everybody, so we flit from this bar to that taverna, downing cervezas and tapas at each, being introduced to smiling tanned Spaniards and nodding a lot. It's amazing how much communication you can establish in a foreign language with the use of a smile, your eyebrows, and interrogative drinking gestures with your hand.

Last conscious thought: write to Dulux to suggest new product line – Soft Sheen™ With Hint Of Pig's Blood.

DAY TEN | THURSDAY 9TH APRIL

Vejer de la Frontera

James has disappeared to work, so we set out to wander round this fascinating little town. Perched 700 feet above the plain, it seems very small and compact, but actually 10,000 people live here, and they seem fairly affluent compared to similar towns we've passed through. Part of that is because about twenty years ago the town won *El Gordo*, Spain's annual state lottery. Held just before Christmas, everybody plays, and the tickets are very expensive – up to a hundred quid each – so there are lots of syndicates. About a dozen of the town's worthies had clubbed together and bought several tickets, and one came up. 700 million pesetas. That's nearly 3 million quid; and twenty years ago too, when 3 million quid was considered a colossal amount of money.

Having picked themselves up and made sure each was quite comfortable thank you, they then gave millions of pesetas to the town, rebuilding churches, schools and hospitals. The sleepy, bright white character of the town is still there of course, but it's newly painted, tidy and content.

The main church, at the highest point of the hill, is the focal point, and as in Cordoba, it's thrice-faithed: the spire is the minaret of the mosque that used to stand here, and the stone Star of David, carved high above the secondary door, is still there 400 years after you'd have thought it would have been chipped off.

Before lunch, a pre-arranged meeting at Radio Vejer FM, scene of a previous triumph. Last time I was here it was just before Christmas, and James had asked me to voice a radio commercial for his shop. In Spanish. Having voiced thousands at home in easy English, I couldn't resist the challenge, so James wrote a script featuring *Papa Noel* – Father Christmas – who would be extolling the virtues of the shop, and letting listeners know that Magnum is where he would be buying all his presents this year – providing he could get mountain bikes and surfboards down good little girls and boys' chimneys. My appalling accent was only slightly masked by the gruff ho-ho-hos of *Papa Noel*, but James, and Paco the DJ, were falling about with laughter, so on-air it went. To universal acclaim; I later learned that it had won Best Ad of the Year in a listeners' poll. It even produced a few sales – pity purchases, I've no doubt.

This time I'd promised to voice a few jingles for Paco, but in English. *"You're listening to Radio Vejer FM!"*. *"With The Best Music, Seven hours a day, THIS is Radio Vejer FM!"* I was up for going out and doing a roadshow, but Ali was on the phone trying to hire the local hitman, and it was time for lunch, so we met up with James' business partner Regli, and her sisters Anna and Amalia, down at the beach.

Sitting under the vine-covered trellis at Reyas we had superb tuna croquettas and mounds of fresh grilled languostinos, washed down with several bottles of Barbadillo. They take lunch seriously here – the shops close from midday to four.

After a windy walk along the sand, and a visit to a pot shop for Ali to stock up on terracotta dishes, I began to feel like I'd made an enemy at lunch. One of the languostinos had marked me down for death, and my usual dustbin-like constitution was fighting a losing battle. Which is why this journal now jumps from the ninth of April to ....

DAY TWELVE | SATURDAY 11TH APRIL

Vejer de la Frontera to Marbella

Oh dear. Oh dear oh dear oh dear. Ouch. Normally I get on fairly well with seafood; I love eating it, and I'm sensible about discarding unopened mussels and so on, but one tiny prawn had utterly levelled me for thirty six hours.

Respect.

I was still pretty weak, but we had to move on to our next port of call, so we gently packed the Jensen, said goodbye to James and Rulo, and drove gingerly along the coast towards Marbella. We'd toyed with nipping into Gibraltar as we passed, but the Spanish were doing one of their periodic works to rule at the border ("So, Senor, your mother's maternal aunt's maiden name again *pliss*?… and I'll need to see the deeds to your house also.") so any nipping was likely to take several hours, and I've not heard anything about Gib to make it worth it.

We are booked to spend Easter in the Hotel Rincon Andaluz in Marbella. It turns out to be one of those amalgams of low-rise fake stucco villa apartments clustered around three pools of suspiciously copper sulphate blue. It's like a posh Butlins.

Our room is pretty good, though – a suite, with large bedroom, comfortable bathroom and sitting room. The bedroom is my first stop, for five hours of collapse, with occasional visits to the comfortable bathroom the details of which you don't want to know about. Ali No-Mates, meanwhile, abandons her fainting fiancé and racks out under the sun to begin her miraculous transformation from olive to mahogany.

By early evening I'm feeling much better, so we don our linen jackets and Ray-Bans and walk along the beach path to Puerto Banus to get in with the gin crowd. This is apparently the mecca for the fake tan and hair/espadrille/gold Rolls & credit card set, so we find a harbour-side bar table and watch.

This section of the marina is so exclusive, it's lined in every way – lined with the poshest shops, the most ostentatious yachts and cruisers, the flashiest cars, and anything white in lines you want to buy – this is the recreational drug capital of the western Med. To bring your car onto the quayside you have to pass a sort of car bouncer – a guard on the gate who vets your Vette or refuses your

Reliant. Only beautiful cars here, *por favor*. I would have brought the Jensen, but what if – oh shame! – it had been turned away because of the *gringo blanco* driving it?

We make do with the last table at Antonios's for a dinner of breathtaking expense, made bearable only by the lines of self-important and self-made millionaires being turned away while we eat.

A late drink at another quayside bar, watching the rich and famous at play. Rich, without doubt – the vast gleaming cruiser moored opposite us had a flying bridge with its own flying bridge – but famous? Well, I suppose that is Gilbert O'Sullivan sitting at the next table. Suddenly I'm feeling much better.

DAY THIRTEEN | SUNDAY 12TH APRIL

Marbella

Easter Day, which we spent by the pool, Ali basting nicely and me trying to take a few layers of blue off my skin, instead taking just layers of skin off, so finding shade to write postcards.

Lunch in the hotel's restaurant, served by waiters who were surly or incompetent, or both.

In the evening, we wandered along to the casino, then wandered away, having uncoolly forgotten our passports. Cheap day.

DAY FOURTEEN | MONDAY 13TH APRIL

Marbella to Granada

The Jensen is having starting problems, which Frank, consulted by phone, thinks is something to do with the Park Inhibitor Switch. Of course, how stupid of me. Anyway, it takes a lot of jiggling and cursing before it will start, and I'm reluctant to stop too often in case it refuses altogether. We have a long drive today – to Granada – so we set off early as we want to go via Ronda, high up on the plain. The road from Marbella winds up through the Sierra Blanca mountains on smooth twisty roads – makes me think of the opening sequence of

The Italian Job, and I half expect to come across Raf Vallone driving a JCB and saying, "Signor, ees a long way back to England, and ees thataway."

Into Ronda, which I carefully neglect to tell Ali is the home of bull-fighting. Francisco Romero laid down the rules in the early 1700s, and the Ronda School is to this day the cradle of slaughter for spectacle. It's a very attractive town though, with superb views from the bridges across the gorge.

We daren't stop the car, so we burble through the tiny streets, and then find ourselves with a problem. Ahead is an impossibly narrow bridge, the other side of which is a sheer cobbled path going straight up to a pair of church doors. I'm about to try and back up when tooting behind me indicates a couple of cars and a van, who obviously expect me to get on with it and go up.

I can't see that the road continues past this church, but they obviously, and with increasing irritation, know better, so wincing, and with visions of the Jensen stuck at 45°, wedged forever in the history of Ronda, I gun the throttle and off we go – across the bridge, a paint layer's width either side, up the cobbled north face, to the church doors, where yes, the road goes right, so turn and up again, steeper still, left, right, mind the old bloke, scrape the kerb, scatter pedestrians – who are cheering now as we pass – more power, sharp *left*, hairpin *right*, and finally, against all the odds, we emerge wide-eyed and laughing at the top, into an old plaza.

Leaving Ronda behind, we set off across the high plains of Andalucia towards Granada – home of kings and popes in the shadow of the magnificent snow-capped Sierra Nevada.

"Yes, yes, Senor, you will find us easily", the receptionist of the Hotel Saray had said that morning. 'No, no', I said to myself after nearly an hour stop-starting around the city of Granada, 'your directions are crap'. Still, our room is okay, and has a view of the mountains. The hotel is clean and antiseptic – lots of marble and caramel-coloured mirrors – and is obviously a conference hotel. This would make sense, as it's next to the Palacio de Congresos, though how any delegates ever find it beats me. Perhaps they all get bussed in from the airport, and no one ever actually has to find it for themselves.

It's quite late by this time, so we have a fairly poor dinner in the hotel (neither my steak nor Ali's salmon had been ordered tartare, so we sent them back) and I get trounced at Scrabble in the bar. Again.

DAY FIFTEEN | TUESDAY 14TH APRIL

Granada

A beautiful spring day, so we decide to leave the Alhambra until tomorrow and make the most of the weather by driving up into the Sierras. A smooth and deserted road takes us up. The guide book says this is the highest road in Europe – presumably when the snow has gone and the road goes right to the top.

The snow is still here now though, and we arrive in Spain's main ski resort to find the season still going strong. After lunch on a sunlit and crisply cold balcony, we buy tickets for the gondola, part of me wishing I'd hired some kit and could do a bit of skiing.

This is a part of our lives together that will need some careful handling. I love skiing, and have done it since I was a teenager. There is certainly a drug-like quality to the sport; if you love it, you'll try and go whenever you can, even at the expense of other holidays. Or food. Ali on the other hand has never been, and being a sun baby can't understand how it might possibly take precedence over a beach.

The gondola swings (alarmingly for Ali) high over the pistes, and we get out at the top, where we stand out by being in jeans and shoes instead of coloured skisuits and gravity boots. It's much colder up here, and I take a wistful look at the slopes before we sway back down. Ah well, I'm on the trip of a lifetime, and what if I twisted something? This is only Day Fifteen; it would be a bit of a waste.

A long swooping return journey, with the Granada plain spead out before us, and back to the Saray, where after dinner Ali loses her famously good nature for a moment, when the barman tries to turn the lights off in our section of the lobby bar while we're still playing Scrabble. I mean, don't these people know who we are?

Oh, okay then.

DAY SIXTEEN | WEDNESDAY 15TH APRIL

Granada

In the winter tourists come to Granada for the skiing in the Sierras. All year round, but particularly in spring and autumn, they come for

The peaceful wonder of the Generalife's water gardens.

the Alhambra, the magnificent fortress of castles and palaces on one of Granada's three hills. We set out about tennish, but arrived at the main entrance to see seventy-five coaches and a two hour-plus queue in the blistering sunshine. My lack of tolerance for queuing is a matter of public record, so I set about trying to find a way round it. A taxi driver said we could also buy tickets at the Tourist Centre in the city, so I hire him to take us down there.

Normally I carry a small pinch of salt around with me so I've got something handy to take when taxi drivers promise me something, but amazingly enough we are able to buy tickets as advertised, and he drives us back up the hill to another gate – the Palacio de la Justicia – and we're in. Twenty minutes and a few extra pesetas well spent, say I.

The Alhambra is absolutely stunning – a cool oasis of palaces and churches amidst ancient gardens of cypress and pine. We started with the Palacio de Carlos V, designed by a pupil of Michelangelo's – a perfect and dignified circle of great columns within a square palace. It's rather cold and bare now, but must have been amazing when full of bustling courtiers and red-robed clerics. On to the western end of the walled complex, and the Alcazabar, the 9th century castle. The huge keep remains, and you can climb up to the flat roof with its incredible views of the city and the mountains, but the barracks are only floor markings and low ruined walls.

Back towards the gardens, and time for a glass of wine in the Parador. Yes, there's even one inside the Alhambra. It's the most expensive of the chain, naturally, but if you're coming to 'do' the Alhambra, it's the hotel to stay in. We took our glasses out onto the wide terrace, and sat overlooking the valley towards the Generalife – no, not an insurance company, but the summer palace of the Kings of Granada, which sits on the next hilltop. Ali goes off for a wander in the gardens, and I get siezed by a mad moment and start drawing the Generalife in my diary. I haven't picked up a sketch pad for years, and the result bears that fact out, but I enjoyed doing it – might have to see if I can buy a Fisher Price watercolour set for later in the trip.

Ali came back, helpfully pointed out that I seemed to inadvertantly have made a big smudge in my diary, and we wandered over to the Generalife. Built as a sort of summer house, it's a gorgeous spread of cool corridors and collonnades, designed to catch the slight breeze around the hilltop, and all centred around its crowning glory – the water gardens. Fed from reservoirs up on the hillside, the waters flow, bubble and tinkle all around you – down channels in the rock, over stones and waterfalls, in and out of pools, ending up in a long ornamental pond out of which sprays of water dance across each other, flashing in the sunlight. Utterly bewitching.

There's even a long flight of stone steps where the handrails are inverted terracotta half-pipes, with the water coursing down inside them. It must have been one of the most relaxing places to be in the heat of ancient Andalucia, even though very few people were ever allowed to see it. Now, we can all enjoy the enormous effort and love that must have gone into its creation. Worth the trip to Granada just for this.

What most people come to see though, is the Palacio Nazaries, the Nasrid Palace. The Nasrids founded a new dynasty in Granada after the Muslims were kicked out of Cordoba in the 13th century, and it was during the next two centuries that Granada flourished and the Alhambra was built.

Their palace is constructed around two enormous courtyards, with dozens of richly decorated rooms surrounding them. Stunningly ornate low relief carvings and incredibly complicated tiling mosaics greet you in every room. Most rooms have windows with eagle-eye views, and you end up in the Salon de Embajadores – the Hall of the Ambassaors – where the Emirs would greet their guests under the domed cedarwood ceiling. The palace really is two eyefuls of splendour, and every man hour of the 130 years it took to build and carve is on show, but it was the simple joy of the water and wonder of the Generalife's gardens that I'll remember longest.

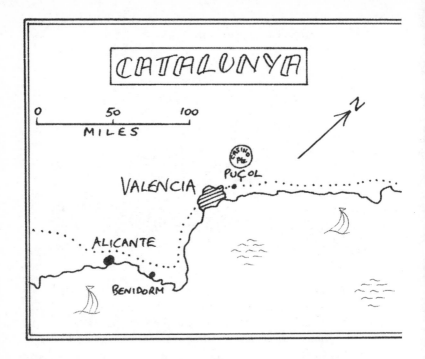

CATALUNYA

Valencia

In which we stay at a strange hotel, the vast lobby of which is straight out of 'Where Eagles Dare' – all dark panelling, suits of armour and enormous mooses staring down at the punters.

Just North of Valencia

In which a disaster of calamitous proportions descends on us, threatening to destroy our holiday and very nearly us too. No, really, we almost died.

Barcelona

In which we begin to lick our wounds and re-build our shattered lives. We explore this amazing city, stay in a fabulous hotel, start our battle with insurance companies, and visit the eagle-high monastery of Montserrat.

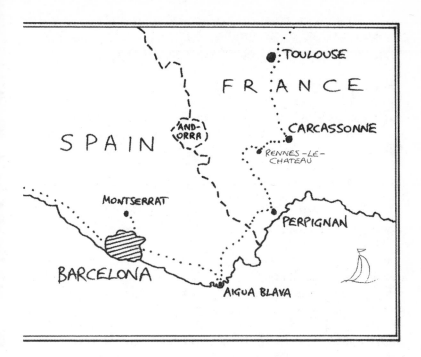

Aigua Blava
In which we relax in a Frank Lloyd Wright-esque Parador, overlooking Paradise Bay.

Rennes-le-Chateau
In which we visit a tiny hilltop village in the French Pyrenees which claims to conceal dreadful secrets of earth-shaking religious import.

Carcassonne
In which we stay in an awful hotel, have a superb dinner, and visit the largest ancient fortified city in Europe.

Granada to Valencia

Being away from home for three months has a number of consequences that you don't get from a fortnight's holiday. Apart from not earning money – only spending it – which is a worry in itself, there's the post collecting at home (bills, bills), and, for me, a lack of news. I like to know what's going on in the world, and you tend to get out of touch. Once in a while I'll be a grockle and buy an English paper, but that's a comfort luxury only, as it'll be two or three days old, and have cost you more than your lunch.

So, in hotels that have it, I found my anchor on the world was CNN. This is presumably exactly what Mr Turner had in mind – pushing his way into hotels everywhere, so that despite its somewhat brash approach and American influence, CNN has, for English speakers away from home, become indisputably the TV network of record. And of course it has as its linking anchor the world's finest male voice, my old showbiz mate James Earl Jones.

This morning CNN gives us the cheering news that Pol Pot is dead. Wishing him nothing but torment on his journey to hell, we continue our journey with our longest leg yet – 350 miles north up the coast to Valencia. We're actually aiming for Barcelona, in a desperate attempt to stay on some sort of schedule, but 600 miles in this heat is too much for me, and probably for the Jensen, so we've arranged a stop-over.

It's hot and sunny as we pass Benidorm (always a good idea) and arrive in the small Valencian satellite town of Puçol where we check in to the Hotel Monte Picayo – a vast edifice set into the side of a mountain. And the comparison to *Where Eagles Dare* doesn't stop there.

The hotel seems too modern to have actually been designed by Albert Speer, but walking into the lobby felt like walking into the Great Room of the *Schloss Adler*. A huge baronial hall with dark panelling and dozens of suits of armour and entire bison hanging from the walls. I fully expected to see Richard Burton holding a Luger to the heads of the German High Command, with Clint Eastwood ready to jump out of the window onto the cable car. It was utterly extraordinary, and would even have looked over the top in Berchtesgaden. Reception were very welcoming though – not a heel click in sight – and showed us to a large pleasant room with a balcony. They even helpfully pointed out to the *senor y senora* that the hotel casino was at their disposal, and here was a free ticket of entry.

Now I saw their dastardly plan. The senora's eyes lit up, so, suited and booted, we walked down the hill to the casino building, where we had an excellent dinner and allowed the Reich's treasurers to accept a further donation towards their next Blitzkrieg.

Afterwards we wandered back up the hill for a last nightcap under the larger of the two elk.

DAY EIGHTEEN | FRIDAY 17TH APRIL

Valencia to Barcelona

I'm writing this entry at about eleven at night, knees drawn up under the sheets, with one eye on Ali's head on the next pillow, as she tries to get to sleep.

I can't sleep. I can still hear the crackle and roar; still smell the acrid carbon stench; still feel the anger and frustration; still shake from the nearest I've knowingly been to death.

However, we're alive, and that has to be the most important thing. We are whole, physically undamaged, together, and although very shaken, we're alright.

The Jensen blew up.

I mean it turned into a fucking *fireball*, which we escaped by seconds.

Today was to have been another long journey – 230 miles on up the coast to Barcelona – but we hadn't gone three miles when it happened, without warning. We'd just come off the slip-road onto the Autovia north, and were doing I suppose forty miles an hour, when suddenly the car was full of smoke. I swung across onto the hard shoulder, shouting at Ali to undo her seatbelt, and screeched to a halt. Checking Ali was on her way out of the car, I leapt out of my side. As I got out, I looked back through the windscreen over the wheel and saw, through the louvres in the bonnet, an orange-red inferno in the engine bay. I saw Ali was past the boot on her way back to safety, and I then did the stupid thing they always tell you not to do – I went back. I pivoted on one foot, and reached back into the car, swept my wallet and phone off the central console, and then made a dash for it.

I suppose I'd just passed the rear bumper, moving well, when I heard a sort of 'whump!' from behind and felt a blast of heat on my shoulders. Not looking back until I'd got twenty yards away, I then saw a huge ball of flame erupting from the front of the car, and within three or four seconds the whole car forward of the front seats was engulfed.

The next few minutes remain a bit of a blur. Ali says I was leaping up and down shouting "No! Fucking *NO!!*", and then running back up the carriageway waving my arms to stop the traffic, shouting "Emergentheea! EmergenTHEEA!" It's funny how even one's rudimentary grasp of language fails one in a real emergentheea.

I was waving my arms like a mad thing, and cars and vans were stopping – well they would, by now the flames from the Jensen were thirty feet long and spewing across all three carriageways, blown by a strong sideways wind. I was making 'lend-me-a-fire-extinguisher-would-you-be-so-kind' hand gestures, as if I or anybody was actually going to get near the inferno.

By now the motorway was jammed, and several people had their mobiles out. While we waited for the *bomberos* to arrive, all we could do was stand and watch her burn. Ali couldn't watch – she sat in tears on the crash barrier. I could hardly watch, except that I had this awful feeling that the tank was going to blow, lift the car off the tarmac in slow motion, execute a few graceful movie-like pirouettes in mid-air, and land splintered and crisped on the southbound carriageway.

I tried to explain to cars wanting to edge their way past that the Jensen was full of petrol (we had filled up moments before) by shouting "Gazolina completa!".

I have no idea what that means. Nevertheless a few cars made a dash for it, while all three lanes behind us began to turn into a major jam.

The fire began to eat its way back towards the tank – the whole cabin was now ablaze – and I really thought it was a matter of seconds before she went up. The bonnet was producing great gouts of flame – like the footage you see of the surface of the sun – and I knew that it was all beyond saving.

Everything we had for three months was in that car – clothes, cameras, shoes, hats, CD player and CDs, diaries, money – dear God, our *passports!* I just *couldn't believe* this had happened, and it was much too soon for all the implications to sink in.

Eventually – actually I don't suppose it was much more than seven or eight minutes – the *bomberos* arrived in force and efficiently and methodically doused the flames. The Guardia Civil were there too, and soon had at least two carriageways open for people to continue on their way with a juicy story to tell.

It was a mess.

The front of our beautiful car had melted into the tarmac. Most of the paint had burned off, and the inside was just a charred skeleton of metal and seat springs. Here the blackened remains of a Nike trainer, there a melted CD. The seats were gone, and on what had been the back seat were the dark misshapen lumps that had been our carry-around bags. Mine was prised out by one of the firemen, and we took the sorry remains over to the hard shoulder while Ali's was disentangled from the wreckage.

As expected, the DV video camera, my Nikon 35mm, all the spare tapes, batteries, films, tripod and cables had melted to buggery, but unbelievably the very inside pocket, with all our documents, travellers cheques and the passports had escaped the worst of it, and although singed and brittle with heat, they were usable. Even this very diary was a trifle blackened, but had survived. All of it must

43

have been mere seconds from destruction when the *bomberos'* foam had puffed into action.

The same could not be said of Ali's bag. Tragically, her diary and the beginnings of her book about the trip had burned. What she was most worried about, apart from that, were her rings and bracelets, including her engagement ring, all of which had been in her make-up bag in the main bag. The make-up bag and its contents were no more, but the rings, again blackened and tarnished, were intact, and later polished up fine.

But everything else in the main cabin of the car had gone. Hats, shoes, maps, guide books, car manuals, a box of spare parts Frank had lent us for the Jensen, the portable CD player, a soft carry case with 36 CDs in it – all consumed by the awesome power of the fire.

Now for the horror of the boot contents – our cases. The Chief Bombero wielded his crowbar, and we opened the boot. The vast rear windscreen of the Jensen had fallen in on the hard tonneau cover, so we cleared that away, then, amazingly we saw two smoke-blackened but whole suitcases. Again, there must only have been seconds in it, but they seemed intact. We had to cut them open, as the plastic zips had fused, but inside the clothes seemed whole. They stank of smoke and fuel, but we could at least take them away to see what was salvagable.

Ali, with huge presence of mind, remembered that her little camera was, unusually, in one of the cases. Would it be a good idea to fish it out and, if it was still working, take lots of pictures of the car and the scene? For insurance? It would indeed be a good idea, so I rummaged, found the camera and Ali began clicking away.

While she was doing that, and seeing that if we'd thought of that we might actually now be capable of rational thought, the chief cop wandered over with his clipboard. Music-facing time. The Guardia had been very Civil indeed so far, considering we'd mucked up so many people's day, but what helped oil the wheels considerably was AA Five Star.

Before leaving home, I'd followed some advice and taken AA Five Star cover. They needed some convincing that we required cover for three months at a stretch, rather than the usual two or three weeks, but we were sorted out with the package, which got us 24-hour English speaking roadside assistance and a number of other benefits, including a phone number. What impressed me was that I dialled that number from the hard shoulder outside Valencia, got a very young-sounding bloke in Hemel Hempstead or wherever, who said

"Pass me over to the officer in charge", and then proceeded to sort the whole thing out. In Spanish.

When he'd finished, he was passed back to me with a smile, and he told me it had all been sorted. We just had to sign a couple of papers, and the cops would help us on our way back to the hotel, where he would talk to us again. Hugely impressed, I asked what would happen to the car, which needless to say was a total write-off.

At this point it appeared that one of the vans that had been first on the scene, and seemed to be still hanging around, was the local *desguacio* – scrap metal merchant. He must have thought it was Christmas, and before long the cops had given him the nod, and he was back with a flatbed to scrape our pride and joy off the public highway. The cops whistled up a taxi which took us and our remaining remains back to the Monte Picayo, where we arrived in reception, a soot-stained and sorry sight, steaming gently.

They were delightful, and gave us back our old room, and at a much reduced price. This wasn't charity – it was what the room should have cost us the first night, but we'll pick up this story, about us being stung by UK tour operators, when we get to the Dordogne.

We unpacked, and unpicked, the suitcases, and threw away the most damaged clothes, hanging all the rest out on the balcony to try and get rid of the worst of the smoke smell – acrid and horrid. Then we sat down, still queasy, with a large beer to figure out the next move.

To go on, or not to go on?

We'd lost our car, well over half our possessions, and escaped death by seconds. We'd lost thousands of pounds worth of camera equipment, tapes and films, Ali had lost her diary, and the insurance and sorting out would take ages and cost money. And we'd been badly shaken up. Wouldn't it be more sensible to admit defeat and go home? Had it all been too ambitious after all?

On the other hand, bugger it. We were alive and unhurt, we had passports, wallet and phone, we *should* be well insured, and we were only three weeks into a trip we'd taken a year to plan. Were we going to allow the first little hiccup to deter us?

Were we, bollocks!

Sleep now, and try not to dream... about what if the accident had happened in one of those long, dark, narrow tunnels through the Spanish mountains.

DAY NINETEEN | SATURDAY 18TH APRIL

Valencia to Barcelona

The AA supplied us with a Citroen Xantia for ten days until we could sort out some insurance, and see about getting a car organised for the remainder of the tour. We loaded our smart executive traveller's bin liners into it, and set off for the long drive up to Barcelona, where we had already had to cancel last night's hotel. The car was rather weird to drive after the Jensen – left hand drive, kilometers per hour not miles, gears, and a fifth of the power – but we gently made our way up the coast, arriving in the capital of Catalunya in the late afternoon.

Perhaps fate had smiled on us, because it so happened that this was one of our treat hotels. We'd heard about how wonderful it was, and saved up to stay there while we explored this beautiful city. How much exploring we'd get done while we had all the shit from the accident to sort out we didn't know, but as soon as we set foot in the Hotel Arts everything seemed to be that little bit easier.

From the first moment, we were impressed. We turned our dusty Citroen into the imposing entrance roadway, easing past Mercs and Porsches, and pulled up outside the marbled main doors. Out we got, dressed not in Armani or Nicole Fahri, but old T-shirts and shorts, and carrying our luggage in three bin liners. Not an eyebrow was raised by the green-tunic'd commissionaires, who ushered us upstairs into reception and made sure a receptionist was on hand immediately to check us in.

Now I've been fortunate enough over the years to stay in some pretty nice hotels – mostly for work, but occasionally for holidays and because I *like* nice hotels – and I can be a picky old bastard. I tend to expect that what's been advertised is actually on offer, and of the standard advertised too. I'm quite prepared to admit that mistakes are made, but the test of any hotel is how quickly they rectify a problem. I'm in danger of beginning to sound like Michael Winner, but the point is that we stayed at the Arts for four days, and in that time I couldn't find a single fault.

Not one.

Bernard Levin, the finest journalist of his time, has many things to say about hotels. In the past he has given it as his opinion that the Mandarin in Hong Kong is probably the finest hotel in the world, and that the Brenners Park in Baden Baden is probably the finest in Europe. I haven't been to Hong Kong, and wonder if the Mandarin is the same post-handover, but, as you will see later, we did stay at the Brenners Park. It was indeed superb, but I felt that the Arts scored higher. For your information, and for my interest and amusement, you will find at the end of this book our Hotel Rating Chart – every one of the forty one hotels we stayed in rated and commented on in ten categories, and with an overall rating and value comment at the end. Sad, yes, but interesting and utterly objective.

Like-for-like comparisons are difficult of course, and opinions can be subjective – the Brenners Park is an imposing old building surrounded by mature stream-edged gardens in a sleepy spa town; the Arts is a ten year old thrusting glass tower in a bustling cosmopolitan city – it's what's inside, and, to a very large extent, who's inside, that counts.

At the Arts we were received with as much welcome as the richest rock star or the most crowned head. Nothing was too much trouble, and arrived instantly and efficiently. Every member of staff looked you in the eye with a confident "Buenos Dias", and more often than not asked if there was any way they could assist you this morning. The rooms were cleaned, changed and fresh-flowered twice a day. All this, and the most comfortable room of our trip, for a room rate of, in some cases, half what we paid in other leading hotels.

Then, above all that, the true measure of a hotel – the concierge. His name was Paco, and more of his efforts shortly.

I've just cast my eye over the above, and realised that you might have formed the opinion that I have shares in Ritz-Carlton – who own the Arts – or that the hotel knew we were coming and that I was writing a book, or that we got some special rates or favours. I must refer you to the Author's Note, where I point out that, being nobodies, we planned out and paid for every step of our trip at punters' rates, and we were, to every hotel, just another very ordinary pair of guests. So when I praise one hotel and slag off another, it was my actual opinion at the time. You won't find any small print in italics at the bottom of *this* article saying, *'Jonathan Booth flew as the guest of Biggish Airways and stayed at Posh Hotels International, call 0033 555 7767'.*

Our room was superb – all cool creams and white wood, a huge bed with wide side tables and fingertip controls for lights, curtains, TV etc. On the fourteenth floor, it had an excellent view of the sea and the Olympic Marina. The bathroom was an experience – vast and marbled throughout, it had separate glassed off cubicles for shower and loo, the shower had a seat and four multi-angled shower heads, there was a huge bath and double-fronted basin.

Back in the room, TV and Video (vast English video library available from the concierge at hire rates less than the video shop back home – and delivered, too) B&O CD player, huge minibar... the list goes on.

That's it, I said, I'm not leaving. I'm never leaving.

We gratefully dumped our bin liners, which within moments were taken away to have the contents cleaned. (They were back, each item cleaned and ironed in its own cellophane wrapper, by noon the next day. Yes, that cost a bit, but by no means excessive, and the insurance should pay.) By this time, it was nearly eight, so worn out by our trials, we had a light room service supper (simple and superb), and went to bed.

Neither of us slept very well. Ali has a bad headache and stomach ache – probably delayed shock. It will take us a few days to pick ourselves up, but it appears we have found the right cave in which to lick our wounds.

DAY TWENTY | SUNDAY 19TH APRIL

Barcelona

Insurance is a vicious circle. You pay a company a premium to cover you if you lose stuff, but the previous chap has claimed for something he *didn't* lose, so the company has to either put your rates up or spend a lot of time trying not to pay your claim. Or both.

I don't know what the real figures are, and I don't suppose it's possible to find out, but I think that most people now believe that most insurance companies see it as their job to avoid paying out anything unless they absolutely have to. And since they're vastly bigger and more powerful than you are, if you pick the wrong one, you're stuffed.

In our current situation we had picked a right one and a wrong one. The Jensen was insured with a classic car specialist called

Boncaster, based in Essex. From start to finish they were excellent. They'd insured the car since I first got her 18 months before, and had done a special three month extra premium for our trip. I rang their Steve from the hotel and gave him the bad news. He was genuinely concerned – for us as well as for the car. He arranged for a local agent to go and look at the car, assess it, and then, in the fullness of time, we'd get a settlement. The fullness of time turned out to be 15 days – cheque for the full amount of cover. Thank you Boncaster; if Ali ever allows me to have another classic car, I'll be right round.

And then there was the contents insurance. Oh dear. I won't go into detail about the dozens of phone calls (many trying to find someone with a brain), letters, affadavits, photographs, legal threats and general heartache that we experienced dealing with Suretravel, but at the end they frankly refused to believe that we'd lost what we had actually lost, and eventually, and *six months later*, we got about 60% of the value back.

But for now, we had to go shopping. Our list of needs was long, and so we needed some advice. Enter Paco, the Arts' consummate concierge. If he was disappointed to be on duty when the *gringos* who'd blown up their car came to the desk, he didn't show it, and was charm itself. Certainly, he could advise us on the best places in town to get luggage, cameras, music equipment, clothes, shoes, new documents and so on. Here was a map which he would annotate for us, here were the phone numbers of the best value places. Of course, he would be delighted to fax these four different documents to their destinations, and by the time we had returned he would have made extensive inquiries about car hire for the rest of our trip. Here is my direct line to the desk, please do not fail to telephone if you need further assistance, I am on until eight. Have a successful day.

Deeply impressed, we headed out into the city of Barcelona to re-equip. We were lucky – this was probably the largest city on our route before Rome in six weeks time, so we were able to get practically everything we needed quite easily. Arpi, the camera specialists, replaced all my kit like for like; we bought basic suitcases and essentials, and soon felt we had most things we would need. Apart from all the phoning and faxing needed to sort out the admin side, we didn't want to waste too much time and miss seeing one of the most beautiful and exciting cities in Europe.

Barcelona is Spain's second largest city, and the capital of Catalunya, which it would probably rather be known as. Catalan is spoken in preference to Castillian Spanish, the more proudly since Franco banned it. The Romans first fortified the hills above the city, and it grew large and powerful from the 12th century. Now it is one of the most thriving centres of art and culture in Europe: opera, theatre, architecture and music, and Picasso, Miro, Dali and Gaudi. The 1992 Olympics gave the city a 20th century boost, and it's now a conference and exhibition first-pick.

Our first stop is the Museo de Picasso, in a Florentine mansion down a tiny side street. Quite a queue to get in, but a Flamenco guitarist entertained us while we waited. Once inside I was pleasantly surprised, and then stunned, by Picasso's very early work. I'm rather ashamed to admit that I didn't know he could actually draw. Amazing life studies when he was a young student – anatomy drawings to rival Leonardo, family and self portraits; incredible use of shadow and line. I suppose it's rather like Les Dawson, who had to be able to play the piano very well first, before he could pretend convincingly to play it very badly. On to more familiar later works, that I have never really got on with, but then another surprise – superb linocut work that I didn't even know he did. Apparently he led the way in this medium in the 1950s and 1960s. A prolific and touched genius.

After lunch we tried to see the cathedral, but it was closed till four, so back to the hotel to do some more phoning. Then out again in the early evening for a walk in the Parque, which was a delight. As in Madrid, Sunday evening in the park seems to be a ritual, and the place was packed with people, musicians, craft and food stalls and entertainers. Florid and Romanesque fountains cascaded down – horses, flying dragons and gargoyles spewing water that sparkled in the evening sunlight. We watched the clowns, listened to the music, breathed the cannabis-laden air and bought a simple bead and leather bracelet for Ali from a stall.

High on a mixture of relief and contentment, we wandered drowsily back to the hotel where we hunkered down in our luxury cave, eating supper and watching Costner and Russo ham it up joyfully in *Tin Cup*.

DAY TWENTY-ONE | MONDAY 20TH APRIL

Barcelona

An envelope under our door with breakfast contained a letter from Paco saying he had some information regarding our car. We had decided after some thought to hire a car for the rest of our trip, rather than buy one, which had been an option. While we would be left with a car at the end of it, it would be left hand drive, and have little re-sale value back home. Despite the expense of hiring – anathema to me – it was probably the best option.

Paco had found a number of deals, despite the difficulty of hire companies understanding that we wanted a car for seventy two days, travelling from Spain to France, Italy, Austria, Germany, Switzerland, Luxembourg, Belgium and back to France, dropping it off in Calais. In the end, he found that none of them would allow us to take a car out of Spain for that long. Two of the majors would allow us to do it from Bordeaux however, so we persuaded the AA's agent to allow us to drop the Citroen off there and pick up a new hiring.

We sallied forth for some more shopping, this time with a more relaxed approach. We started at the bottom of one of the most attractive shopping streets in the world – Las Ramblas. Well over a mile in length, this tree-lined avenue stretches from the Columbus Monument up to the Plaza de Catalunya. Columbus stood atop his column, pointing out to sea, urging us to continue with our journey. Actually we were going north, and he wasn't pointing anywhere near the direction of the New World, but then navigation was never Columbus' strong point; consider the statement that every schoolboy knows – 'Christopher Columbus discovered America' – it's incorrect in every word. His name wasn't Christopher Columbus, he didn't discover America, or even ever go there (he just bumped into Jamaica) and it wasn't called America when he didn't get there.

In Bill Bryson's marvellous book *Made in America* – the one many of his wider readership haven't read, and should – he points out that Columbus is one of the most famous characters from history now, but when he came back from his later travels, he started demanding titles and rewards so that everyone at the Spanish court got bored of him. Apparently he died in such penury and obscurity that to this day no-one knows exactly where he's buried.

Strange – nobody knows exactly where Mozart's buried either.

We wandered up this delightful thoroughfare, which is lined with stalls selling everything from plants and flowers to carved wooden and ceramic objects, to live birds in cages (Ali, look away). Here and there are statue performers, on little plinths in the hot sun, covered with gold or silver paint, standing stock still, only moving or breaking a grin if coins jingle in the hats at their feet.

At the top we go into El Corte Ingles, the vast department store, where we top up with more essentials, and then lunch, rather cravenly, in the Hard Rock Café in the plaza. I suppose we were still in comfort mode, and just wanted to know what we were going to get. Inside it's the usual dark wood and chrome railings, and exactly the same sort of menu – ribs, wings, burgers, bottled beers from Coors to Michelob, and all the trimmings, but slightly less choice on the veggie fron for Ali. As we were to discover even more in places like Austria and Germany, the Europeans haven't really latched on to this no-meat thing. Around us hung the assorted movie memorabilia that make Hard Rocks quite diverting, and have helped cement their place as one of the most successful dining brands around.

When I was first in Orlando the Hard Rock Café was shaped like a huge guitar (they've since rebuilt it) and at the time was the world's busiest restaurant, serving 3,000 covers a day. I was told they take something like $25 per head in the restaurant, and $37 per head in the merchandise shop next door.

Eat the burger, buy the dream.

A wander further north to Altair, the wonderful bookstore, where we stock up on maps. We'd bought every map we thought we'd need before we came, but of course they were now just so much charcoal. Altair provided us with all the maps we needed, and most of the English language guides we'd originally had.

The walk back takes us past Gaudi's 'lalique' house, Casa Mila, all spirals and curves, which is now apartments, but stunning nevertheless. A little further east brings us to his best known work, the Iglesia de Sagrada Familia. Began in 1883, it is a remarkable building, partly because it is still being built seventy years after Gaudi's death.

Antonio Gaudi was brought in as chief architect in the second year of construction, when just the groundwork had been done. He envisaged a huge church, with great vaulting arches and massive tapering towers – all intricately carved with saints and sinners. A huge dome was to rise between the towers, and the finished masterpiece would dominate the whole city from the mountains to the sea.

The building was to be paid for however by donations, alms and fund-raising, not by the city. Gaudi's designs required new techniques and much hand-crafting, and so progress was slow. He worked on it for over forty years, living in a small room in the church, and then was run over and killed by a tram. Moral, please?

Inside, the work continues, but at a snail's pace. The vaulting nave is up, a stunning sweep of white marble and stone, with scalloped columns and high seating – the 'gods' – while the floor is covered in scaffolding, stone-cutters' tools and bunches of fruit; well, the mosaic'd clusters of stone fruit, in a very Gaudi style, that are presumably intended for column tops or finials, when they ever get finished. I think it's wonderful, and if I were Bill Gates, I'd tear off a cheque every month until it was done, just because it *should* be finished.

Mind you, the towers still look to me like four brandy snaps standing on end.

On to the revitalised marina, with its galleries of shops and cinemas and aquaria. One of our sad losses in the car had been our home-made games compendium (I did say sad), comprising a Scrabble board slotted neatly into a backgammon set, which closed to contain all the tiles, counters, dice , pens, scoresheets and so on required for both games. It had turned into mush, so we went to look for replacements.

Lo and behold, a games shop! Backgammon, no problem, and Scrabble no problem either, except of course the mix of tiles was configured for Spanish. This meant lots more 'U's and 'A's and 'S's, no 'K', a 'Q' worth five, and some new friends – a 'LL', a 'RR' and a 'N' with a tilde, all worth eight, and a 'CH' worth five. We soon got used to this new set of challenges, and we still use the Spanish set of letters at home to this day.

Of course the really sad fact was that the only thing we asked my brother to send us out from England when the car blew up was a replacement Official Scrabble Dictionary. Well, one of us would have soon killed the other without a common arbiter.

A last dinner, and then back to our beloved Arts. Paco was still on duty, and beckoned us over for some last minute information he'd discovered (unasked) about our car arrangements. He shook our

Iglesia Sagrada Familia. See what I mean about brandy snaps?

hands and wished us well on our journey. Perhaps he really was going to miss us, with our bin liners, our long lists of demands, and our seventy two day/eight country car hire requirements.

Or perhaps not.

DAY TWENTY-TWO | TUESDAY 21ST APRIL

Barcelona to Aigua Blava

Before heading north again, we have to take a small detour to see Montserrat.

Perched eagle-high in the sawtooth mountains north west of Barcelona, Montserrat is the main religious and cultural centre of this part of Spain, and attracts hundreds of thousands of tourists and pilgrims. It's a long way up, but it's worth it.

Nestling on a ledge at just under 4,000 feet, the hermitage was founded by the Benedictines in the 9th century, and there is still a community of around eighty monks. Inside the basilica a real sense of calm and agelessness comes over you. We wandered round in silence, looking at the gilt work and dark ornate carvings. In a niche behind the high altar is the Black Madonna, the patron saint of Catalunya, and you climb up a small back staircase to wander past her.

I decided not to kiss her feet; I have to do enough of that at home.

You're then taken down and round, emerging in a cool stone cloister lined with thousands of red flickering votive candles. We lit one for each of our dead parents, and stood quietly for a moment, reflecting. Of all the churches and cathedrals we visited on our tour, we thought the Montserrat Basilica – much less grand than most, much less beautiful than many – was the most peaceful.

Back outside in the wide courtyard, the mountains leap up behind the buildings, piercing the blue, for all the world like a huge wooden stockade around a Wild West fort. Unfortunately the craggy massif wasn't enough to stop Napoleon's troops destroying most of Montserrat in the same year he was having Russian troubles at Austerlitz. Although the buildings don't look that modern, they're mostly 19th and 20th century. Nice one, Boney.

Closer to God – the high citadel of Montserrat.

Now for a bit of R&R from the bustle of Barcelona. We head up the Costa Brava to find our last Parador, at Aigua Blava. This tiny fishing village occupies a bay of azure blue, surrounded by olive-strewn hills and rocky outcrops. The Parador is, surprisingly, modern – a three storey long low flat white block right on the edge of a cliff. It's a bit Frank Lloyd Wright, with levels within levels, fish ponds and small waterfalls inside, and terraced gardens outside. I suppose the state had allowed only themselves to build here, and applied to themselves for planning permission and architectural approval. It's actually quite comfortable, with big, balconied rooms, stunning views and lots of light.

We check in and wander down the cliff path to a small cove, where a pre-season beach bar has three customers, including us. The waves lap gently, we sip quietly, and contentment begins to ebb back as the sun sets on our last day in Spain.

France

*"And so, my Lords,
to our French causes."*

DAY TWENTY-THREE | WEDNESDAY 22ND APRIL

Aigua Blava to Carcassonne

On our way to Carcassonne, we take a diversion through the foothills of the Pyrennees to see if we could discover the truth behind the most shocking religious secret ever.

In their book *The Holy Blood and the Holy Grail*, Michael Baigent, Richard Leigh and Henry Lincoln had posited the theory that Jesus hadn't died on the cross, and hadn't risen into Heaven on the third day; that he had instead collected Mary and taken ship across the Mediterranean, arriving somewhere in southern France. Here they raised a family, the direct descendants of which survive to this day, their identities protected by a secret society.

Quite a theory to take on board, let alone try to prove, but these gentlemen were convinced that the truth lay hidden somewhere around the tiny French Pyrennean village of Rennes-le-Chateau. In the latter part of the 19th century a young priest, Berenger Sauniere, took up the parish and went about his ministry. A few years later a rumour began to circulate that he had found something locally. He suddenly appeared to become very rich, building a large house in the village, and a towered folly on the edge of the hilltop. He was summoned to Paris, where he became very in with the higher echelons of the church, and the rumours grew that what he had discovered was of stunning importance and secrecy.

The authors go into exhaustive detail of their research into the mysterious Order of the Prieuré de Sion, one of the secret societies descended from the Knights Templar of Jerusalem. They name the current Grand Masters and say that the Order exists primarily to protect the identities and persons of the descendants of the Holy Family.

One of the more interesting aspects of their research for me, was their contention that one of the possible Holy bloodlines was the Royal House of Stuart, the Kings of Scotland. This would make my friend James a direct descendant of Christ. Did I tell you some of the locals in Vejer call him Jésus?

It was a fascinating story, and we resolved to find this village. And find the vital missing piece of the jigsaw ourselves, of course.

The road wasn't signposted, so it was more by trial, error and triangulation that we found the winding, single lane road up and around the hill. Right at the top, just when we thought there wouldn't be enough hilltop left to put a village on, we turned a corner and there was Rennes-le-Chateau – perhaps fifty or sixty huddled stone houses, a church, and on the very summit, a dusty car park. The wind whipped up from the plain, moaning through the cypresses, snapping at our coats. There was no one about. We walked across towards the church, and there, behind a copse of trees, was Sauniere's house, Villa Bethania – standing back from an unkempt formal garden, shuttered up and menacing – just like the grainy black and white 20s photo in the book which showed Sauniere and his wife in the garden.

Shivering, we walked towards the church. Above the porch lintel, carved into the stone, is the legend TERRIBILIS EST LOCUS ISTE. This place is terrible.

Charming. The urge to leg it was very strong, but, the church being locked, we went back to the edge of the hilltop where Sauniere's crenellated folly, the Tour Magdala, still stands. Sentry? Beacon? Or holder of dread secrets? We didn't know, and it seemed nobody else did either – the place was deserted, and the book now being nearly twenty years old, perhaps it is a story not meant to be uncovered until the very earth cracks and gives up its secrets. Or something.

As we drove slowly away, I noticed the village shop had a few faded copies of the book in the window. We didn't look back.

The foothills of the Pyrennees melted away, the plains flattened out before us, and we came to Carcassonne. A couple of one-way system hiccups later, we found the Hotel Montsegur, and our first accommodation disappointment of the tour.

I don't know if you've ever tried to get things out of the bottom of a tightly-packed suitcase when it's standing up – believe me it's not

La Cité – a thousand years of defence

easy – but when your room hasn't enough floor space to lay the case flat, you've got to try. The bed had laid claim to 89% of the space, with the rickety side table clinging on to another 7%. There was just enough room for me to turn round and ask Ali if there was space in the bathroom to put the other suitcase. She took one look and burst into fits of laughter.

When you hear the phrase 'wall-to-wall carpeting', you assume a room has a carpet on the floor, and that it touches the walls all round. Not that the walls themselves are carpeted. And the ceiling. Seriously, every inch of wall and ceiling was covered in that sort of rough grey nylon carpet tile. Except the floor, which was a shellac-pink lino. It was like standing inside a Brillo Pad. Goodness knows what horrors the carpeting was put up to hide – and we'd paid over fifty quid for this! Well actually, we'd paid a UK tour operator over fifty quid. No doubt Madame downstairs could retire on the maximum of £8.50 she'd been able to charge them.

Downstairs was not much more cheering. The single public room looked like a funeral directors' laying-out parlour, so we set out to explore the only thing people come to Carcassonne for – La Cité.

It is magnificent – a 10th century fortress, little changed since the Middle Ages – and absolutely gargantuan. I don't know if it's the largest fortified city of its kind in the world, but I wouldn't be surprised; it dominates the skyline, with double ramparts of amazing thickness, over fifty towers and barbicans, and all in remarkably good nick, considering it's been besieged countless times in its life.

Begun by the Visigoths as early as the 5th century, it was added to and enlarged over the next 800 years, and was the main fortified position on the important route between the Med and the Atlantic. I slagged off the French a few pages back for trashing Monserrat, but of course our record is hardly spotless in the trashing department. Crusaders under Simon de Montfort starved out the city in 1209, and no doubt forced some of their beliefs on the survivors; and our own Black Prince Edward had a crack at it during the Hundred Years War. He took one look and decided it was too much trouble, so he completely destroyed the Lower Town. Life might have been simpler back then, but it was bloody cheap.

We enter the city through the eastern gate, the Porte Narbonnaise. Massive curved side walls prevent a frontal assault by battering ram or troop-rush, and then you'd only be in the no man's land between the great walls, attracting arrow fire, boiling oil and dead dogs from every battlement. Inside the main walls is the town itself – a maze of tiny streets and stone houses – which would be charming but for the fact that every doorway is a shop selling postcards, leather bags and huge gleaming metal swords. Do people actually buy these monstrosities ...?

"But what would you *do* with it, Norman?"

"I thought it would go nicely above the fireplace, dear."

"Well it's going to look a bit silly perched above the two-bar. *And* it'll be me that has to clean it. *And* you won't put it up properly and it'll fall off and kill the cat."

Norman's knuckles whiten briefly around the pommel, then he puts it back on the shop rack, and they buy a nice doll with a ruched skirt instead.

Back at the hutch, with a due sense of doom, we ask Madame's advice for dinner. She directs us to the hotel's own restaurant, a few doors down. Nodding politely, and fully intending to walk past it, a glance at the menu outside indicates splendour within, and we give it a try. Aaahhh! We're in France.

When we started the trip I had expected France to produce the best food, but not by the extent it actually did. The meals we had in France were orders of magnitude better than any other country. And in this case, as so often in France, I'd forgotten that the restaurant and the food come first, and if accommodation is offered by the owners, it's an afterthought – a place to sleep it all off, really.

Anyway we had a delicious dinner of the rarest Tournedos (not *le boeuf fou Anglais*), a Grand Marnier meringue thing and a couple of bottles of Pouilly Fumé. Back in the room, in our happy drunken state, we tried making love passionately against the bathroom wall, but we got terrible carpet burns.

THE DORDOGNE

Bordeaux

In which we discover the most deeply lovely private house I have ever seen, have a memorable dinner in St Emilion, and visit a friend's prestigious and carefully-tended six hectares of prime St Emilion vineyards.

Sarlat

In which we visit the Lascaux Caves (except they're not the real ones), the banks of the Dordogne (except they're flooded), The Gouffre de Padirac (in which I suffer from claustrophobia and vertigo simultaneously), Rocamadour's cliff-clinging splendour; 8-foot wingspan Condors smacking me in the head; feeding popcorn to the inhabitants of the Forêt des Singes; and guilty, guilty amounts of fois gras.

And in which we start to discover how much we have been stung by various UK tour operators. We name and shame them.

Cognac

In which nothing happened except rain – and the worst value hotel on the tour.

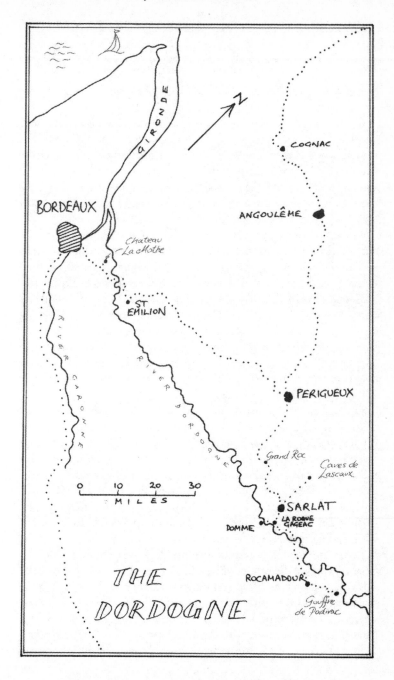

THE
DORDOGNE

DAY TWENTY-FOUR | THURSDAY 23RD APRIL

Carcassonne to Bordeaux

We left Carcassonne early and found the Autoroute de Deux Mers to cross France from sea to shining sea.

We'd arranged to swap cars tomorrow, but we made good time and decided to try and sort it today, leaving more time for wine. We arrived at the *gare* in Bordeaux – not a particularly charming city – and handed back the Citroen Hairdryer. That seems a little cruel – it had done us perfectly okay – but I sometimes think cars should have more interesting names, don't you? The Vauxhall Latrine; The Nissan Smear GTi; the Ford Knob 16v, that sort of thing.

We walked round the corner to the big three – all lined up by the station – to see who wanted our money. After careful research – partly by Paco – and some inquiries into the car insurance situation, we'd said bugger it and decided to hire a Mercedes estate to finish the trip in. Large enough to carry all our stuff, and anything we bought on our way round, but comfortable and reliable enough to actually get us round. Budget didn't live up to their name, and quoted us a silly amount, but Hertz, having finally grasped the concept, hired us a Mercedes 220 Diesel estate for seventy two days (including eight countries and a drop-off in Calais) for what worked out at just over £30 a day. Result, we reckoned.

So, loaded up, we left Bordeaux, which had only been a car-collection point, and headed a few miles inland towards St Emilion. Ali had found, in *Fodor's B&Bs of Charm and Character*, a family-owned chateau that offered rooms. Called LaMothe, we found it just the other side of a small village not far from the lower reaches of the Dordogne. What we found was simply the most beautiful and complete house I had ever seen. An exquisite 12th century chateau, surrounded by its own moat, set in mature parkland. Twin towers, with those gorgeous French blue slate turrets, rose at one end, and the honeyed stone of the rest of the building was covered with ivy, twisting around the bright white shutters.

It's owned by the Bastide family, and they had decided quite recently to renovate three of the rooms and offer them out. We are welcomed by the second daughter, Veronique, who has returned from Paris to help her parents with the new venture. She shows us to our room, which is utterly stunning. A huge jasmine-silked four-poster

Chateau LaMothe. Or something like it.

occupies barely a third of the room, which also has linen-covered side tables, armchairs, dressing tables and wardrobes. Two massive windows open over the moat to the gardens, and the bathroom is hardly smaller, and full of luxury touches. I feel like Marie Antoinette. They have taken a great deal of trouble, and superb taste, to do up these rooms – we asked to see the others, which were no less lovely. All this, and breakfast on the terrace, for under a hundred quid for two. What a find.

We change for dinner (they have recommended a restaurant in St Emilion), and are invited for a drink in the drawing-room before we go out. Monsieur is charm itself, and happy to wait while my French catches up. He bought the chateau in the fifties when it was run down, and, having retired from running the major local Renault dealership, the family is doing everything it can to stay there – and who could blame them? I'd even turn to crime to keep such a treasure. He obviously adores the place, and knows everything about it.

A gentle drive into St Emilion, and we find the Hostellerie de Plaisance, a charming old stone restaurant, where we have the most spectacular, mouthwatering five-course dinner, with wine and coffee, for £62 for both of us. *Compris.*

More of this, please.

TWENTY-FIVE | FRI 24TH APRIL

St Emilion

Wine! Divine miracle, or happy accident of nature? I don't really care, I just love the stuff, and St Emilion is, for many, the wine Mecca. Here, the sun and the rain and the soil combine perfectly to turn humble grapes into a living, breathing wonder; a liquid marvel that has its own infinitely-varied character and expressiveness.

I need to declare two things here. First, I used to be, in another life, a wine merchant, and know a little about it. Second, there's more bollocks talked about wine than almost any other subject. Very few people have the skill and experience to really tell one vineyard's wine from its neighbour's, and talk knowledgeably about micro-climates, the effect of Noble Rot, and what wine you should drink with what, so for most of us, there's only one rule: taste lots of wines, and when you find one you like, buy lots of it and drink it. Jilly Goolden's done a lot for the wine industry, but not much for the language of description:

"*Sniiiiff...* Mmm, yes, I'm getting tarmac, I'm getting the smell of bracken after the rain, there's some molasses in there, *...sniff, sniiifff* ...baby's skin after bathtime, and... wait a moment... yes, blackberry and apple crumble!"

As I said, bollocks. People used to come in to my shop and worry terribly about buying the right wine – whether by label, price or food compatibility. What about taste? Yes, it's a bit silly to slurp a big Chateauneuf with a lighly poached sole, or a thin Pinot Grigio with Steak au Poivre – you won't be getting the most out of any of them – but it really doesn't matter. What matters is to find a wine, or many wines, you actually like drinking, and drink them.

I'd better shut up now – we're off to see a Frenchman who makes world class wine from his own grapes, and I expect he takes it rather more seriously than I do.

A friend of a great friend of mine back home used to work in Life Assurance, but a few years ago she met a French *vigneron* at a conference, married him, and now helps him grow and make some superb wine here in St Emilion. The Moritz family has had six hectares of prime Puiessegin-St Emilion vines, *Pere et Fils*, for generations, and now Jean-Michel is the man in charge. He and Sue greet us outside their lovely rambling farmhouse, Chateau Guillotin, and

Jean Michel Moritz, winemaker.

show us round. Being April still, the vines are only showing the very first flashes of green – *les premiers raisins* – and stand in their neat dark brown rows in the fields around the house. From these six hectares, they produce 40,000 bottles a year of delicious red Bordeaux, which, when they're not pruning, picking or bottling, they drive all round Europe selling at wine fairs and trade shows. You can buy direct from them (we did) or from a number of their agents in various countries, including Britain.

The *vendage* – the harvest – happens in September, and the resulting pressings are taken away in tankers to be bottled. Brought back, they are labelled and capsuled by Jean-Michel and Sue themselves, and placed reverently in the *caves* until they've grown up. Each capsule – the foil seal around the mouth of the bottle – is sold to them as a state tax on each bottle. And another interesting fact – if you grow something in God's green earth, you tend it and water it as required, don't you? Not here – they're not allowed to water the vines. In St Emilion, unlike many other wine areas, growers are banned from irrigating their vines. Apparently it would dilute the noble taste of St Emilion that is famed the world over, or some such bollocks.

They give us a delicious lunch, much of it liquid, and we say goodbye with a glad wave and a bootful of the right stuff.

Not that I'd dream of serving it with cod 'n' chips, you understand.

On our way back to our gorgeous chateau we take a walk round the town of St Emilion. No doubt the streets used to ring with coopers coopering, bottles clinking and carts piled high with juicy grapes rattling past, but now all the actual work is done outside the town, and it's turned very touristy. Attractive it certainly is, with old stone buildings and churches and steep cobbled *rues*, but the wines and *souvenirs des vins* that you'll be sold will be rather expensive. Like the wrought-iron candle holder we bought, and later saw for half the money in Sarlat. Suckers.

Back at LaMothe, I took my diary out into the gardens to try and sketch the chateau. Not too appalling, for only the second sketch I've done in years, but unlike the original, it does look like it's about to fall into the moat.

An American couple are also staying. He's a retired metallurgist, and they travel to France and Italy every year buying pottery and art. At home, when not looking at their collection, they like to go to Las

Vegas. The dollar signs spin in Ali's eyes at this, as she's always wanted to go gambling properly. They give us their card, and say "Now doan y'all come to Vegas without callin' us fer advice furst, y'hear?" They didn't really say it like that, but apparently they know every do and don't about Mammon's home-town, so if we do ever go (100-8 we don't), they're the people to call.

The four of us venture into the village for dinner at a local restaurant, where I dazzle them with my command of the French menu. "Oh, er, don't you like tripe? It's a local delicacy. Try it!"

DAY TWENTY-SIX | SATURDAY 25TH APRIL

St Emilion to Sarlat

Very reluctantly, we wave goodbye to Chateau LaMothe, vowing to return. Jacques Bastide gives us a bottle of his family wine, and we drive away to head up the Dordogne to Sarlat, the weather greying ominously.

We arrive at the Hotel del Selves in the late afternoon. Our room is small and basic, but the hotel has a small indoor pool, and it's only four minutes walk from the centre of this very attractive medieval town.

Market day is winding down as we walk through a very well restored and cared-for town of imposing 15th century sandstone buildings and narrow pedestrianised cobbled streets. Obviously the tourist is king here, and much of the local economy is based around him, and his purchase of walnuts, duck, and of course, fois gras.

Ooh, this is a tough one. I eat fois gras with equal amounts of relish and guilt. I really don't like the way it's made, and don't want more information about its production than I already possess, but I don't quite have the will to ban it from my mouth – it tastes so fantastically, smoothly, creamily, meatily delicious. And since most starters on any Dordogne menu contain a derivative of it, I've got no choice, have I?

I wonder what Ali's going to have?

After a swim and another wander, we have a very pleasant five-course dinner (including fois gras for me) for less than £40 for both of us. Very content, except it has now started to rain.

DAY TWENTY-SEVEN | SUNDAY 26TH APRIL

Sarlat

It's still raining hard, and looks set to continue, but Ali drags me out to look at caves. She apologises for dragging me out, but I love her even more for it, because I (and she) know that I wouldn't normally venture out on a day like this except for a long café lunch.

First stop, the Lascaux Caves, which even I have heard of. We drive up a hill road, through dripping trees to a sodden car park, walk across to a sodden holding area and kiosk, and buy our tickets. The only sound is a low murmur from the queue, and the louder pit-pat of rain on their cagoules. It's only while in this queue that Ali tells me we're not even going to see the real caves, only a Hollywood mock-up of them. Apparently they discovered in the 1960s that the carbon-dioxide breath from thousands of visitors was eroding the limestone and the drawings were fading, so they closed the caves for ten years while they built a complete replica. We would have liked, as with most sites we visited, to wander round at our own pace, but you are led in groups into an antechamber where a guide takes twenty minutes to tell you in French what you've just learned in the guidebook.

The main cave was discovered only in 1940, by a man looking for his lost dog. Inside, untouched and unseen for 15,000 years, they found a rich tapestry of drawings and paintings which led one church leader to describe it as 'the Sistine Chapel of prehistoric times'. One thinks of those dozens of centuries passing by in total darkness and total silence – what's happened in the world since those ancient fingers worked earth and ochre onto their limestone canvases? Practically everything.

After lunch we visit the Grotte du Grand Roc, limestone caverns deep inside a massive bluff at the river's edge. We climb up a steep path, and wait in a bedraggled queue of French tourists for our guide (again). She hands us a limp sheet of paper with what she's going to say, very badly translated into English. It has numbered paragraphs on it, presumably so she can say "And now, for our only two *rosbif* visitors, I am referring to zee number seess. You unnerstan? Yes?" I read the whole sheet in thirty seconds and put it in my pocket.

On we go, into very claustrophobic crystalline caves, glistening and dripping with calcium sludge. Years of misuse and gittish souvenir hunters have forced them to mesh it off, rather like Stonehenge. Did you know that until quite recently, people used to drive to look at Stonehenge, then get back in their cars, drive into Amesbury, hire picks, and come back to hack off a chunk for their hearth?

Here, time's pace has dripped calcium slowly and inexorably into the most unearthly stalagmites and 'tites, and milky, death-white pools and outcrops. It's like *Alien* meets Gollum meets some sort of sugar refining operation. I was beginning to feel like a potholer – the activity I least want to do – so we slipped out of Mademoiselle's lecture and legged it.

We wound our green and damp way back to the hotel, where I managed to find a copy of yesterday's *Times*, and took two coffees and a plate of biccies to read it cover to cover. Ah, Sunday!

DAY TWENTY-EIGHT | MONDAY 27TH APRIL

Sarlat

Still *pleut*-ing, but we're here to explore – so let's explore! Hmm.

We followed the course of this loveliest of rivers, the Dordogne, which no doubt is even lovelier in the sunshine, until we came to Domme, perched above the river on a rocky escarpment. It's a simply charming village that looks like it could have been transported whole from the Cotswolds. We park in the square and suddenly remember that our umbrella is now just so many charred spokes outside Valencia. Can we buy another one here, d'you think? What the hell is French for umbrella? I know it's in there somewhere... er... aha! *Parapluie*, that's it! Even though it's Monday, when most of France is shut, an enterprising lady has put bins of *parapluies* outside her little shop in the main street, so we choose the brightest coloured one we can, in the hope of putting the sun to shame.

Our trusty Michelin gives Domme's panorama three stars, so we wander to the edge of the top square, and there laid out before us, 500 feet below, is the stunning alluvial plain of the Dordogne – lines of poplars and crops, tiny roads and small villages – with the swollen, silvery-brown river gliding at his own sweet will.

Pity about the pouring rain. They'd knock off a star for that.

A coffee, and then on to La Roque de Gagiac, a small village right

on the riverbank, overhung by a vast cliff. And I mean overhung –
most of the houses are actually underneath the top of the cliff. We
have a rather nervous lunch in a small restaurant, and with good
reason – in 1957 a chunk of the cliff came down and flattened part
of the village, and some villagers. And they still live under it.

On to more riverside villages and hamlets. So green, so quiet, so
wet – so we gave it up and returned to the hotel for Scrabble and
some admin; Ali has booked some hotels further on and wants to
check them. And we now realise that all hotels seem to need watching
like hawks.

As we passed through reception this afternoon, I happened to
notice the tariff that was posted up behind the desk. It shows all the
room rates, and I think it's law for it to be up there in plain view, so
everyone knows what they're paying. I did a double-take, because it
seemed to say that our room was 570 francs a night, including
breakfast which was about £60 at the then exchange rate. I checked
with Ali, and we'd paid Cresta, the UK tour operator, £72 a night,
two months ago.

Hang on a minute. I think I might have to get on my high horse
here. Now I wouldn't call myself an experienced traveller, but I'm not
a novice either, and in the past I've made certain assumptions about
hotel rates. I know that there are published 'rack' rates for each hotel.
You call up and ask the rate and they'll tell you their top rate, hoping
you'll be an ordinary punter and pay it. Really experienced travellers,
and companies, never pay rack rates. They know how to ask for deals,
and there are always deals. And of course travel agents and tour
operators have even lower rates, because they're booking in bulk. Fair
enough.

As I've said, on this trip we are just ordinary punters, and I fully
expect and am prepared to pay rack rates. I also fully expect any travel
agent or tour operator to make a profit on any transaction they
perform for me. But I know that they will be getting a fat discount
on any rates they book for me, and that's where their commission lies.
Surely? But it looks like they've been playing both ends against the
middle. After some investigation, I gather that Cresta sends hundreds
of people to the Hotel des Selves every year. Naturally the receptionist
wouldn't tell me what rate they pay, but one would imagine it's no
more than two-thirds of the rack rate. So, say they pay about £40 and
then charge me £72. Over three nights, they make £96 for sending
one fax to the hotel and one voucher to me. I don't know when the

Selves gets its money for our stay (bet it's not in advance), but Cresta had my money two months ago. And we've booked several other hotels on our trip through them, all listed to them in one purchase.

Yes, but, you say. Okay, let's look at the buts. Obviously Quality Travel have got to make their commission, so there's a percentage (15%?), and everyone's got overheads and so on, but as a punter, whichever way you look at it, I feel ripped off. I'm not saying I have been ripped off, because they quoted a price, I paid it, deal done; but I *feel* ripped off.

Digging deeper, I set out to phone each hotel we've stayed in, and each one we've been booked into by Cresta and others, and getting the rack rate for the night or nights we stayed. I then compare it to what we paid, and find to my horror that the Selves is by no means the worst.

Once again I state that they quoted, I paid; and of course caveat emptor, but for the record, here's the list.

Spain

HOTEL	NIGHTS	RACK RATE	WE PAID	WE OVERPAID
Parador, Gijon	1	£88	£110	£22
Parador, Toledo	1	£108	£116	£8
Rincon Andaluz, Marbella	3	£94	£102	£24
Hotel Saray, Granada	3	£47	£82	£105
Hotel Monte Picayo, Puçol	1	£68	£122	£54
Parador, Aigua Blava	1	£80	£98	£18

France

HOTEL	NIGHTS	RACK RATE	WE PAID	WE OVERPAID
Hotel de Selves, Sarlat	3	£60	£72	£36
Domaine de Breuil, Cognac	1	£40	£72	£32
Chateau de Chissay, Loire	6	£82	£100	£108
Le Cottage, Talloires	2	£113	£146	£66
Mont Mellion, Meursault	2	£35	£50	£30

Total paid on these hotels over the top rack rate: **£503**

Having compiled this list, we called Gail at Quality Travel, who confessed herself baffled, and outraged. She said she'd take it up with the tour operators, and meanwhile agreed wholeheartedly with our suggestion that from now on we should book direct.

In many hotel rooms were some of the books their establishments featured in, and whose associations they belonged to – like *Relais du Silence*; *Chateaux et Independents*; *Fodor's B&Bs of Charm and Character*; *Relais & Chateau* (a bit posh); *Leading Hotels of the World*™ (very posh); and the *Good Hotel Guide*. We very quickly learned to pick up the phone and with a mixture of the local language and English, book our own rooms. In some cases, a fax confirmation was required (very easy), but not always, and in every case we were paying no more than the rack rate.

So there you are: as a punter you'll never compete with tour operators on packages, because they include flights and transfers, and sometimes food – but here's my tip for multi-centre travelling: never, ever, book just accommodation via a tour operator. Do it yourself, and you'll save at least the cost of your dinner in each place.

And a decent glass of wine to say up yours with.

DAY TWENTY-NINE | TUESDAY 28TH APRIL

Sarlat to Rocamadour

We leave Sarlat in the rain. I'd like to return in the sunshine, when I'm sure its plumage is brighter.

The weather follows us east on winding roads through villages and communities that have had some bad floods: playing fields and car parks, riverside streets and camp sites are all under water, and the soon-coming and all-vital tourist season will have to be good for them to get through the summer.

We approach the Alzou valley via L'Hospitalité, the only way to arrive in Rocamadour. You wind down off the plateau and this amazing town is there across the gorge, seemingly glued half way up the cliffs above the river. The tiny medieval village nestles against the rock wall, huddled under the towering stones of the castle and chapel above. The 10th century sanctuary, containing seven chapels, has been a place of pilgrimage for a thousand years, and is built over the site where the hermit Saint Amadour burrowed his way into the rock, and away from the world.

From the ramparts of Rocamadour.

We are allowed to gently take our car into the very narrow cobbled street, as we are staying at the Hotel Beau Site, right in the middle. This is a Best Western hotel that Ali found in the French version of the book, and we are shown to a very comfortable suite with great views over the valley. This is costing us £39 per night. Yah boo, Cresta.

The village street (there's only room for one) is lined with the inevitable souvenir, ceramic and art shops, but has a certain charm, and the buildings are lovely. Near our hotel is the Ascenseur – the lift that takes you up to the chapel level, and then a further lift, this time an Otis 45° funicular, which takes you up through the cliff itself on to the plateau. You walk along to the castle, built to protect Rocamadour from overhead attack, and then ten francs lets you out on to the ramparts, which jut out over the town and the valley.

It really is a very long way down. Dr Vertigo here had a few lumpy moments, but it is stunning – as much the view as the mind's attempts to comprehend the courage and techniques of the men who built this sanctuary all those centuries ago.

Ali had picked up a flyer in the village which called to our attention the Rocques des Aigles – a wild bird sanctuary a little further along the plateau. Rather reluctantly I allowed myself to be dragged along, expecting a couple of sparrowhawks and a dyspeptic owl. Actually it was great. They do a lot of research and breeding, and you can walk past big windows full of incubators and laboratories and earnest men in white coats. A snide remark about the French trying to find another bird to get fois gras from earns me a slap.

You walk on to where the cages (large and airy) contain dozens of breeds of hawk, owl, falcon, eagles, kestrels and so on, and then to a stand of trees surrounded by what looked like lots of huge dog kennels. This is where the big boys live – enormous vultures, eagles and some simply gargantuan Andean Condors. As big as sheepdogs, you can hear these birds breathing. We were concerned to see they were tied to their tree stump perches by heavy chains, with only a few square feet to move around in, but we soon learned that they are all let out to fly free around the valley four times a day. And you can watch. The next show for us gawking punters was just about to start, so we lined up to stand around the edge of a large paddock, at either end of which was a wooden grandstand. 'How much to sit in there?', I said, reaching for my wallet, but no, they were for the birds and their handlers.

Monsieur le MC donned his lip-mike and the show began. The great birds were brought out by the handlers on their forearms, and with a sort of discus-thrower's action, the bird was flung into the air. Almost as an afterthought ("oh, al*right*, then!") it lazily unfolded its massive wings and floated effortlessly across the compound. They were magnificent, and once they'd done a couple of across-and-back flights, they were allowed to fly high and free above the valley and the forests. After a while, the air was thick with birds of prey, our host encouraging them and telling us all about them. "Ici Robert", he shouted, pointing to a vast condor flying back towards us from the treetops, "Regard! Robert arrive!" We turned to see, and suddenly it was upon us, growing impossibly large in my camera's viewfinder – then the vast bird flew between us at head height, the tip feathers of its twelve foot wingspan brushing the camera lens. I don't know what its lunch would feel like, running from those talons, but I was scared shitless. What amazing creatures. I hope their life wasn't too awful, and that the stated conservation aims of our hosts were true.

A hawk was brought round to sit on people's heads. Ali backed away, but you can't back away from this sort of audience participation. Then they brought out a large snow-white owl, and bade us listen as it flew across the compound. Nothing. All the other birds had made a soft whooshing sound as they flew, but this owl made absolutely no sound in flight. Utterly silent. If you're a shrew or mouse, at least I suppose you don't know you're lunch until the owl is dabbing its beak with a napkin and calling for coffee.

The skies began to cloud over again, so we walked back down the cliff for an excellent dinner, including scallops in pistachio sauce; you'd have thought the rich sauce would obscure the delicate univalves, but they were wonderful together.

DAY THIRTY | WEDNESDAY 29TH APRIL

Rocamadour

Ali's list of caves continues, but she has left the best till last – La Gouffre de Padirac.

Only two years before the dog-seeker had discovered Lascaux, another cave finder, this time a professional, found a way into what was thought to be a vast underground watercourse and cave system a few miles east of Rocamadour high up in the Massif Central. How large, and how impressive, was to become clear as they probed and roped and slid their way down into the most incredible hole on earth.

You arrive at the site, unfortunately surrounded by nasty cafés, and next to the main building, there's a hole. One hundred feet wide and 250 feet deep, you look down to see tiny people emerging from a lift and walking into a tunnel at the bottom. Oh dear. I've already mentioned my terror of potholing. I wonder if there's a bar down there.

You descend in the lift, and across the bottom of the chasm, and walk down a steep dark tunnel for what seems like ages. With its naked hanging lightbulbs, metal handrails and rough hewn construction, the tunnel looks like a Spielberg film set – I expect to see Indy come running full tilt round the corner chased by a battalion of crack SS stormtroopers. It then flattens out to a path, when suddenly there's a river next to you. And boats. What? We're going on a boat? Oh yes, and you can't back out now. We are piled twenty strong into a shallow canoe, and a guide punts us away along the underground river. We brush the rock and the low light flickers off the water around the cavern. The only sound is the dripping from the walls and the swish of the punter's pole ("*Where iss it, my precioussss? We wantss it.*"). After a few minutes we reach another landing stage, where we pile off and start walking up. The paths here are slick with calcium water run-off, and we can hear the sound of waterfalls ahead. Finally we emerge into the most amazing cave I've ever seen. Cathedral-sized, 300 feet from top to bottom, this is the Hall of the Great Dome, and we have come upon it half way up the walls, on a railed ledge. I never thought it would be possible to suffer from claustrophobia and vertigo at the same moment.

Lit by strategically placed spotlights, this massive cavern has a truly unearthly feel. Sheets of subterranean water flow down calcite-encrusted walls, and milky aquamarine pools gather at every level. Great stalagmites, huge as Cleopatra's Needle, thrust roofwards, and everywhere the drip drip drip of damp, inexorable time.

It was deeply impressive – again for the dedication and courage of its discoverers and developers, but mostly of course for its creator; nature at her most quietly awesome.

DAY THIRTY-ONE | THURSDAY 30TH APRIL

Rocamadour to Cognac

We left Rocamadour with one short visit to make – Le Forêt des Singes – which allowed me to do my Eddie Izzard impression: "*Les singes est dans l'arbres.*" And they were too, although they didn't look too happy in the drizzling rain. We walked alone around this monkey sanctuary, feeding them popcorn (supplied), and thinking it was all a bit seedy. I don't know what they thought.

On, and northwards, to Cognac. I'm not sure why we included Cognac on our intinerary – neither of us are very fond of brandy – and to be brutally honest, we needn't have bothered. The rain didn't help, but there didn't seem to be much worth seeing. There were the great brandy houses of Cognac – Hine, Martell, Hennessy – but they were closed to the public, so we went to find our hotel.

The Domaine de Breuil occupies an imposing building in mature gardens, and it looked as if it had once seen glorious days. But not for a long while; the paint was peeling, the staff were unappealing, and our room was barely above DSS standard. This is only worth about thirty five quid, I thought. Sure enough, the tariff billed it at FF390. Pity we'd already paid P&O Ferries £72 for it. Grrrrr!

Into the town centre to find alcoholic succour. Actually the town centre is rather charming, with pleasant squares, shops and cafés, in one of which we had a coffee and a cognac. Nope, still wasted on me.

Back at the hostel, sorry hotel, we had a remarkably good dinner (food first, remember) which was constantly, and sweetly, interrupted by a five-year-old Dutch girl called Anna. We knew that was her name because she came and told us so every few minutes. We told her our names and said hello, but that was the extent of our knowledge of the others' language. Well, I did know a phrase in Dutch, taught to me at the age of twelve by an au pair, but I didn't think Anna would appreciate it.

Or her parents.

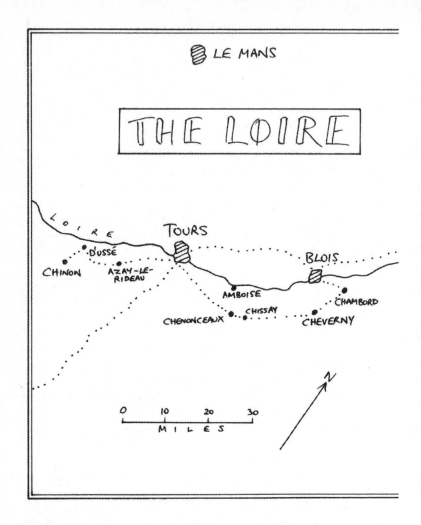

THE LOIRE

The Chateaux
In which we bag seven chateaux, all of which are damper than billed. The Loire and the Indre have burst their banks. We also visit the Futuroscope theme park, Tours and Blois.

Disneyland Paris
In which we drive 150 miles out of our way to get mugged by the Mouse.

Chartres
In which there's a nice window.

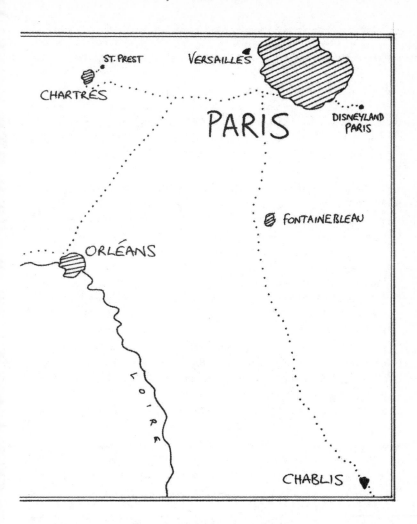

Versailles

In which we wander awestruck around the most glorious expression of France at her most majestic.

Chablis

In which we discover this most French of villages, and stay in a charming hostellerie where our room (for two) costs about the same as our main course (for one).

DAY THIRTY-TWO | FRIDAY 1ST MAY

Cognac to The Loire

We joined the queue of guests waiting to check out of the Domaine de Breuil at 06.30. We didn't really, but there wasn't much to keep us there, so we hit the A10 early. We arrive in the Loire valley shortly after lunch, and check into the Chissay, our hotel for the next six days, while we bag as many chateaux as we can. I've never 'done' the Loire, and have always looked forward to it. Hope the weather clears.

The Chateau de Chissay claims it's in the shadow of Chenonceau – it would have to be a very long shadow – but is an imposing hunk of stone around a large courtyard. We are shown to a room right at the top (no lift), which is alright, but not what I'd call £100 worth. Of course, it's not, it's top-priced at less than £80. Here we go again.

Left to explore, we find a rather charming bathroom, actually inside the eastern tower. It's circular, with mosaic walls throughout, and has all the usual cons, except... where's the loo? What's in here?... aha! Oh. A small cupboard, the opening no more than 5'10" high (I'm 6'5") leads to a flight of four steps, right at the bottom of which is a loo. And I mean right at the bottom – the porcelain pedestal touches the bottom step. Apart from the fact that the door doesn't fit the jamb, and should be re-named 'piece of wood that's slightly in the way', I genuinely can't work out how either of us is going to use this in-convenience. Ali is laughing so hard she has to sit on the bath. Asking her to wish me luck, I start down the steps. Now... what you probably have to do ... *oof* ... is hunch over (minding your head), shuffle round backwards ... *ungh* ... while standing on the second bottom step, grab hold of the loo roll holder, and sort of ... *aargh* ... fall backwards onto the seat. Sorted. Now, how the hell am I going to get my trousers down?

It really was going to be a problem, so, what with the room rate gap, I venture down to reception to make a bit of a fuss. The rate isn't the hotel's fault of course – they've had to accept a lot less than rack rate from P&O Ferries – but I explain our worries, and that we are going to be here for six days. Monsieur apologises, but he is full this evening. He will try to move us tomorrow if he can. Fair enough.

Again, the hotel's restaurant is of a much higher standard than the rooms and we have a very good dinner, and because we're now in the Loire, a couple of bottles of Ladoucette Pouilly Fumé.

DAY THIRTY-THREE | SATURDAY 2ND MAY

The Loire

Chenonceau is France's second most popular attraction, second only to Versailles in terms of tourist numbers, and welcomes 9,000 people a day in the summer season. This is a holiday weekend, so even though the weather is grey and there are floods all round the Loire valley, there are already many hundreds of cars in the car park when we arrive shortly after ten.

It's a very slick operation. Owned for several generations by the Metier family (apparently of chocolate fame), the whole experience, from manicured and lawned car park to brisk and efficient ticket office shows that ancient and noble surroundings don't have to be unbusinesslike.

You walk up a long tree-lined avenue, and there, rising from the lawns and flowerbeds, are the honeyed stone walls and blue slate roofs of the chateau – not the prettiest or most symmetrical, and by no means the biggest – but perhaps the most richly satisfying of all the chateaux of the Loire.

We swing left along the great square of slightly sunken formal gardens, to widen our view of the building. The main body of the chateau rises from the banks of the Cher river, with a drawbridge over the moat to a small gravel yard in front of the main door. Towers and turrets climb the corners of the building, and then we see the wonderful triple-storeyed flying wing reaching across the river to the far bank. Several arches support these halls, and the foresight of the designers is obvious as we see the swollen Cher, perhaps as high as it's ever been, rushing headlong at the stone arch supports, bulging waves of brown water trying to carry it away downstream.

Inside, very chic white-gloved and grey-suited girls are in attendance to answer questions, but they leave you alone to wander around. Highlights include the kitchens – although rather precise – the delightful chapel, and the superb long gallery over the river. The stone flags in the window bays are worn down into dips by centuries of people stepping up to the leaded panes to look out across the water. Apparently, during the First World War, old man Metier housed over 2,000 wounded soldiers in these halls, looking after them with his own doctors.

Upstairs the grand bedrooms, where so many crowned and self-crowned heads have slept, are impressive, particularly the third floor chamber of Louise de Lorraine, who, widowed from Henry III, came here to meditate and die. It took her fourteen years, which considering the deep black silk drapes and dark panelling seems a long time. I'd have topped myself on the first night in that room. My brother, who has a sixth sense for the eerie, wouldn't have been able to walk into it. Very creepy.

Outside again, we walk round to the other side of the gardens to see the chateau from the back. Looking over the stone parapet edging the river, I can see the banks of floodlights, screwed to the wall below me, that obviously cover the building with light at night. Not for long, if they don't unhook them – the swift-flowing river is only a few inches from the lowest cable.

Leaving Chenonceau – hoping they're all as impressive – we head north to the town of Amboise, with its chateau perched on an escarpment on the edge of the Loire itself.

Lunch first, in a pleasant bistro in the old town, under the very walls of the chateau. It was built as a Royal Residence by Charles VII, but he died at the age of twenty eight after hitting his head on a low beam (I know how he felt). Francois I carried on with its decoration, bringing a certain Italian artist from Florence to help him – Leonardo da Vinci. He was installed in a house in the town; the ultimate 'little man from the village'. Actually, he didn't do much. By now 64, the great man mostly sat in his shed sketching hovercraft and helicopters and other ludicrous far-fetched machines.

The chateau itself is rather ghostly, being neither as complete or as furnished as many others. Large parts of it were destroyed by various Republiques, and the only really interesting part is the amazing spiral horsecase that rises from the river level up into the castle 250 feet higher – a cobbled path that could take mounted cavalry riding up or down to defend against, or retreat from, attackers. If it wasn't lovely old stone and cobbles, I could descibe it as like the exit ramp from a multi-storey car park.

We followed the river downstream to Tours, the main city of the Loire. Large and bustling, it contained nothing of architectural interest, so we shopped. Kickers for Ali, and tape and film for me.

Back to our chateau to find they had very kindly moved us to a room more in keeping with what we'd paid. It was lovely – huge and airy, big bathroom with easily accessible facilities (room to swing your pants once you'd got them off) – and situated in the other corner of the castle, where there *was* a lift.

"*Merci, Monsieur le patron.*"

"*Je vous en pris, Monsieur.*"

The Loire

To the south west today, to visit what I've always considered (in photographs, anyway) the most beautiful of the chateaux – Azay-le-Rideau.

Unfortunately, the Loire basin has had double its usual ration of rainfall this spring and small tributaries, like the Indre, have burst their banks. Azay result, Rideau's normally tranquil moat has disappeared somewhere beneath the wide brown river that is now flowing across the lawns and up to the castle walls. Most of the gardens are underwater, and the mill race past the front of the building is a raging torrent. It seems like a matter of minutes before it will start flowing over the bridge instead of under it. All the water lilies have drowned, and the floodlights, unlike Chenonceau, have actually been covered.

Inside, Azay is not actually very interesting, except for the King's Bedroom, which has a stunning 17th century parquet floor. The open staircase all the way up the front of the chateau is visually fascinating, but must have been hell to heat.

On to Chinon, a pretty town on the banks of the Vienne, dominated by the massive ruins of the castle on the hill above. We have lunch in a restaurant overlooking the river, and then walk on up to the chateau. In the dry moat, as we cross over the drawbridge, are a trebuchet and a mangonel – the large wooden engines of ancient beseigement. You've seen them in movies – you put a large boulder or flaming ball of tar into the cup, pull the lever, and the counterweight flings the projectile up over the castle walls. If you were feeling particularly nasty that day, you'd strap a couple of diseased cows on, and try and poison the defenders. Or if you got really pissed off that they wouldn't surrender, you'd burn their surrounding town and families.

These machines were obviously fake – used for ceremonies and demonstrations – but they were full size and interesting, and gave Ali the chance for a short sleep while I told her the above.

Inside the ramparts it's mostly a ruin, with very few whole buildings. Henry II of England and his wife Eleanor of Aquitaine built the castle, and it was their favourite residence. Richard the Lionheart is supposed to have made his way here in 1199, wounded and dying, and died in a house in the town below.

However the main importance to the French is that it was in a hall of this castle (the floor and some pillars remain) that Joan of Arc came in 1429, and picked out from a row of anonymous courtiers the Dauphin of France, who was rather cravenly hiding from his destiny.

"You are the heir of France and true son of the King," she said, "So get your aristocratic shit together and show some backbone!"

Or something like that.

Shortly afterwards she showed who had the real bollocks in France, and got her tootsies toasted for posterity.

Anyway, it's a good story, thoroughly spoiled by the utterly nauseating waxwork tableau they've installed next door to show how it all happened. Madame Tussaud would be ashamed by the motley collection of shop dummies in gaudy pink and yellow chiffon costumes. Yuk.

From our guide book, and a glossy brochure we'd picked up in the hotel, we thought Chateau D'Ussé would be interesting. This is supposed to be the original Sleeping Beauty castle, proud and high-turreted against the backdrop of the enchanted forest. The chap who wrote the original fable is rumoured to have stayed here and, inspired, written his story. Well, it's certainly attractive, and it does back on to a forest, but we weren't impressed by their efforts to impress us.

First, they charged us 65 francs each to get in – double what any other chateau wanted – then we were made to wait outside for fifteen minutes until the previous tour had finished. This better be good, I murmured, not quite under my breath. It wasn't. A rather apologetic young man spent half an hour shepherding us round very few rooms, full of desperate *objets* and faded tapestries, none of which were original. We finished by going up a staircase dotted with more appalling waxwork mannequins, this time depicting the Sleeping Beauty story. I began to feel rather sorry for our guide (we had come to suspect he was a junior member of the family, who had to rally

The temporary island of Azay-le-Rideau.

round and give the punters a show for their six quid) and he ended our short and lukewarm tour by thanking us and *holding out his palm* as we filed out! Alright, he can't have been a member of the family. Then again, the only way out was through the shop, so....

We left Chateau D'Useless to count our money, and returned to the hotel for another excellent dinner. I had *l'escargot profiteroles* with quails eggs (don't try this at home), a superb Carré D'Agneau, and a mouthwatering chocolate thingy. Ali had a small green salad.

Well, we were getting married in three months, and she felt her nineteen inch waist needed a trim.

Girly.

DAY THIRTY-FIVE | MONDAY 4TH MAY

The Loire

A complete change of time and pace today, as we headed 100 kilometres south west to spend a day at Futuroscope.

We'd passed it on the A10 on our way up from Cognac, and since most of France is closed on Mondays, including many of the chateaux, we decided to give it a go.

The vast car park was only a tenth full, which boded well – I don't like crowds – and indeed there weren't that many people about. The park is huge, and is basically a showcase and fun park for futuristic entertainment technology, a lot of it based around film. Dotted around the campus are large buildings showing various films at twenty or thirty minute intervals. Highlights included a stunning film shown on a huge screen, about Alaska, narrated by Charlton Heston; a film about fish, where they have screens under your feet as well, giving an excellent floating impression; and a 360° cinema, where you stand in a big circular auditorium. The walls all around you have the film projected on them, which they shot with a special cylindrical ten-lens camera. It's a weird sensation as you are carried round on your heels by the action, but very impressive.

Then the one I was looking forward to – the IMAX 3D. I'd always wanted to see this, and the film they were showing was *Wings of Courage*, directed by Jean-Jacques Annaud, and starring Val Kilmer and Tom Hulce. The story is of the remarkable courage (and frankly stupidity) of the pilots who flew the mail across the Andes, and the 3D effect is absolutely stunning, particularly (and surprisingly) in the close-up personal bits as well as the action sequences. However the whole thing was spoiled for me by a piece of collossal French arrogance. Annaud had shot the movie in English, to cater for an international market, and they'd dubbed it into French for this audience. Fair enough, but they'd put the French dub straight onto the film, and the headsets we were provided with, to give us the English, had obviously not had the original soundtrack fed to them. It was patently on another track, and at least a second out of sync.

I would love to see it as the (French) director intended.

Outside in the emerging sunshine – *incroyable* – we climbed into what looked like a ferris wheel lying on its side. It was a large circular observation platform which rose up a massive tower to a height of 200 feet and revolved, so you could see the whole park laid out below. It was like being on Kubrick's space station in *2001*.

Eyes wide from screen-staring, we wandered out of the park, pausing only not to buy any merchandise. Unfortunately there hadn't been a Star Wars ride, otherwise I'd have been able to say to Ali, "May the Fourth be with you."

A long sunny return drive, through fields shining bright yellow with oil-seed rape, and back to our comfortable room.

DAY THIRTY-SIX | TUESDAY 5TH MAY

The Loire

The jury is still out on this hotel, but it received a shock piece of evidence this morning. They have four stars plastered over all their headed paper and literature, but when faced with laundry, they folded like a damp *mouchoir*. We only wanted a few shirts and pants washed and ironed, but Gallic shrugs all round. They said they'd see what they could do.

I sometimes think the number of stars some hotels have has something to do with how bored the local signwriter is.

Today, chateaux six and seven.

Sorry, but I must pause here to tell you where one of our oldest

Chateau Cheverny – inspiration for Marlinspike Hall.

expressions comes from, because I bet you don't know. You've heard of the Guilds of the City of London – Goldsmiths, Silversmiths, and so on; they were founded as trade associations hundreds of years ago, for the various master craftsmen and their apprentices – and they still process through the city behind the Lord Mayor every year. Well, back in the 15th century the Lord Mayor's Procession happened on the Thames, with each of the twelve great City Companies having their own barge. In 1485 there was a fight over precedence. No one disputed the order of the first five Companies, but both the Skinners and the Merchant Taylors thought they should be sixth, and that year there was a pitched battle on the river – they rammed each other with their barges, and several people were killed.

The Lord Mayor of the day, Robert Billesdon, said "Okay, chaps, that's enough of that. I hereby decree that from henceforth one company will be sixth in precedence one year, and the other shall be sixth the next. And in each year of their precedence, the sixth shall entertain the seventh to a banquet." The companies still exist today, and still hold the Billesdon Banquet every year. And hence the expression 'at sixes and sevens'.

Well, any excuse for a good story.

Right, back to our sixth chateau – Cheverny. It's a delightful 17th century Louis XIII building of white stone and pleasing symmetry,

Chambord – Francois I's little place in the country.

but what delighted me most was that it's Marlinspike – you know, Captain Haddock's ancestral home in the Tintin books. And it actually is; apparently Hergé either stayed there, or visited, and based Haddock's house on it. A long tree-lined gravel drive between verdant green lawns leads arrow-straight to the house, so we did our Tintin and Haddock walk up it, feeling like the Start-Rite kids.

Inside it's been beautifully restored, and is full of interesting furniture, suits of armour and some fearsome iron killing tools. The place is still owned by descendants of the original family, and looming over the sweeping staircase is the largest moose's head I've ever seen. It must have been very pissed off. Probably still is.

In the large grounds there's an orangery with an arty crafty shop in it, selling contemporary paintings and sculpture, while further round, by the river, is a tethered balloon where they offer 'flights' over the park, with great views of the chateau. Apparently. Of course, it was too windy to fly today.

And now, finally, for Chambord. An ambition to visit since I did a project on it when I was twelve, this is the most massive, arrogant, stupid, bottom-wincingly wasteful building in the world.

It's simply magnificent, considering it's just a hunting lodge.

When Francois I came to the throne of France at the age of nineteen, he realised how rich he really was, and, like all French kings, having a liking for hunting in the forest of Sologne, decided to build a dream palace at the forest's edge with which to impress his guests.

Begun in 1519, many of the greatest French and Italian architects worked on it, including, rumour has it, Leonardo. Certainly the massive double-helix open staircase in the centre of the building has the stamp of genius. However, not long after major construction had begun, Francois was captured in battle, and after his ransom, deemed it more prudent for the king to live nearer Paris. The chateau was eventually finished – it took most of his thirty two-year reign to complete – but he only ever spent twenty seven nights here.

It is a house of Brobdingnagian proportions (I've always wanted to say that in context – never been able to). The four great corner towers enclose an incredible amount of floor space, and there's nothing in it. Never furnished, the house is just vast room after vast room – the odd tapestry here and there – and everywhere, carved into stone lintels, mantlepieces and ceilings, is the twisting symbol of Francois' salamander. They say the house has 365 chimneys, one for every day of the year. So, 338 more than Francois ever needed.

One final piece of trivia – I'm not saying this is a big estate, but the park in which Chambord stands is surrounded by a stone wall that is the same circumference as the Periférique road around Paris.

It was wonderful to finally see Chambord, but the dreams of childhood are never as golden in reality, and the sheer scale and uselessness of it made me want to cheer and weep at the same time.

DAY THIRTY-SEVEN | WEDNESDAY 6TH MAY

The Loire

Today was rather frustrating on many fronts. We had to do a fair amount of admin – still sorting the fire insurance, and booking ahead for hotels – and to cap it all the Mercedes developed a rattle. Hertz sent a man out to look at it, who shrugged charmingly and could do nothing, so Hertz said would I please take it in to Blois and get it looked at by the local Merc dealer. Cheek!

Actually, it quite suited us. We needed to get the Jensen-aftermath photos developed, and buy a few things, so in we went. The car got sorted quite quickly (loose exhaust), and we got the photos developed

– at more than twice the price they'd be at home. "I know", said the white-gloved man behind the counter, "Many British say this, but this is what it costs me."

Back to Chissay, where we discuss an itinerary change. Tomorrow we are due to take a leisurely drive to our next stop, Chartres, but since the French have another Bank Holiday on Friday, I thought we'd go tomorrow instead.

"Go where?" says Ali.

"Where I'd planned to take you on Friday as a surprise."

"WHERE?"

"Disneyland."

"Wheeeeeee!!!"

So that went down well, then. It means a long, looping drive around the bottom of Paris, and then back again at the end of the day, round to Chartres – but anything for a shag.

Just a couple of momentos to carry away with us. In Montrichard, the village near the Chateau Chissay, is an inn called Tête Noir – it might be an idea to avoid eating at the Hotel Blackhead – and when I rang the Hertz Emergency Line to tell them about the Merc, the on-hold music was *Song for Guy*. Well, it tickled me.

DAY THIRTY-EIGHT | THURSDAY 7TH MAY

The Loire to Disneyland to Chartres

"*Hi there, ho there, hey there, it's a Disney kinda day.*"

Oh dear.

Actually I've got a sneaking admiration for The Mouse and his empire. Although I don't like crowds (nothing would have induced me to come tomorrow, on a Bank Holiday), I do acknowledge that the Disney quality is orders of magnitude higher than other 'attractions', so you have to queue.

We got to Marne-la-Vallée at eleven, after a two hour drive around Paris, and parked in the largest car park I've ever seen. With Ali writing on her hand whereabouts we'd parked, we went up the central walkway towards the park. Forty-five quid lighter, we enter the Magic Kingdom, Ali's eyes shining with delight.

There are a thousand stories about Disney. One I liked was that when the park was nearly complete, the French said "Of course, the signs will be in French first and English second, n'est ce pas?" Disney said "Oh, no you don't, buddy, and if you insist, we'll level the park and build in England instead." It's obviously not true, as the signs are in French first, but I don't doubt for a moment that they'd have done it. Everyone in any sort of related business knows you don't mess with the Mouse.

The other story, which is true, is one of the smartest pieces of business I've ever come across. In the American parks, you can buy Disney Dollars. As you go in, there are kiosks selling these Dollars, which are nicely printed, look like real money, but have Mickey and Donald on them. They cost a dollar each, and they are legal tender inside the park for everything you want to buy – food, drinks and merchandise. So, as a father, you buy a fistful for your kids, don't you? Doesn't cost you any more, and they think they're cool. They might even think you're cool too, but let's not push it. So you all have a wizzo time, and at the end there's a few Disney dollars left in the party. And you can cash them in, of course – one Disney Dollar for every green back. But you don't, do you? Each kid wants a couple to take home – stick on their corkboards, show their mates at school – so you let them keep a few, as a reminder of a great day.

You paid a dollar each for them. What d'you think it cost Disney to print them? Three cents? Five? They make tens of thousands of dollars (real ones) a day – just from pieces of paper. Very smart.

We start on the paddle steamer, which makes its gentle way round the lake, so you can get a good look at all the other rides you'd like to try. Thunder Mountain is a must, and we queue for forty minutes (grump!) to go on it. Ali's not sure about it – the train thunders and rattles in, around and through the centre of the mountain at great speed – but she's soon whooping and laughing with everyone else.

Pirates of the Caribbean is good fun – they do this sort of thing supremely well – and then lunch in Walt's, the slightly posher restaurant on Main Street, in which I had one of the best-cooked pieces of salmon I've ever had. Remarkable.

When I first went on Star Tours, in California, it had only just opened, and I had to queue for two hours. Yes, it was fantastic, but practically nothing's worth queueing two hours for. This time there was virtually no queue, so we went on it twice – unheard of, and great fun. Then Ali made me go on It's A Small World After All, a mistake

Sleeping Beauty's castles – Disneyland Paris, and (inset) Chateau D'Ussé.

she's yet to live down. You sit in a tiny plastic boat (I should have been warned by the fact that I could hardly get my arse in the seat, so designed was it for small bottoms), and then you're floated gently through an aircraft hangar stuffed with twenty-five thousand cabbage patch dolls singing "It's a small world after all". After about thirty seconds I'd have handed over to anyone who asked my bank details, deeds to the house, first born male child – *anything* to make it stop.

And finally, the Disney Parade. "*Hi there, ho there, hey there, it's a Disney kinda day,*" blare the loudspeakers, as the dancers dance and the floats float. Or don't, actually. The driver of Sleeping Beauty's float – presumably hidden behind all the papier maché with two tiny eyeholes to steer through – didn't make the corner onto Main Square and dinked a lamp post.

The song through the speakers is synch'd to whichever section of the parade is in front of you, so there was some rushing about, and uniforms with walkie-talkies trying to sort out the traffic jam, Disney smiles fixed in place. The trouble was, the float was a two-piece, and backing it up took more skill than our chap had. They sorted it out eventually, with shunting and shoving – Beauty and her handmaidens swaying on their heels on the platform above – but combined with the Thunder Mountain train breaking down earlier in the day, it was a poor display. It would never happen (or not so publicly) in America. Walt would not have been amused.

All in all, of course, it's a very entertaining day. Ali got her Mickey balloon and Disneyland Paris beach towel, and we wandered out contentedly into the evening sunshine.

I still smell the whiff of Stepford, though.

A long, and pre-holiday traffic-jammed trip back around Paris to the tiny village of St Prest, a few miles short of Chartres, where we check into Le Manoir Pres du Roy, a charming old farmhouse. Our room is fine, and we end a long and happy day with l'escargots in garlic butter, seafood panache and orange-flower crème brulée.

And so to sleep ...

...."*Hi there, ho there, hey there, it's a...* "

Shut UP!!!

DAY THIRTY-NINE | FRIDAY 8TH MAY

Chartres

A long lazy morning reading a *Telegraph* I'd picked up somewhere, and completing the insurance claim form, then into Chartres for lunch, with the sun high.

The window is stunning of course, and the cathedral is vast and cool inside, but altogether less soul than Monserrat. It does look impressive from a distance, though – from almost any direction you approach Chartres, the spires rise from the flat plains, piercing the sky like a tall ship.

I sat in the cathedral square attempting a sketch – which spectacularly failed to capture any of the majesty of size or artistry of the building – while Ali wandered around the little shops and cafés that border the close.

Back to our rustic and peaceful Manoir for tea and Scrabble on the lawn.

Very civilised.

DAY FORTY | SATURDAY 9TH MAY

Chartres to Chablis

Our destination this evening is Chablis, turning south again, and heading down the wine route to the Cote d'Azur.

But first, like moths to a flame, Versailles.

I can't put it better than Michelin, so I won't try: 'Versailles is the creation of the French monarchy at the moment of its greatest splendour...the definitive monument of French classicism.' They go on to quote Pierre Gaxotte: 'Versailles taught Europe the art of living, good manners and well-bred behaviour, wit, love of truth, tolerance, human values, a love of beauty and of work well done, the secret of being rather than merely seeming, and a concern that all should shine.'

That should be enshrined in the European Constitution.

We arrive in Versailles via a rather tortuous route, and some odd signage, eventually joining a traffic jam composed entirely of vintage

Renaults. I suppose I'd never really thought of there being any Renaults much before the Alpine, but there were some wonderful old bangers chugging along, on their way to, as we discovered, a rally in the wide open fields to the south of the palace.

Once we'd got past them, we eventually found a parking space in a small square a few yards to the north of the main entrance, only to find that the meter had gone to lunch.

As I expect you know, most of France takes a two hour lunch – very civilised if you live there, very frustrating if you're travelling (they also seem to have dozens of extra Bank Holidays, not just Mondays either, and of course Paris hangs a sign out during the whole of August saying, "There's nobody here to sell you anything or feed you, so you might as well sod off").

What we didn't realise was that parking meters take lunch too. From twelve to two you can park for free. Very nice thank you, but you can't feed them, so if you arrive, as we did, shortly before one, wanting to stay the stated maximum of four hours, you can't – they won't take your money. They're happily moving onto the cheese, and are damn well going to have a little nap before opening up again.

We decided to hope that *les wardens de traffic* took even longer lunches, and legged it.

Versailles is awesome on an altogether higher plane of awesomeness. I'd always thought of Chambord as the ultimate expression of French culture and over-the-topness, but Versailles dwarfs it in panache, exuberance and blinding gilt – if not in arrogance.

We walk up the wide expanse of the Ministers' Court, over cobbles the size of footballs, and past the great statue of Louis Quatorze, horse and king rampant in oxidised green. You're then faced with a choice of house or gardens, and the queues looked fairly hefty for the palace, so we decided to start outside.

You wander through the archway to the gardens, which open out onto a stunning vista of the parkland and lakes. Unfortunately we turned round to look at the main façade of the palace, which had looked spectacular in the brochure. Today – 400 feet of scaffolding all across it.

Bien sur.

We then – further irony – discover that the wonderful water music and fountains display, *Les Eaux de Musique*, happens on Sundays. Ah well, the sun is shining, and the lawns and flowers are at their most spring-like, so we wander tranquilly through the most stunning formal gardens on the planet.

Down the sweeping cascade of steps to the Apollo Basin, the vast fountain pool centred with a spray of bright gold horses and figures, Apollo in his chariot dominating. Beyond stretches the impossible length of the Grand Canal, seemingly going on for ever – which was probably the aim of its designers in 1667, to mirror the illimitable depth of the King's domain. From the round pool at the start of the Grand Canal you can take *un petit train*, which hums its peaceful way around the garden paths. We got off at the Petit Trianon, where the Queen had a private suite of rooms, and could escape, or be quietly sidelined, from the Court and the affairs of state. It's the most perfect Georgian style house, and unlike anywhere else in Versailles, one can imagine living there. Yeah, right.

And now for the main palace. It's so huge that for a short visit you have to ration yourself to just the state apartments in the North Wing, and the Hall of Mirrors. You also have to adjust to shuffling round, sheep-like, with 10,000 other punters. The trick is to look up.

The ceilings and chandeliers are quite breathtaking. Vast canvasses of sweeping majesty dominate the main rooms – acres of classic figures, cherubs, nymphs, shepherds and angels cavorting or reclining against pink and orange fluffy clouds. Not quite the Sistine Chapel, but more for your money. Each niche and bureau-top has a bust on it, usually of the Sun King himself, and then you are herded at last to the Hall of Mirrors. Built over twenty-something years from 1670, this vast long gallery is a blinding testament to the excesses of the monarchy. Every tall smoky mirror and every shard and filament of the massive chandeliers catches the light, and the rays of the setting sun, so that no courtier or visiting foreigner then, nor slack-jawed tourist today, could be in any doubt that they were in the presence of majesty.

Standing by one of the twenty-foot windows that overlook the gardens, I watch as a large American, in shorts and gaudy T-shirt, enters at one end of the Hall and walks slowly down its entire sparkling length to the far door, and exits, never once having raised his eyes from the viewfinder of his camcorder. Perhaps he's been through lots of times, seen it with his own eyes, and is only now coming back to video it.

By all that's holy, I hope so.

Lining the southern aspect of the palace, facing the sun, are Marie Antoinette's apartments. Her bedroom and its ornate facilities and decoration (all for one person) gives tangible understanding to the Revolution, the music from which is still reverberating around our heads from our twentieth exposure to *Les Miserables*: "*No song unsung, no wine untasted*", sings Fantine, summing up the life of those chosen, golden, few.

And so, south again, avoiding Paris. Perhaps this was a travesty on a European tour, but we'd wanted to try and see as much as we could of less accessible places while we had a car, and Paris is now so near on the excellent Eurostar. So down the smooth A6 to Chablis we go, as the clouds melt away and at last it is summer.

Long comfortable and prosperous on wine, this sleepy town was perhaps the most outwardly French we'd visited. Pleasant market squares, a classic Hotel de Ville with tricolour flying, lovely stone buildings, and willow-draped river, all surrounded by undulating hills of precious vines.

We found our hotel, Le Hostellerie de Clos, in a side street near the main square. A delightful lawned courtyard is edged by a huge stone barn, containing the breakfast room, and the main building with its shuttered windows and smart green awnings. The rooms themselves are small and functional – ours is only £30 – because once again the main glory of the establishment is its restaurant. Michel Vignaud owns and presides – he is featured in a bedside booklet of leading French chefs – and indeed a glance at the menu's prices confirms his reputation. We change, and amble downstairs for a pre-prandial snifter in the garden.

On the basis that the room is only thirty quid, we decide to splurge. Ali has a starter of the most delicate *saumon tartare*, beautifully presented with a raw quail's egg placed upturned in its half-shell in the centre. I have *escargots au epinards*, simple and superb. Ali then follows with *langoustines de maison*, and I have lobster, huge and perfectly grilled, with drawn butter and a panache of exquisite vegetables. A crème brulee of Elysian lightness is my pudding choice, while Ali has a chocolate marquise she professes to be "fab". Coffee and hand-crafted petit fours follow, at which point the maestro himself, M. Vignaud, comes out of his kitchen to walk round all the tables enquiring after his clients' digestive wellbeing. We nod, almost in supplication, and this god of gastronomy, having flit, moves on.

The lobster was, at £28, the most expensive main course I've ever ordered. I thought of having it stuffed, but then that would make two of us.

DAY FORTY-ONE | SUNDAY 10TH MAY

Chablis

A gorgeous summer morning, with a freshly-laundered blue sky entirely free of clouds – can this be set now?

Breakfast in the garden, followed by a walk through town, and a bustling market in the main street. Rather too many recently-deceased rabbits and pig's trotters on display than Ali would like, so we ducked into the cool tasting rooms of Daniel Defaix, maker and purveyor of fine Chablis. Defaix is represented exclusively in the UK by my old friend Max Graham-Wood, whose wine merchant shop in Burnham Market in Norfolk is a treasure-house of rare and delicious finds. He has recommended that we call on his friend, so, not needing much prompting, we taste a variety of golden glasses, emerging with a mixed case of nectar Premier Cru.

After lunch I establish myself at a table in the corner of the garden, sketch pad and charcoal pencils arranged just so, and attempt to look as if I know what I'm doing while I have a crack at some of the chateaux it was too cold to draw on the Loire. Occasionally a guest wanders over, is polite enough not to wince audibly, and wanders away again.

In the evening, another mouthwatering dinner from the skillet of M. Vignaud – the *beurre au Chablis* sauce with my *truite de saumon* is a poem – and then an early night. Ali falls gently asleep during the CNN evening news, and I flick over to TNT to catch a few minutes of Brando, chin high and accent clipped, having fun with the script in *Mutiny on the Bounty*:

"I believe I did what honour dictated, and that belief sustains me.... apart from a slight desire to be dead, which I'm sure will pass."

SAÔNE AND RHÔNE

Beaune

In which we refuse to stay in our booked (and paid for) horrid hotel, and find instead a lovely one a few miles away. Vast old stone buildings, pool, and the best dinner of the tour. We wander around this charming wine town, soak ourselves in glorious Burgundies in tiny villages with world-class names, and are persuaded to buy one or two. Cases.

Lake Annecy

In which we discover a stunning lake-side village with a peaceful hotel and superb food. An old friend joins us from his Geneva work conference, and agrees to transport our wine home. We take to the waters in a hired dinghy with a worrying name, and drive up into the mountains to Courchevel, where one of the world's busiest ski resorts is utterly, and spookily, deserted.

DAY FORTY-TWO | MONDAY 11TH MAY

Chablis to Chagny

A short journey this morning down to the start of the wine region proper, and a turn off to Gevrey-Chambertin, where we have *croque monsieur frites*, and a glass of the '95.

On through Beaune, which we will explore tomorrow, to tiny Meursault, home of my favourite wine, and, it turned out, my least favourite hotel.

The Hotel Mont Mellion has no stars that I can see, which is quite an achievement; usually running water gets you two stars. Madame – a cross between Kathy Bates and Norman Bates – shows us to a dank room with iron bedstead and faded pink curtains. We've already paid Cresta, nearly three months ago, over fifty quid for this. A quick conference (lasting, oh, ten or eleven seconds; enough time for me say, "You have to be joking"), and we're downstairs again telling Madame that – *je suis desolé* – we find ourselves unable to take up her offered accommodation. She shrugs Gallically – the room is paid for anyway – and we leg it. It's not her fault; the tariff shows the room at FF280 – about right – but we were, quite reasonably, expecting fifty quid's worth.

At the back of this book you'll find a list of the associations and accommodation directories we found on our trip. Please, if you're travelling in Europe, use them, or any others you find where you can book direct, rather than ever, *ever* giving half your value-for-money away in commission to a tour operator. Promise?

Feeling only slightly guilty, we sit outside in the car thumbing through the above books, looking for an acceptable alternative. We find one situated a few kilometers down the road, outside Chagny, and phone ahead for a room. It's called the Hostellerie de Bellecroix – a 12th and 18th century chateau, with mature gardens, a pool, and a delightful Madame, who shows us to a huge stone room in the *vieux chateau*, with its own door to the gardens and poolside.

It didn't cost thirty quid, or even fifty, but it was too late to go looking for anything else. No, really, it was getting on for four o'clock, we'll just have to rough it.

I'd turned round for a second to get something out of my camera bag, turned back, and Ali had disappeared. It had taken her a nanosecond to strip off, slip on a bikini, and dive straight into the

Hostellerie de Bellecroix, Chagny. The oddest room, and the best meal, of the Tour.

pool. Well, it was the first pool on our trip that hadn't had a cement mixer and a pile of blue tiles on the bottom of it, so I picked up my sketch book and wandered out to join her. She'd had a dip and was just calling for the de-fib cart because it was so cold, so I decided to dangle my legs only. After a minute or so I pulled my feet out, counted my toes, and ordered some tea, which shortly afterwards was delivered and set on a linen-clothed table in the late afternoon sun.

Better.

Our room is extraordinary. Quite the largest of our tour, it's one of the old stone rooms from the original chateau, huge and cool, with stone flags and a ceiling that you have to peer upwards to see. The bathroom is circular – the bottom of the tower – with the wedge-shaped arrow-firing positions still intact, although the slits are long walled up. Lying in the bath, you hope the great weight of the tower isn't going to entomb you while you do your pits.

Dinner at the Bellecroix is an experience, and like so many hotels, obviously attracts as many non-resident diners from the town as it does guests. We start at a table on the lawn outside with a bottle of Chassagne-Montrachet '93, a simply sublime white Burgundy, perfectly set off by the canapés brought to us by Monsieur. Then (*aah, le cuisine!*) six courses – Ali counted – including seared scallops, feather-light asparagus soup, the pinkest rack of lamb, a mini crème brulee and finally hot strawberry soufflé – all washed down (if one can used such a pedestrian term for such a wine) with an Âloxe-Corton '91.

I wonder what they're serving at the Mont Mellion?

FORTY-THREE | TUES 12TH MAY

Chagny

Into Beaune, the centre of the Burgundy region, for a look-see. We parked in a side street and spent a very pleasant couple of hours wandering around this lovely medieval town. The main square and radial streets are lined with restaurants and shops, many selling a full range of the famed names of the region – Gevrey-Chambertin, Vosne-Romanée, Pommard, Meursault, Puligny-Montrachet – together with cheeses and mustards. We have a *pression* under a parasol in the square, just a few yards from the famous Hospices de Beaune, with its multi-coloured tiled roof.

This hospital for the local sick was founded in 1451 by a man called Nicolas Rolin, who had gained fame and fortune by rising fairly meteorically from the position of Chancellor to Philip the Good, Duke of Burgundy. He was one of the men instrumental in re-uniting Burgundy with the crown of France, the Duchy having been an ally of England and of Henry V for many years. (Agincourt, where the French should have let Harry go, is on our itinerary for the last leg of the tour). Rolin, having lined his own pockets during his long life, founded a free hospital at the age of sixty-six, and left a vast amount of land – 3,000 acres – to its perpetual benefit in his will. To this day nearly 150 acres of great vines support the charity.

We wander up the main street to the northern gate, near which there is an art shop. Ali questions my temerity in even considering entering an establishment with art in the title, but in we go and I buy some watercolours, brushes and paper. Even Ali relents and buy some pastels; well, she reckons, she can't be worse than me.

And now, for our cellar. Up till now, it's consisted of a couple of cases or so of Max's excellent, but short-lived, house plonk, a few bottles of champagne, and some lovely claret that my uncle gave me years ago that we daren't drink. What we'd like to do is start collecting a few bottles to lay down, and actually wait more than a week before chugging them.

So, to Aloxe Corton, one of the tiny medieval villages that line the wide Saone valley. As in all these villages, the vineyards seem to go right up to the edge of the houses, and sometimes beyond. Just when you've passed a couple of houses, there's a low stone wall enclosing another twenty or so vines. Each one is so ancient and precious, I suppose, that it's worth nurturing. We park in the tiny square and wait a few minutes for one of the *degustation* cellars to open up. This is where you can roll up, and taste and buy the wine from the people – sometimes the actual person – who made it.

A charming lady – Madame perhaps? – opens up, and brings out some sample bottles for us to try, which she puts on a table under a parasol, with tasting glasses, some Evian and bread, and a price list. After humming, hawing, slooshing and swallowing (that's why I left the wine trade), I pore over the list, and we plump for six of the Beaune Premier Cru '95, and five of the '96. Bottles, that is, not cases – what were you thinking? At £13 a bottle, even from the guy who made it, that's three quid more than I've ever spent on a bottle from a shop.

But not, oh deary me, for long. Because just down the valley, south of Beaune, is Meursault. Pulling up short of yesterday's hotel, and hoping she hasn't put out an APB on us, we pull in to the imposing gates of Chateau de Meursault. Ali has never been down into the *caves* of a wine house, and I not a great one, so we take the tour. Beneath the neat gravel drive and white walls of the chateau are nearly a million bottles of wine – 200,000 still in wood, and 800,000 in glass.

We walk down dark stone corridors past rank after rank after rank of racks – the bottles seeming black in the gloom, half moons of light reflecting off their bottoms. Each bay and rack has a slate on which is chalked the wine – Meursault, Beaune, Puligny-Montrachet, Aloxe-Corton – and its year. Then we come to the cask cellars, low vaults as long as three cricket pitches, containing hundreds of oak barrels. Our breath plumes in the cool air – wine should ideally be kept at 56° – although really it's constancy that matters; wine likes to be the same temperature. That's why you hear about wine 'not travelling well' – it means it might have been through several temperature changes from its home caves to your glass.

Eventually the arrowed route leads to the tasting cellars, where, temptingly, bottles of the good stuff are sitting open on upended barrels waiting for you to try. And the chateau's charming and English-speaking staff are waiting to help you buy.

Well, it seemed rude not to. The chateau's own Meursault Premier Cru '96 was stunning, so, well alright, a case of that *s'il vous plait*; and, oh alright then, three bottles of the Aloxe-Corton since you've been so kind as to pour me a glass. Merci, merci.

I mean, it's not as if we're going to get home and simply *drink* the stuff, is it?

We return, laden, to the hotel, with me devising a cunning plan to get our new cellar home to England without us having to cart it round Europe for seven weeks. Ali begins serious work on her tan, while I make the first childish daubs with my new watercolours.

"Don't call us", Tony Hart would have said, "we'll call you."

DAY FORTY-FOUR | WEDNESDAY 13TH MAY

Chagny to Annecy

We say goodbye to Hostellerie de Bellecroix, perfectly situated for an overnight stay, or more, on any drive to the South of France, and continue our journey in that direction. Today, though, a detour to Lake Annecy.

Nestling in the armpit of France – geographically that is – Lake Annecy is a gorgeous, glacier-fed oasis surrounded by wooded and snow-topped mountains. On its eastern edge are a number of lakeside villages, and it is to one of them, Talloires, that we are headed – a small community of around 1,500 souls, nestling on gentle slopes between the jagged molars of the Alps behind, and the smooth waters of Lake Annecy in front.

We find our hotel for the next two nights down on the waterfront – Le Cottage, a large chalet-style house set slightly back from the promenade, with its own tree-lined terrace and secluded pool in front. We are welcomed by the owners, Monsieur and Madame Bise, and shown to a lovely room on the first floor, with a balcony overlooking the lake. It is quite stunning, so we set out for a short explore before lunch.

The delicate and exquisitely beautiful harbour is shaped like a sickle – the long sharp end a high wooded promentary poking out into the lake, the gentle inner curve the harbourside, and the elbow and handle the pier and beach, before the lake continues on south. Bobbing contentedly in the quiet waters of the harbour are small yachts and dingies, and arranged a few paces back from the water's edge are the village's most prestigious houses, four or five of which are hotels. The grandest is L'Abbaye, a large stone building that was the first to become a hotel. A plaque tells you that Cezanne stayed here, but it doesn't say whether he was a guest of the hotel, or of the house's owners before it became a hotel.

We wander round the towpath as far as you can walk, and look up at the very neat, and no doubt desirable, houses that perch on the slope. Many have beautifully kept gardens, with superb green lawns – but all at a good 40°. How on earth can you play croquet on that? Or put up a marquee? And how d'you mow it? With a block and tackle?

The other side of our hotel is the jetty, which supports a regular small ferry service that potters up and down the lake, and another large chalet house called the Auberge du Pere Bise, which proudly occupies the very best site right on the water. Yes, it appears the family Bise own the two best-positioned hotels, and, so I gather, shops and houses as well. One glance at the menu posted up outside Pere Bise explains how they can afford to buy property like this. Most of the starters are fifteen quid each, most of the mains are twenty five and up, and one of the set menus is 820 francs. That's eighty five quid for one person's food, before you've had a glass of Evian! I'm sure it's completely fab fare, but for that money I'd expect the lobster to do twenty minutes' stand-up before hopping on my plate.

Although owned by the same family, Le Cottage is obviously not in the same pricing league (it doesn't have Relais & Chateau membership dues to pay for a start), so we wander back for lunch. It's not cheap, of course, no decent food in France is, but reasonably priced and delicious. Afterwards, it's time to explore the thing that binds this whole area together – the lake.

Right in front of our hotel is the man who hires out the boats. As we walk over, he's working away sanding the upturned bottom of a wooden dingy – the season is only a week or so old – and he greets us warmly. Ali has persuaded me to take out a rowing boat, as opposed to my choice, one with a little bladed engine that does the rowing for you. She assures me she'll pull her weight, but, knowing she won't, I negotiate a promise for a trip in an outboarded dingy afterwards.

At school at the age of eleven, I seem to remember winning some sort of prize in one of these. Yes, a similar shaped, dark-wooded dingy with two rowing positions, Geoff and I going flat out for the line, cheers and treble orange squashes all round. What did we win, I wonder? A newt in a jar, probably.

I take the stroke position, my back to Ali, so she can follow my lead. That's the theory, at least. After a few oar-clashes, much laughter and much lake water in the boat, I take sole control. I don't understand this – how come girls can do co-ordinated step classes, which boys are crap at, and yet they can't follow a simple rowing action? I look over my shoulder at Ali, lounging in the bow trailing one elegant hand in the hissing water, looking at me with her wide Bambi eyes.

I have a sneaking suspicion that... no, she wouldn't.

We have a contented three-quarters of an hour rollicking our way across to the cave in the rocks and back, and then, after a restorative

Le Cottage, Talloires. Sleepy and content, like a cat on a cushion

tea, I declare it's time for another voyage – this time in a proper, powered craft.

The majestic lines of the great ship take the breath away. Freshly painted, her white sides and varnished decks shine in the sun. The people on the dock gaze in wonder at this queen of the seas – surely, they gasp, nothing can harm this mighty vessel? Aft, the transom, towering a full thirty centimetres above the waterline, proudly displays her name – "TITANIC".

I know you don't believe me, which is why I've included a photograph of her.

Ali stops laughing long enough to check the number of lifeboats on board (none) and the number of life jackets (two), I fire up the mighty engine, with both of its strokes, and we steer the huge liner out into deep water with slim hope of return.

We burble across the lake, pushing further this time, now that I don't have to row back. The other side of the lake from Talloires, where it narrows between the Grand Lac and the Petit Lac, is a wooded promentory with a castle on it, so we float over. It's called the

The great ship at anchor, before her epic voyage.

One of those lunches that needs to last till five.

Chateau de Duingt, and we sail round it until it is perfectly framed by the snow-capped Alps, and take some pictures. So impossibly pretty is the scene, we'll have to sell the pics to a chocolate-box maker, or a jigsaw company.

We return the Titanic, dent free, to the boatman, and go back to the hotel for a shower and change. A phone message tells us that Jono will be here about 6.30.

This is part of my cunning wine-running plan.

Our mad friend Jono is attending a trade conference in Geneva this week, and we've arranged to meet up. I happen to know he's driven over from the UK, so we've suggested he nip down here to Talloires this evening – only about an hour – and we'll treat him to dinner by the lake. And, just casually by the way, would he be a sweetie and take all the cases of wine we've bought back to England and stick them in our cellar? Hmmm?

He arrives shortly before seven, borrows my trunks for a swim, and declares the journey down worth it just for the chance to cool off after a hot day in a suit in the Geneva Conference Centre. Suit, I think to myself? What's one of those?

The three of us have a wonderful evening in the warm and tranquil hotel dining room; he hearing about our adventures, and us catching up with news from home. The dinner was excellent, and then we loaded him up with our wine and best wishes for his trip back to Geneva, and then England.

To bed, with the soft lights of the harbour and the gentle frapping of the boats wafting over the rails of our balcony.

DAY FORTY-FIVE | THURSDAY 14TH MAY

Annecy

A long time ago, when I first knew we would be coming to this part of France, I'd planned to take Ali up into the high Alps and show her Courchevel, my favourite ski resort.

Being May, of course, there wouldn't be any snow for us to ski on, but I'd hoped at least to be able to take her up in a cable car or chair lift and give her some breathtaking views. And I'd only ever been to the Alps in winter, so I'd never seen an Alpine meadow, or heard a cowbell. So we set off south to Albertville, and on to the new dual carriageway they built through the pass to Moutiers for the 1992 Winter Olympics. From Moutiers the road climbs ever steeper and ever narrower up the mountainside. Tiny villages cling to the grassy slopes, looking somehow shabbier and older in the spring sunshine – not covered with three feet of bright snow, as I've seen them before.

My suspicions are first aroused when we pass through Courchevel 1650 (the village has four centres – positioned, and named after, their elevation in metres), which is eerily deserted. And then we swing into 1850, park in the tiny lay-by at La Croisette by the main lifts (which you never, ever can normally), and switch off the engine.

Silence. Absolute silence.

There's no one about. Not a single human being, and only a couple of cars in sight in the village. Anyone who's been here in the season will find that hard to picture, as usually the place is humming with activity – thousands of people on the move all the time.

I'm very disappointed, partly at the total lack of anything to show my girl, partly at my stupidity in not checking whether this was one of the Alpine resorts that offered summer facilities.

We walk across the scratchy gravel surface around the lift stations – usually a couple of feet of packed snow – and look up at the mountains. A light breeze moans gently though the massive cables that loop their black-threaded way up the mountainside. All the gondolas and cars must be stored away – some in underground bunkers – while the huge glass lift stations stand silent against the blue sky. A church bell tolls midday, the sound echoing off the hills and rocks.

If it wasn't a bright sunny day, this would be very creepy indeed.

All the expensive shops, restaurants and hotels are shuttered up, and in our whole time there we see just one man, sweeping a pavement. He didn't look up. We drive up the hill, past the expensive private chalets and apartments, until we reach the Jardin Alpin side of the main piste. I take the car out across the grass of what, in a few weeks time, will be the golf course, but which I remember as the final *schuss* home to tea. I park, and we get out so I can show Ali the main mountain peak, La Saulire, which divides this valley from its *Trois Vallées* sisters, Meribel and Val Thorens. The great bowl, one of the best skiing experiences there is, curves down from the summit to the centre lift station, and then the wide piste glides past to our right, back down into the village. There is some heavy snow still in the bowl, and in the Grand Couloir where the spring sun has not yet penetrated, but most of the valley is brown grass turning green.

From here I can just see the balcony of La Soucoup, the mountain-peak restaurant where many a *vin chaud* has warmed me in a white-out, but the lifts are closed, and my hopes of lunch are dashed.

We get back in the car and drive round to look at one of the most startling sights in the valley – the Altiport. It's the airport for the villages, and it's on a very steep slope. The runway, that is. There's a flat ramp and apron area at the top, surrounded by small hangars and the control tower, and then the runway drops away like a child's playground slide – straight down the mountain slope – and it's not very long. When you're arriving, you fly straight at the mountain, and pull the nose up at the last minute, using your brakes and gravity combined to slow you enough so that you just hop over the lip of the top ramp and power down coolly, as if to say, "Well, that was a doddle".

Taking off is lap-of-the-gods time. You simply park on the edge of the ramp, your nose pointing out into space, spool up the props and flip the brakes. You surge over the top, plunge down the slope, and hope that by the time the tarmac runs out you're flying. If not you'll just be a horrified expression smeared all over the opposite valley's rockface.

Pleased we saw it, even in very different clothes, we leave Courchevel and wind our way back down the valley to Moutiers, the town at the juction of the three valley bottoms, where I once spent a very painful week.

It was back in 1989, when I'd organised a skiing holiday for a group of mates. I hadn't been skiing for a few years, and this was going to be the big one – a decent chalet, eight mates and new kit.

We arrived in Meribel, as many packages do, at about one in the morning on a Sunday. The coach hissed to a stop outside a small hotel, and we were told to walk down a short lane to our chalet. Glad to be off the coach, I strode ahead, down the little road, which hadn't been gritted. I felt my feet slide from under me, and I began to fall. My right trainer then re-gripped the surface, and instead of both feet whizzing out and me landing hard on my arse, the right ankle and foot stayed underneath and my body wound its not inconsiderable weight down onto it. Crunch.

Oh, fuck.

In fact, fuck, fuckity FUCK!!!

Oh yes, and OUUUCHH!!

I knew instantly it was broken, but I couldn't tell how badly. Actually it didn't matter – Game Over.

We'd been in the resort for six minutes.

As I waited, not very patiently, for the ambulance, I asked the head resort rep whether I'd set a record. "No", he said, "someone fell off the steps of the plane at Geneva Airport last week. Sorry".

Anyway, to cut a very painful (not to say embarrassing) story short, I then spent a week in the hospital in Moutiers. The doctors didn't speak (or refused to speak) any English at all, the food was totally inedible, even for me, and I was sharing a ward with four very old locals who stank, and a young biker who's attitude hadn't been improved by his smash. Medically, I'm told, they fixed me up good and I got pinned and plated, fed and fed-up, and shipped back home. I walk fine now, with full movement, and as a souvenir I still have a plastic Ziploc bag of three-inch steel screws and plates.

Half a Meccano set, that is. Do for the kid's third birthday.

Having found no food at all in the mountains, we arrive back at the lake in time for a late lunch. After that we get back in the car and drive along the lakeshore to have a look at Annecy. Once the capital of the region, it's a gorgeous town – or rather it's in a gorgeous position, which helps. The large 19th and 20th century conurbation spread out at the lake's end is a fairly standard collection of no-personality flats and offices, but the 17th century old town is largely intact. We walked towards it along the path at the edge of the lake, through the open parkland of the public *jardins*. Hundreds of boats, pedalos and kayaks line the lake edge, and at weekends, this must be a focal point for the town and its all-important tourists.

The old town is a delight. Lifting our eyes from the souvenir shops and pizza parlours, we look up at the superb old gables and beams of the 17th century buildings that line the river. Arches and overhangs, mullions and dormers – it has a look of Sarlat and a feel of Salzburg. The river flows swiftly and shallowly, and it's criss-crossed by tiny foot bridges like Venice. Unlike Venice, the water is gin-clear, even when flowing at speed. It must be all that glacier water, running off the mountains, through the lake, and out through the town.

We drive back as the sun dips behind us, and just outside Talloires, at the edge of the mountains, we stop to watch several gaily-coloured parascenders wheeling and floating on the rising thermals. They seem to stay up for ever, slowly sinking, then catching a warm lift up the rock face again. One by one they gradually float down, aiming for a mown landing field, where they swoop in and, at the last second, pull a guy rope and lightly put their feet down on terra firma. It looked easy and effortless. Bet it wasn't.

A lazy evening, with a delicious dinner on the terrace – the shimmering lights of the lake spread out before us, and the cicadas chirruping in the grass at the water's edge. We'd just finished our main course, when a city floated round the headland; a great slab of lights that just kept on coming. I wasn't sure what was approaching us in the dark, but then I realised it must be the enormous restaurant ship we'd seen moored up in Annecy. It edged into our harbour and then out again, like the Great White cruising off Amity, and then the lights slid away round the corner.

We could still hear the low rumble of her engines, and the tinny sound of the on-board band, for many minutes.

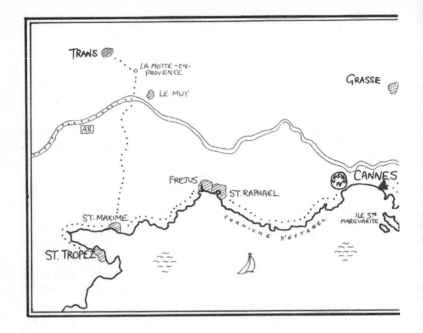

THE FRENCH RIVIERA

Le Muy

In which we take a villa high in the Provençal hills, and are joined by friends from England. It's a glorious small villa, utterly private, with pool and boules terrace, barbecue and be-vined arbour. In between lazing and swimming and langostines, we visit the Gorge de Verdon, St Tropez, Nice, Cannes and Monaco.

Cannes

In which we find ourselves staying at the coolest hotel in Cannes during the Film Festival, and have to fight our way through the barricaded movie

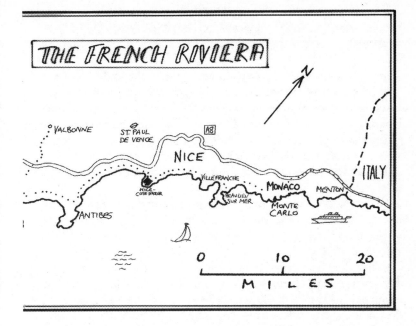

fans to get to our balconied room overlooking La Croisette and the Med. We shop, we lig, we wave graciously at the punters, we visit Villefranche and Beaulieu-sur-Mer, we only mildly trouble the bank at the Casino, and on Sunday we blag our way into...

The Monaco Grand Prix

In which we manage to find ourselves in a five star private apartment just a hundred feet above the Royal Box and the start line. The best view in the whole country, and lunch thrown in!

DAY FORTY-SIX | FRIDAY 15TH MAY

Annecy to Provence

Time to leave this very peaceful corner of the world, and head down to the noisier environs of the Cote D'Azur. We say goodbye to the Bises, who seem to have an excellent life – six months in Talloires looking after (fairly) civilised guests, then six months in the Caribbean to get over it. Their staff all go up into the mountains to work in the ski resorts. This sleepy, but somehow very organised and civilised village, is prosperous, comfortable and well fed – like a cat on a cushion.

Tip: if you don't mind ambling along while driving in France, with no itinerary to keep to, take any road you like. If you actually want to get anywhere, and especially by any required time, take the autoroute.

Unlike the UK, where if you know what you're doing some of the dual-carriageway A roads can be just as fast, if not faster than the motorway, in France the N roads (nice and red and fast-looking on the map) are strictly for sightseeing. The French built the autoroutes for those who wanted to get places – at a price, of course. But I don't mind paying tolls when I know I'll get there on time, and with far less traffic around me, too. On which British motorway, and especially on the main ones like the M1, could you drive stretches in daytime where you don't see another car?

I bring the above up because we had decided to take the Route Napoleon down from Annecy to Valbonne, a few miles north of Nice. Well, it was one side of a triangle on the map – the autoroute went south west all the way to Marseilles before curling back along the coast to Nice.

I didn't spend sufficient time wondering why.

So, down the lovely open motorway to Grenoble, then we intended to head for Gap and Digne, and then across to Grasse, and down to Nice. Looked a bit wiggly on the map, but it's all red N roads, isn't it. Be there by two, easy.

The road began by getting narrower, then windier, then steeper. The Merc, while quite happy on the flat, is rather like me – ask it to go up a hill and it just doesn't want to know. We take ages crossing several medium-sized Alps, and it's well after one when we limp down the switchback into Gap. Nothing looks very enticing for lunch in the town, so we find a roadside café to the south and stop for fuel and food.

Just on from there they've started some roadworks, and we pass a sign saying **NICE 180km**, right next to another sign that says **NICE 280km**. A little confused, I ask the petrol attendant which is quicker, and he looks at me sadly, as if to say, "Why d'you think they built this bloody motorway, you ignorant *rosbif*?"

As it's now nearly two o'clock, we opt for the safe option, and are soon cruising along at ninety, with no caravans or lorries in front, and a fair chance of estimating our arrival time to within closer than half a day. We cruise effortlessly past Aix-en-Provence, Frejus and Cannes, before turning up into the hills. At last, the weather is truly warm, the trees are truly palm, and we are in the South of France.

The Hotel Golf Valbonne is a group of stucco villas around a golf course, up in the thickly wooded hills above Nice. Our room is pleasant, with a mezzanine seating area, and French windows onto the 15th tee. I wish it was early enough in the day for a swift hack round. We make do with a bottle of Sauv Blanc and a smirk at others' efforts to leave the tee gracefully.

I once played golf with a group of rather laddish lads, who stated that their house rules were that if your tee shot didn't get past the ladies' tee, you had to play the rest of the hole with your knob out.

Must have been members.

DAY FORTY-SEVEN | SATURDAY 16TH MAY

Valbonne to La Motte

A change of accommodation, and of pace, today. Back in the misty days of planning, Ali and Gail came up with the idea of building a week's villa rental into the itinerary. It would provide a half-time pause, give access to nice places (and Nice places), Ali could work on her tan, and it would also work out cheaper than hotels. So they booked a villa in the hills between Frejus and Draguinan, and it was there we were headed, after picking up Karen and Gerald from Nice airport.

Karen is one of Ali's best friends, and she and her man had thought it a great idea to come out for a long weekend, and a welcome break from their busy lives. We met them at Nice/Cote d'Azur at about ten, and set off back west along the A8, towards Draguinan.

Through the little village of La Motte-en-Provence, and on up the hill, we follow the printed directions. With no signs at all, it's a challenge, but eventually, up a ridiculously steep earthen track, through a pine forest, and down an equally steep driveway, we find the villa.

I don't know about you, but booking almost any holiday accommodation is something I find a real lottery. Unless you've been there, or you know someone who has, you have no idea what it's going to be like. You already know, dear Reader, my views on tour operators, but more often than not, the brochure photograph has been professionally cropped to cut out the glue factory, the blue sky has been airbrushed in, and the block of flats that overlooks the pool has been airbrushed out. The copy in the brochure is usually a joke too – full laundry facilities means washboard; barbeque means a small one-touch foil tray, and sleeps six means you'll be quite comfortable if two of you missed the flight.

Well I'm sorry not to feed your schadenfreude, but this time we fell on our feet. It was lovely. Cut into the hillside a good 800 feet above the valley, the little plateau had a large single-storey house built on it, with low sloping terracotta tiled roofs, and a vine-covered terrace at one end. Set into the flagstoned forecourt was a bright blue pool, and the whole garden was surrounded by mature trees, bushes and shrubs. Flowers in pots lined the edge of the pool, and the views across the valley were magnificent.

Well, the inside will be horrid, we thought.

It wasn't of course – an enormous living room, with huge beamed ceiling, sofas and chairs and large dining table; good-sized kitchen with all mod-cons (including a dishwasher, washing machine, fridge-freezer and microwave); and three bedrooms. Being utterly selfish and gittish, I bagged the master bedroom for us, but Karen and Gerald's was large and bright, with french windows out to the pool.

The master bedroom looked like the set from *Jason King*, or *The Persuaders*. Apart from driving a Jensen, I didn't really want to be associated with Peter Wyngarde, but this was seventies heaven. A huge bed made of stone and stucco, with the mattress on top; two sets of French windows; steps up to a mezzanine bathroom, with sunken bath, double basin and mirrors, separate loo and shower, the whole suite in matching purple, with gold accessories. Yuk, of course, but very comfortable, and everything at your fingertips. What a result!

We've been let in by the Brit couple who look after the villa – Fred and Sue Maybank – who tell us the place is owned by an English family, who let it for most of the summer, and come here themselves too. They price it very reasonably, and it's always booked out by the end of March.

Fred and Sue moved to France about eight years ago, looking for work and warmth, and have now found a sort of equilibrium – Fred works as a plumber and caretaker, and Sue cleans and teaches. They found it very tough at first – Fred was seen as taking locals' work (especially if he was far more efficient at it), and neither spoke French well. But they put their three children into school, and kept their noses clean, and are now being accepted as part of the community. Their children's French is now native standard, and their efficiency has won them many clients – particularly among British villa owners.

Certainly our villa is spotless, and everything seems to work fine.

We all pile back in the car, and head back down the steep track to visit one of my favourite types of shop – a French supermarket.

Supermarkets at home have got immeasurably better over the last ten years, but they still don't seem to have the exuberance and flair of a French one. The *Continent* in Trans, a few miles away from the villa, is typical. Huge and hangar-like, the entrance is a dreadful brick arch, and the surrounding shops and stalls are not pretty, but once inside, the whole gastronomic world opens up. Fish counters the length of a cricket wicket, meat and cheese the same, acres of vegetables and fruit, chilled cabinets stuffed with goodies – all lovely, oozey, unpasteurised dangerous stuff.

We spend a happy half hour wheeling our trolley round, buying steaks and huge tiger prawns for the barbie, fresh veg and cheap wine, chocolate and crisps, and, of course, a lilo. At the checkout I proffer my Visa card, and the girl asks for ID. I'm not carrying my passport, and my driving licence apparently won't do. Eventually she accepts it anyway, and apart from wondering whether it's now policy in France to ask for ID with a credit card, or I've been picked out for being an obvious outsider, I reflect on her astonishment that somebody should be wandering around without picture ID. Are we the last country in the world not to have it? I know Blair has been trying to introduce an Identity Card, but I think it'll take a while to be accepted.

Laden with Provençal provender, we head back to the villa. The barbeque is gas-powered, so I don't have to go through my 'men are here!' routine and spend hours getting a charcoal one going. Time for a swim before supper – or it would be if it wasn't still a little early in the season for the pool to have warmed up to 'sober' temperatures. Perhaps we'll dive into the wine first, and wait till the pool has warmed up to 'drunk' temperatures in a couple of hours time.

We marinade the prawns and stuff the mushrooms, and as the sky goes the colour of blue-black Quink, we barbeque them – the sweet fumes joining the evening scents of jasmine and wisteria – as the four of us get quietly, contentedly, companionably and utterly pissed.

DAY FORTY-EIGHT | SUNDAY 17TH MAY

La Motte

The sun streams in to our bedroom, stretching warm rectangular tongues across the terracotta tiles. I lie in bed and watch it for a while. A small gecko flits, in fits and starts, across the floor and out of the French windows. Quite right, I think, can't be inside today.

I make myself an enormous French breakfast vat of coffee and carry it out onto the terrace, and find three sun-loungers stretched out on three sun-loungers.

This lying about in the sun lark – never understood it. I'm like Billy Connolly, who said that being Scottish, his skin is actually blue and it takes him a week in the sun just to go white. My skin will go bright red and fall off if I walk too close to a naked light bulb, so I have to be careful. Ali sometimes persuades me to strip off and rack out like a big chip, but the whole slapping up and Factor ninety stuff is all too much effort – I prefer to sit quietly under the vines, wearing a panama and doing my Dirk Bogarde impression.

After the coffee has begun to have its effect on my system, I politely make enquiries of the assembled company as to what they'd like to do today. Three individual hands flap feebly, conveying quite succinctly the message, "listen, whitey, the sun is shining, the pool is warming, the wine is chilling, and it's Sunday. Sod off".

Fine, then, suit yourselves. I start devising a set of rules for my newly-invented pool game, Pop The Lilo.

After lunch the weather starts to close in a little, so the sun-loungers agree to a little sightseeing. Not far up the road is one of the most spectacular bits of geology on earth – the Gorges de Verdon.

Europe's Grand Canyon, the gorge is sixteen miles long, and up to 2,000 feet deep. It was first fully explored, during a very tough three day trip, by the same chap who discovered the Gouffre de Padirac, Edouard-Alfred Martel. The trip along the canyon floor and down the river is still fairly gruelling, I imagine, but we stick to the southern road that winds its way along the cliff edge. Unfortunately the weather is quite grey, and we can't see a great deal. At one point we stop and walk out to a stone viewing platform, and there below us – a long, long way below us – is the milky-blue ribbon that cut this massive abyss.

It's getting a little late to attempt the round trip, and being Sunday, the hostelry at the edge of the Gorge is closed, so we make our way back, hoping the weather will clear for tomorrow.

DAY FORTY-NINE | MONDAY 18TH MAY

La Motte

Today the committee decide to head over to St Tropez, so we take the car down the hill, under the A8, and wind through the cypressed hills towards St Maxime, where, for the first time since Aigua Blava, we hit the Mediterranean.

You then have to start the long loop around the bay to St Tropez, the single lane road putting you at the mercy of the holiday traffic. Except, it's a Monday, and not even the season yet. What must this be like in summer?

I relieve the boredom by diving into Michelin again, emerging with a gruesome nugget of legend: St Tropez is named after a Christian centurion called Tropez, or Torpes, who lived in Pisa in Roman times. Old fatty Nero took a break from violin lessons to order him executed, and he was beheaded and set adrift in a small boat, strapped upright with his head on the seat beside him. Also placed in the boat were a dog and a cock, who were supposed to devour his remains as the boat drifted over the horizon. Whether on the grounds of taste or principle, the beasts didn't touch him, and the boat was carried by wind and current to the headland where St Tropez now stands.

Charming. When's lunch?

After a jog-jog entry into the town, we follow the signs and find ourselves in the finest multi-storey car park I've ever seen. I've talked before about this – and the sad-ometer is twitching – but it was wonderful: bright and airy, freshly painted in soft pastels, and so clean I was reluctant to drive on the floor. It was like a Park Lane showroom, and the cars already parked there completed the illusion – I've never seen so many Ferraris, Porsches and Royces in my life. There was even a Lamborgini Countache; our dowdy Merc estate quite lowered the tone. Paying much less than the Chinatown NCP, we were borne upwards in a huge glass lift, and out into landscaped gardens with fountains plashing – and we were still in the car park.

We wander through the streets past glittering shops, towards the harbour. The actual buildings are very pretty, most in honey or orange stone, with green or white shutters from the first floor up, but at street level, it's all wide gaudy awnings and hundreds of grockles at café tables.

I'm sorry, but despite its car park I really don't like St Tropez – it's all scuzzy rich showing off, and scuzzy poor watching them. I'm writing this while sitting at a pavement café watching billion dollar yachts – that I couldn't even afford to paint – squatting fatly at the quay, but I feel like a piece of meat in a sandwich; caught between the indefensible and the unspeakable. The indefensible are these gas-guzzling gin palaces, huge and bloated (and their gin-guzzling gas bag owners, huge and bloated)... and yet here next to me, watching the boats, is a family from Belgium (the kid's knapsack is be-flagged). The child is picking its nose, the mother's holding her youngest in her arms and smoking, and father is trying to fit a vast crusty sub-sandwich into his mouth, oozing salami and sauce. All three are slouching, round-shouldered and slack-jawed, watching the boats, their mouths chewing slowly and openly, like cows. Unspeakable.

We eat, rather more tidily I hope, in a covered harbourside restaurant, and then the crew decide they need a beach. Collecting the car from the pristine car park, we head over the hill to the southern beaches, where the biting wind and freezing water don't deter three of us from charging Reggie Perrin-like into the Med – see if you can guess who remained on the sand to guard the cameras, and his sanity? They warmed up in a beachfront bar where the bill for four coffees made my eyebrows recede into my hairline – a remarkable feat for one so follically challenged.

It took even longer for us to nudge our way back round the bay road, past the obligitory drive-in MacDonald's, and wind up through the hills to home, only stopping to buy more big prawns. Oh, and a few more just in case.

DAY FIFTY | TUESDAY 19TH MAY

La Motte

Karen wants to have a look round Nice before they fly home this afternoon, so we set off along the A8, arriving on the Promenade des Anglais in time to park up for lunch in one of the pedestrian lanes.

Nice is the grand old lady of the Cote d'Azur, rather like Brighton used to be, only with palm trees and sunshine. Like many attractive places, especially in Europe, it's been fought over and occupied by several different powers. For centuries it was part of the Gallic lands, but then the Italians and Austrians nicked it in the late 1300s and held sway for half a millennium. In 1860 Napoleon III helped drive the Austrians out and the people of the Nice area were asked if they wanted to become French again. The result was as follows: YES: 25,743 NO: 260

Not even the Tories would ask for a recount on that vote.

The buildings are formally French, but with a Mediterranean laid-back faded look – all iron shutters and peeling pastels. We had a long lunch under a huge parasol, during which a British TV crew tried to interview us – were we here for the Cannes Film Festival? Where were we from? Did we like the South of France? Please say something interesting, we're desperate.

I'm sorry, no pictures – call my agent.

The shops are no less classy than the buildings they occupy, so we have a wander, and Ali discovers Blanc Bleu, which looks like it will prove expensive. Is it the range of very smart ivory white and Cambridge blue clothing, or the fact that they're not in Britain yet that appeals, I wonder? The huge glossy stiff carrier bags, with hand-braided rope handles gave me a clue to what the bill would be, but Ali had bought me a pair of striped swimming trunks to ease the blow. Next door, Karen had opted for fushia pink in the gaudy underwear shop, and we have a last coffee before heading for the airport to send them contentedly home.

It's a gorgeous blisteringly hot Riviera afternoon, and we drive west along the coast road. Past the huge curved beachfront apartment blocks, shining white in the sun, with plant-draped balconies, we reach Juan-les-Pins and Antibes. A slow circuit of Cap d'Antibes takes us past the Hotel du Cap – no doubt full of Tom Hanks, Steven Spielberg and other Hollywood luminaries. Even if we could have afforded to stay there, film festival fortnight is booked out years in advance.

And so to Cannes itself. Both movie nuts, although with no connections, we'd semi-planned to be passing through Cannes during the festival, just to have a lig. Fortunately we'd been well advised by Gail before the trip, and had booked a room in the Martinez – smarter and cooler than the Carlton, and a few steps away from the noisiest stretch of the Croisette. We weren't due until Saturday, but we thought we'd wander round the town and check out the action. We parked in the underground car park a block away from the Palais des Festivals – and no, it wasn't quite as smart as the St Tropez one, but still clean and safe and odour-free.

I've always been crap at blagging my way into special events, restricted areas, cool parties and so on (not once have I been able to get upgraded on a plane), so I had no expectations here, at one of the most security-conscious events in the social calendar. Everyone who's anyone is in town – and they're all dealing, *darling*-ing, partying, photo-calling or power-breakfasting. Since I'm no one, we make do with a walk along La Croisette, past the marquees and endless glossy movie posters.

The British Pavilion manages to look dignified but rather sad at the same time, and as we walk we pass hundreds of people with festival badges round their necks. The range of expressions and looks on their faces was fascinating – worried, starry-eyed, eager, jaded and even pissed off. You'd have thought that here in the palm-fronded sunshine, in their glamorous and hugely-paid industry's event of the year, they'd at least *try* to be having a good time.

The beach at Cannes is usually wide and sandy, lapped by the soft waters of the bay, but not this week. Almost every inch of golden sand has been covered by duckboards and huge marquees, each one dressed and themed for that night's studio party – you know, the one we're not invited to, the one Liz and Hugh's people said they *might* turn up to. Vast gantries laden with TV lights and scaffolding have been erected, and on the wide white stage beneath a daytime TV show is being transmitted live, the Med as its backdrop. Perfectly-coiffured presenters sit behind desks and emote about the fabulous films in and out of competition for the Palme d'Or.

The vast edifice of the Carlton Hotel looms into view, with its white stone balconies and vaulting French roof. Just below this is the largest poster I have ever seen. Running the entire width of the hotel, and a full storey in height, the poster proclaims loudly that Godzilla is longer than the Carlton. Our ears draw our eyes up into the sky, where a light plane is towing another poster, even bigger, saying SIZE MATTERS.

Cary and Grace would turn in their graves.

And finally, The Martinez. Set back slightly from the Croisette, the hotel has a dignified and mildly Deco air to it, apart from the huge permanent cut-out sign on the roof – not dissimilar to the Hollywood sign – saying MARTINEZ. Around the front door, like triffids pressed against fences, stand a huge crowd of photographers and film fans, six deep.

But we're not due to arrive till Saturday, I say to Ali, who *can* they be waiting for? Smiling, we join the liggers, craning for a look, but after two total nobodies step grandly out of limos on the forecourt, we feel a little better about our impending arrival, and repair to a bar opposite to sit and watch the watchers in comfort.

A couple of lattés with Chardonnay chasers later, we wander back along the Rue d'Antibes for a window shop, Ali gearing up for next week's gear up. A brief stop at the small but excellent supermarket, and then a drive back along the A8 into a blazing orange sunset.

DAY FIFTY-ONE | WEDNESDAY 20TH MAY

La Motte

An utterly blissful day. Lay around in our private hilltop paradise, with no need for clothes – just hot sunshine, cool Chablis, crystal blue water, barbequed langoustines, Scrabble, *Les Mis* and each other.

It really doesn't get any better than this.

DAY FIFTY-TWO | THURSDAY 21ST MAY

La Motte

Another sparkling Provençal day, beginning to make up for all the rain-soaked ones earlier in France.

I dug out the paintbox again, but this time had a go with pastels. Since Ali was racked out on a sunlounger, all bronzed and lissom, I had a stab at portraiture. After an hour or so of trying to de-mystify the curves of the female body, she complained that I'd drawn her breasts too big. Just wait till you have children, I said, then you'll have something to complain about.

By way of revenge, she posted a new record at Scrabble that evening – 471. Perhaps it was her insistence that 'bastard' was spelt with a 'z'.

We have a frog. He is only about the size of my thumbnail – which is why it took me half an hour to find him, perched behind the chrome rail on the top step of the pool ladder – but he makes an amazingly loud 'ribbet'. Le Muy, the village in the valley, lets off a noonday klaxon – don't ask me why – and Philbert, for that is the frog's name, competes easily come dusk. His friends try to join in from the bushes, but we belong to him, and he lets them know it.

Careful JB, your legs are glowing.

On days like these...

DAY FIFTY-THREE | FRIDAY 22ND MAY

La Motte

In the film *White Mischief*, set in colonial Kenya's Happy Valley, Sarah Miles emerges from her villa into a sparkling African dawn, the parakeets chirping, the dik-diks dikking, and the red sun rising over the savannah. She stretches languidly and says, "Oh God, not *another* fucking beautiful day!"

I agree with her because so it was here in Provence; and also because my great-great-great(?) uncle Jack Soames, the ultimate black sheep, was played by Trevor Howard in the film. Did I say I had no movie connections? Hah! In fact, come to think of it, I was actually *in* a movie once, *Aces High*: I played a wide-eyed schoolboy listening to John Gielgud tell us how heroic it would be for us all to get killed for our country in the Royal Flying Corps. Two quid I got for that, and all the cheese sarnies I could eat. Eat your heart out, Harrison.

Anyway, we were just eating our first watermelon of the day, when Freddie Maybank popped round to do the pool. Out of interest, we asked him about the owners, and whether they were thinking of selling. You can do that sort of thing casually when you know you haven't a hope in hell of buying it. He said that the place was owned by a Brit living in Hong Kong, who'd owned it for years, bringing his family here a couple of times a year, but now they had all grown up and flown, so he was thinking of selling. His problem was a limited market, because apparently no local would buy it as its hilltop, pine-forest location and tiny steep track meant no fire engine could get to it.

Hmmm, well, I *was* tempted... but maybe not.

Our last night in this oasis of peace – silken swimming under the stars, and are there langoustines still for tea?

DAY FIFTY-FOUR | SATURDAY 23RD MAY

La Motte to Cannes

Reluctantly but excitedly, we pack up the car and head south to St Raphael, wanting to approach Cannes on the coast road. St Raphael has a nice harbour, but the bulk of the town, like Frejus next door, is a grid of concrete holiday apartments. Still, it all looks attractive in the sunshine, and like many hot places, can get away with it. We leave the harbour and soon find ourselves on the corniche of the Massif D'Estorel, winding its precarious way east towards Cannes. The road plays chicken with the railway, darting in and out of tunnels and hanging off precipices, and before long we're descending into the *ville de festival*, where the traffic grinds to a complete halt. The gendarmes have their white gloves on.

It takes us nearly an hour to edge our way into Cannes, past thousands of punters, hundreds of traffic cops, rows of metal crowd barriers and miles of flags and bunting fluttering in the Mediterranean breeze. Very glad of our advance reservations, we shuffle along La Croisette towards the Martinez, to find the crossroads blocked by police waving cars on. The hotel is once again surrounded by crowds and photographers, and Ali starts to get embarrassed and suggests we go round the back and in through the kitchen. No way, I say, this is worth the room rate alone!

I nudge past the police and join the queue of limos and convertibles wanting to drive into the Martinez's sweeping forecourt. A very chic woman in a Nicole Fahri suit walks up brandishing a clipboard. I lean out of the window and say confidently "checking in!" This is obviously the password, as she instantly softens and says in perfect English, "of course, Sir, welcome to the Hotel Martinez."

Yes!

We are swept in to the drive, and Ali immediately does her Liz Taylor impression – cramming on the D&G shades and rushing through the revolving doors into the foyer. Timing it to perfection, I step out to a blizzard of flashbulbs. Well, alright, not quite a blizzard, but there were certainly a dozen before the assembled paparazzi realised I was an utter nobody and stopped wasting Fuji. The crowd let out a groan of disappointment, and I let a knowing smile play about my lips as if to say, "of course you don't recognise me, fools. If you really knew your Hollywood you'd know I was a major studio bigwig who can greenlight a hundred million dollar movie before breakfast."

It didn't cut any ice at all of course, so I wandered into the hotel.

Inside was all cool marble and calm bustle. Our room was on the sixth floor and had a stone collonaded balcony overlooking the bay. For the money we were paying I wanted our own pool on the balcony too, but it was fine. Of course they nearly double the rates for the film festival, and it was easily our most expensive hotel on the trip – even more than the Gritti – but we were *here*.

I've hardly tipped the bellhop before Ali is stripped and into her bikini, so we cross the road to the only bit of sand that isn't covered with tarpaulin – the Martinez's private beach. Their own pier, with obligatory MARTINEZ sign at the end, stretches out into the calm water, and is covered with bright pink loungers and parasols. After a short dip, we chuck on a shirt and have some lunch in the hotel's beach restaurant. The bouncers check your face first to see if you're important, and then, crestfallen, have to let you in with your room pass. We utterly betray ourselves by looking around to see if we can spot a star, but in vain. Of course, it's only 1.30, they'll all still be in bed.

After lunch we promenade back along Croisette to check out Cannes. Like many good French things, it's an English invention. No more than a fishing village in the 1830s, it was an unscheduled overnight stop in 1834 for Lord Brougham, then Lord Chancellor of England. He liked it so much he returned every winter, making the village fashionable for the British aristocracy, and leading to the development of the chic resort it has become. It's good of Michelin to admit the Brit involvement (but then they *are* fiercely correct) – you'll find it hard to find a Frenchman who'll admit that we invented skiing, and that we brought it, and huge prosperity, to their mountains.

Outside the Palais des Festivals, a distinctly ugly concrete building, the crowd barriers, and the ten deep crowd around them, prevent us from seeing anybody noteworthy, but the festival TV station in our room tells us about all the stars and celebs we've missed by being here in person. Later, we wander along the front looking for a restaurant that can seat us anywhere but in the hat rack, and the only place that doesn't laugh Gallically in our faces is Planet Hollywood, who sell us a bright green cocktail and tell us to wait forty five minutes. Wait three quarters of an hour for a burger? Oh, alright then, so we sit looking at Arnie's spare jacket from *Terminator 6*, and then have a surprisingly good rack of ribs and a bottle of Pouilly.

We stroll contentedly back to the hotel, the sound of deals being made on mobiles emanating from every open-front restaurant we pass, and think about tomorrow, which could, if it works out, be a rare day.

DAY FIFTY-FIVE | SUNDAY 24TH MAY

Monte Carlo

Both of us had always been fans of Grand Prix racing, but had never been to one – for myself mostly because I'd been reluctant to spend a hundred quid to queue for six hours, sit on a far corner, have my ears rebored out, and spend eight hours queuing to get home.

However, here we were a few miles from the Monaco Grand Prix, and this time, for the first time, I had an edge – my friend JC. We've met up a couple of times a year for quite a while, and always got on well, but I hoped I wasn't going to stretch our friendship too far with this one.

JC's partner Michael's mother had an apartment in Monte Carlo, and every year the family gathered to watch the race. I'd casually mentioned that we might be in Cannes this year at the same time, and he very graciously said, "Oh, well, do pop along and join us". Now, do you push it, or don't you? I'm not one for asking big favours from people, especially close friends, but for this – hell yes. And anyway, I'd done him and Michael a favour a few years ago.

He'd said to call us on his mobile on the Sunday morning if we were going to be there, and he'd sort something out. That's a little more tenuous than I like for big events, but we thought we'd give it a try anyway.

I was rather concerned about the best way to get to Monaco from Cannes. Obviously driving was out of the question, and surely the trains would be packed – how about a helicopter? Yeah, right. The Martinez's concierge, Francisco, did his best, but they were all booked out, and it would have been hugely extravagant. Fun, though.

So we took the train, which actually wasn't too bad, and we arrived, only slightly squashed, in Monaco at about 11.30. The place was a heaving, seething, writhing mass of humanity – I was reminded of the roomful of snakes in *Raiders of the Lost Ark* – with chequered and red flags everywhere. Every square inch of building and hoarding was covered with Marlboro posters, and every square inch of balcony and hillside was covered with people. You couldn't walk down the streets, you had to do that sideways-inch-through-crowds shuffle to get anywhere. I was amazed to see that Bernie's boys block off every street-end and alleyway with ten foot high boarding, so unless you've got a ticket, or a friend with a balcony, you can't see the race from anywhere in the city. I hope JC remembered his casual invitation of a couple of months ago.

The Principality of Monaco occupies an area of less than a square mile, but is one of the richest per capita places on earth. Every square foot of that square mile is devoted to making, or in most places keeping, your money. The Société des Bains de Mer will be quite happy to take some of it off you in their casino, or any of their hotels, shops and apartment blocks, but mostly you'll be wanting to quietly sit and accumulate.

The Grimaldi family have been doing just that since 1308, when they bought Monaco from the Republic of Genoa. I don't know what they paid, but the whole deal sounds a bit like when Peter Stuyvesant buying Manhattan Island from the Indians for seventeen dollars. Anyway, the Grimaldis have held sway over their private fiefdom ever since, the longest ruling family in the world. And why not? The place is clean, pleasant, sunny and relatively crime-free (well, violent crime), the food is French and the service isn't, and once a year the entire country goes to the races.

We edge our way through milling crowds of mixed nationalities – there can't be many sports that hold sixteen events a year which attract fans supporting over a dozen nations. Monaco is of course fairly central, so there are Germans, French, Brits by the thousand, Italians (only a few miles from home) by the tens of thousands, Spanish, many Finns come to support their new hero, and even Argentinians and Brazilians. For one weekend, Monte Carlo becomes the world's melting pot. The red Ferrari flags dominate, many waved by Germans. Schumacher has won here many times, and expectations are high.

At one point we find ourselves down by the apartment blocks on the harbour, and as we watch a convoy of limos and police cars sweeps up to some crowd barriers behind a large building. Out gets Crown Prince Albert of Monaco, followed by Princess Stephanie, and together with assorted flunkies and followers, they go inside – presumably for a spot of lunch before watching the race from the best seats in the city.

At this rate, we'd be lucky to get a burger and stand around *listening* to the race. JC had said to call his mobile, and I'd been trying for an hour from my mobile, but obviously the population has increased by a factor of fifty today, and everyone was using their mobiles this morning – the transmitters up on the mountain peaks were jammed solid. We had a beer in the hot sun, and I kept dialling, hopes dwindling. At last I got him.

"JC, it's JB – er, I don't know if you remember, but…"

"Hello mate, we'd been wondering what had happened to you! Lunch is ready, where are you, I'll come down and get you."

What a star!

After a few minutes, his huge jolly form emerged beaming through the crowd, all smiles and welcome. How were we? How was the journey in? Were we hungry? Had we got our headphones yet?

Headphones?

Being race virgins we hadn't realised just how much noise these super-powerful machines actually make, and JC explained that the thousands of bright red and yellow ear-defenders we could see hanging from every street stall weren't toys – the cars' engine noise *shreds* the air, and your eardrums too.

Just how close were we going to be?

Clutching our newly-acquired headphones, we found out. JC led us back through the streets towards the same building we'd seen the royal family go into… and inside we went too, JC smiling at the ranks of police guards and indicating that we weren't potential assassins. Up in the lift, our eyes growing wider, and into a huge apartment with a wide balcony.

Above the Royal Box – five minutes to race time.

We were on the sixth floor. Directly below was the royal box, and smack in front of it, not a hundred feet away from us, was the start line of the Monaco Grand Prix. Holy shit.

Above the silver, red and blue cars, shining and throbbing on the grid, the whole harbour and sweep of the city was laid out before us. Hardly able to speak for excitement, we were introduced to Michael's family, who were very welcoming, and keen to hear about our tour over the sumptuous lunch they'd laid on. I spared a passing thought for my Aunt Jane, who's a Grand Prix fanatic, and would be chartreuse with envy. After lunch a sweepstake was organised – I was pleased to draw David Coulthard, and Ali got Pedro Diniz, so perhaps she'd have to make do with winning at roulette instead.

Outside we could hear things beginning to hot up, so we took our places on the balcony. Down on the start line, we could clearly see Mika Hakkinen getting ready on pole, surrounded by a wasp's nest of technicians and officials. Behind him, the scarlet Ferraris of Schumacher and Irvine, and then Coulthard in the other McLaren, each with a dozen or more worker bees buzzing round the cars. As we watched, Liz Hurley and Hugh Grant were escorted out to meet the drivers – Hugh in very Brit blue blazer and Panama, Liz in not a great deal. I bet *they* didn't arrive by train.

Finally it was race time. The officials melted away, the cars revved up to screaming pitch, the lights began to wink through the start sequence, and we all put on our headphones.

It was quite incredible. I've heard loud noise before, but nothing remotely approaching the crackling, howling, air-rending banshee scream that now assaulted us, bouncing off the shimmering tarmac, reverberating between the apartment buildings, slamming back off the stone.

In an amazing four seconds, the whole grid of twenty two cars had flashed away. Foolishly, like a child touching a hotplate just to see, I'd lifted my headphones off for a second, because they didn't seem to be keeping the noise out. In the nanosecond it took for the unmuted bone-jarring cacophony to liquify my skeleton, the cars were gone, and round the first bend up the long hill into the Place de Casino.

My God.

Shaking my head to try and clear the shards of pain, I decided to keep the cans on for the rest of the race. Ali was beaming, and leaning out over the rail to see how much of the track she could monitor as the cars went round the tortuous city circuit.

Just how loud is this going to be?

In the minute or so before the leaders emerged flying out of the long curved tunnel back into the harbour area again, I took in the view. Every square inch was covered with people – hanging off balconies, perched on street lights, sipping Moët in hospitality marquees, or standing on the deck of the hundreds of boats, yachts and ships in the harbour and the bay. High on the vertiginous hills behind us, where faceless apartment blocks formed a vast amphitheatre, every balcony was a riot of coloured flags and pink faces. For two hours every single eye in a whole country was focused on the same screaming stream of metal.

Down to our right, just beyond the start line, we could see the last two positions in the pit lane, and watch live the co-ordinated wonder of the pit stop that has always amazed me on TV. For the first stop, I'd hardly got my camera raised and ready before the car flashed away again – ten mechanics, four new tyres, twenty gallons of high octane and a new side panel in 8.2 seconds. Remarkable.

It was not the most exciting race of the season – Monaco is a difficult overtaking circuit – and in the end Hakkinen won easily, his fifth win of the year, and surely now he is unstoppable. As he flashed past the line, the chequered flag whirling above him, the most incredible sound began to build. From all over the harbour, from the airhorns of a thousand small boats, a hundred yachts' sirens, and a few massive ship klaxons, rose a cacophony of whoops and hooooo-hahs, as every vessel in sight sounded their own tribute to the winner. It was like the final scene of *The Guns of Navarone*, where the six British destroyers, their cargo of troops unsunk by the guns, let out a stream of triumphal whoops while the town of Mandrakos burns.

After all the finishers had flashed past, Hakkinen's silver-grey McLaren coasted to a stop right in front of us, joined shortly by Coulthard and Irvine, and they danced across the grid, playing to the massive bank of photographers in the opposite stand, and washing champagne out of their hair. Unlike most of the world, we had no need of television to see this glorious moment – it was happening right here in front of our eyes.

Michael had won the sweepstake, and he collected our bundle of francs with a grin. Ali and I showered thanks all round for a fabulous day, and made our way down through the crowds to the station. We waited for an hour in the hot sun, surrounded by ecstatic Finns waving blue and white flags and good-humouredly taunting the Germans and Italians – Schumacher had spun off half way through the race. Eventually we were packed onto the train, like the Tokyo subway, and clanked our way back along the coast to Cannes.

We arrived back in time to join the thousands of movie liggers crowded round the Palais des Festivals to try and spot the stars as the limos inched their way towards the red carpet for the Palme d'Or. We could see nothing and nobody, so, resting on our Grand Prix laurels, we strolled back to the Martinez and watched the highlights of the race, and a Greek director emotionally picking up the Palme, on our room TV. Finally another superb room service dinner on our balcony, as the winking lights of the promenade and the lively bustle of the streets filtered up beyond us into the blue-black Mediterranean night.

DAY FIFTY-SIX | MONDAY 25TH MAY

Cannes

For all the stars, moguls, executives and liggers, another Cannes is over, but for the town there is little or no anticlimax – today the World Perfumery Conference begins setting out its stalls. *Plus ça change, plus ça la même chose.*

We wander round town watching de-riggers de-rig and riggers rig, and Ali begins to salivate at the intended shopping marathon this afternoon. But first, lunch on the island.

The Ile Sainte Marguerite sits basking in the Cannes bay, and we'd decided to take one of the little ferries across to have a wander round and a bite of lunch. We bounce across the glittering waters, and have a chance to see up close the vast yacht that's been anchored off the beach all week. The *Lady Moura* is one of the largest private yachts in the world – much too big to berth in the marina – and she sits in full view of the town, screaming money. Every morning we had watched from our balcony as a hole opened up in her side, letting down a wooden deck platform just above the water, where linen-covered tables and parasols were erected by the crew for the owners' breakfast. The helicopter sits unobtrusively on a rear deck, and every inch of the paint and brightwork gleams in the morning sun. By tonight she will be gone, slipping away to the next playground destination.

The little ferry drops us at the jetty on the island, and just after it's gone we read the notice board that says the next one back isn't for three hours. Even though the morning and afternoon ferries run every half hour, this is still France, and everything stops for lunch – even ferry drivers. Ali accuses me of knowing this, thereby curtailing her shopping hours, but soon we are strolling along a deserted rocky beach, and after the frenetic activity of the last few days, the peace and quiet is very welcome.

It appeared that we hadn't entirely escaped the film world however, as round a headland we came upon a group of people with film cameras and lights. They were concentrating on something happening out of our sight behind a rock, and it soon became clear from the sounds we could hear that they were shooting a porn film. Amused, Ali dragged me by the ear back onto the path and we continued our walk.

Sainte Marguerite is only a couple of miles long, and surrounded by waters of the most azure blue we'd seen since Aigua Blava. Most of it is covered with a pine and eucalyptus forest, but there is a ruined fortress on the northern side and I'm just thinking, 'is this it?' when Michelin comes characterisically to the rescue and informs us that this is where the Man In The Iron Mask was imprisoned.

We know the embellished story from Voltaire, and endless Hollywood movies improbably starring Leonardo DiCaprio, but no-one can really tell us who the masked unfortunate was – disgraced nobleman, a betrayer of secrets, too important to kill, illegitimate brother of Louis Quatorze (the favourite story), or even Napoleon's great-great-grandfather: one theory is that the Man fathered a child in prison who was entrusted (*di buona parte* in Italian) to foster parents in Corsica and became Bonaparte's grandfather.

All we do know is that the man was imprisoned and masked here in 1687, and remained in this dank cell until the Governor, one Monsieur de Saint-Mers, bored shitless with island life, got himself appointed Governor of the Bastille and took his prisoner with him to Paris, where he died, still masked, in 1703.

Suddenly this quiet glade, with its hunched fortress – walls yards-thick and ivy-covered – has taken on a very sinister air. We walk on.

Before long we have returned to the small settlement of houses and boatyards, where we have a long lunch in a restaurant overlooking the water, with the thin white line of Cannes and the hills beyond on the horizon. The ferry, having had its lunch, graciously deigns to turn up and bounce us back over the bay. Time to shop!

We had discovered Blanc Bleu in Nice, and they had a much larger store on the Rue d'Antibes. I'd bought some swimming trunks from there, but of course I'm a mere amateur at this retail therapy lark. Ali had been saving herself, and bought a huge amount of superb clothes – shirts, trousers, a cool jacket fastened with caribiners, and a beautifully-coloured light blue cableknit sweater that seemed to be backlit. She looks sensational in it.

On we go, to shoe shops and film festival souvenir shops, collecting prezzies for folks at home, until I can no longer bear the weight of glossy carrier bags. Enough, I cry, and we hit a bar.

A pleasant dinner in the Martinez's waterfront restaurant, and we manage to resist the casino. We've been saving that for tomorrow night in case we get run out of town on a rail.

DAY FIFTY-SEVEN | TUESDAY 26TH MAY

Cannes

Today we drive along the coast to the gorgeous bay towns of Villefranche and Beaulieu-sur-Mer. Parking by the old fort in Villefranche, we walk round this stunning horseshoe harbour, with its pastel-coloured buildings and pavement cafés, the steep cypress-covered hills surrounding us. Ali racks out on the beach for an hour while I attempt a watercolour. Still way too much detail, and not enough expression. Or talent, really. Sigh.

Back in the car for a slow circuit of Cap Ferrat, where the villas are in the billionaire bracket and life moves slow, and oh, sooo easy. I imagine the heady days of the Riviera, with David Niven water-skiing in the bay before another long lunch under the vines.

Now to Beaulieu-sur-Mer, sleepier and fatly richer. This is where they shot one of our favourite comedies, *Dirty Rotten Scoundrels*, with Michael Caine and Steve Martin conning the rich Americans out of their diamonds. We have lunch in a vine-covered restaurant near the casino, trying to spot locations, and then wend our way back along the corniche to Cannes. As the evening sun covers the bay in gold, we order some nibbly things and play Scrabble on the balcony, planning our strategy for our night at the tables. There is of course no strategy. You take in whatever money you have, and hand it over. They're in business, aren't they? How else do you think they pay for the wood panelling and dozens of croupiers? Yeah, but maybe, just maybe™.

We'd decided not to gamble in the Carlton, where they claim you can play for the highest stakes in Europe. Our entire stake would probably not buy us a single chip, so we wandered along to the Croisette Casino, behind the Palais. It's a huge and rather impersonal room, with a dining area and an unfortunate butterscotch colour scheme. We hand over £150 and get a fairly small pile of chips in return, but hopefully enough to last a few minutes.

Who could ask for anything more?

Ali, normally the smiliest of girls, goes into Mrs Serious mode. She orders a Coke and commands me not to bother her, so I wander off to the Blackjack tables. They want a minimum stake of £10, so I wander back to see Ali's pile of chips has already grown. Quite the lowest roller at the table, she is nevertheless doing steadily rather well. She puts out only about seven or eight chips for each play, and studiously fills in her numbers card as they come up. I'm rather more casual about it, flipping chips across the baize, but amazingly we both start to win. It's all very small time stuff of course, but by 1.30, after nearly three hours of fun, we walk away, happy and hungry, £250 up!

A very late, or early, room service dinner tops off a memorable day, when we had turned the tables just slightly back on the robbing Cannesois. I drift off to a contented sleep, rewriting in my clouded brain some old lyrics:

As I walked along, towards Toulon
With an independent air
I could hear the wife declare
"Now you be careful, dear"
I could hear her sigh, and wish to die
I could feel her close the other eye
Of the man who didn't unduly trouble the bank at Monte Carlo.

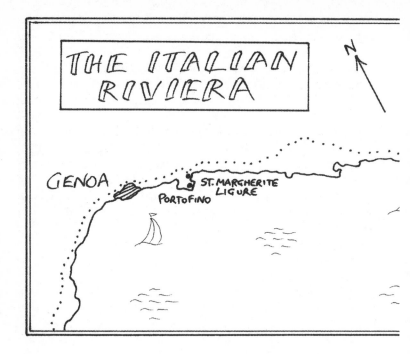

THE ITALIAN RIVIERA

Portofino
In which we discover this jewel of the Italian Riviera, and the storms wash the deckchairs away from the rocks below our hotel.

Pisa
In which we marvel at how the tower stays up, wonder whether they've

cleared a long enough fall path, and are astonished at the world record attempt for the most number of tourists per hectare.

Florence
In which we manage to secure a genuine 'room with a view'; sit under the stars listening to music on the Ponte

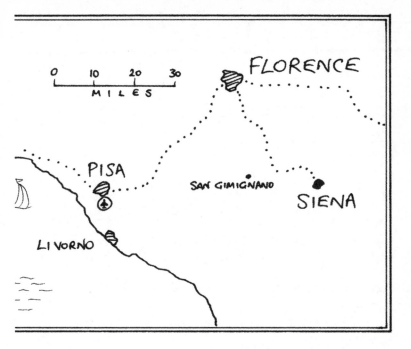

Vecchio; light candles for our parents in the Duomo; marvel at the flawlessness of David in the Accademia and Botticelli in the Uffizi; see the panorama from the Belvedere, and are generally swept away by the beauty of the ultimate Rennaissance city.

Siena
In which we have a fabulous lunch overlooking the shimmering fan-shaped piazza, and buy a leather bag (of course).

Italy

'O mio babbino caro'

DAY FIFTY-EIGHT | WEDNESDAY 27TH MAY

Cannes to Portofino

Our last morning in France until the end of June. We have a final swim off the Martinez's beach and then pack for our drive round to Italy.

We stop in Monte Carlo for lunch. The Grand Prix circuit is still in place, the bunting and endless cigarette ads coming down, and I can't resist having a little burn round; oh, how I miss the Jensen, she'd have loved this.

We park in yet another spotless underground car park, eight floors beneath the Place de la Casino, and have an excellent lunch in the Café de Paris – the food is just as good as France, but the service and attitude is much more pleasant and efficient. We resist a visit to the grand old casino, and tunnel our way into Italy.

From autoroute to autostrada, the road sweeps through mountains and across gorges, and down towards Genoa, surrounded now by industrial mines and factories. Passing quickly through, we arrive in the late afternoon in the Italian Riviera town of Santa Margherita Ligure. The tiny village of Portofino is what we've come to see, but it's so small that it's very difficult to stay there, unless you're Michael Winner and you take a couple of suites at the Splendido.

We check into the Hotel Continentale, an imposing building overlooking the sea. Our room is rather old-fashioned but has a tiled balcony with trim, chest-high dividing hedges – half private, half privet – and a couple of loungers, which will make Ali happy. Between the hotel and the sea is a lovely semi-formal garden, with gravel paths and cypress trees, and as the sun sets over the terracotta roofs of the town, we have a bottle of Pinot Grigio at the water's edge.

Portofino – the ultimate fishing village.

The hotel is so old-fashioned that its restaurant closes at 8.30, so we wander down the hill into the town, where we have a couple of grilled monkfish and watch the Vespas buzz along the front. Ah, Italia!

DAY FIFTY-NINE | THURSDAY 28TH MAY

Portofino Peninsula

Today the storm had come to this corner of the Med. We awoke to crashing waves on the plateau of rocks below the hotel. This was a worry as these rocks had had thirty or so wooden loungers still stretched out on them at nine o'clock last night, and possibly a few guests too. Now, the foaming turquoise seawater was on final rinse, and it even looked too rough for the lifeboat, if they had one.

After breakfast, determined not to let the weather deter our golden-tinged renaissance tour, we set off for Portofino. We had intended to go round the headland on the ferry to avoid the traffic and parking problems, but the water was far too rough for our delicate breakfasted stomachs, and the rain looked promising for crowd control, so we drove.

The corniche road is only a few feet above sea level, and twists its attractive way around the base of the cliffs, past a tiny sandy bay with obligatory restaurant, and then you enter the village of Portofino. Your Sense-O-Park™ is first alerted by Cinquecentos and other diminutive cars squeezed into every conceivable square centimetre of space – between the yellow line and the cliff face, in the bus shelter, inside a wheelie bin – and you begin to worry badly about where you're going to stick the car. Portofino is at the end of the line and the road finishes in the main piazza, where every space is permanently taken (it's rumoured that many cars have been there for years – the owners daren't take them out for a drive for fear of never being able to park in their own town again), and a couple of Carabinieri are moving traffic either on, or back out.

Luckily it's pouring with rain, and it's only 9.30, so we get the last parking space in the huge multi-storey they've built under the hill. I don't know why they don't have a permanent huge red electric sign six miles back in Santa Margherita saying 'Portofino Full'. Perhaps everybody knows.

Catch it on the right day, and Portofino is the most complete, the most romantic, the most idyllic fishing village in the world, let alone Italy. Some would argue that the right day would have been in early May sometime in the 1970s, when nobody could afford to travel and the place wasn't overrun with tourists, as it is most days now.

Yes, on any given sunny day, during an increasingly long season, the village is fairly heaving with visitors, but visiting in late May in the rain is still one way of getting across the harbour piazza without bumping a shoulder, and getting a restaurant table from which you can actually see the boats.

From the car park you emerge into the upper piazza and walk down a narrow alley of shops and restaurants towards the harbour. Under an arch, and you're standing inside the shimmering, pastel-coloured jewel of the Riviera. Directly ahead is the tiny square bay, no more than a hundred feet wide. The smooth stone flags of the piazza slope directly into the black water, small wooden fishing boats tug gently at their painters, and the slick side steps down to the water are dotted with barrels and lobster pots and coils of rope.

On three sides of the harbour, the honey, jasmine, fuschia, willow and ochre-coloured houses rise five or six storeys from the piazza, topped with flower-edged balconies and terracotta roofs. Washing lines drape between high windows, their green louvre shutters pinned back against the stone. Below, canvas awnings jut out over shops and cafés, with little iron tables and chairs beneath – at which, during the season, is seated most of the population of Nebraska. Today though, the rain has allowed humble Brits to be able to sit at the water's edge and sip a calmer cappuccino.

To the left the bay curves round, carrying the line of houses with it, and comes to a stop a couple of hundred yards later, where the stone breakwater falls into the sea. From there you can look across the Gulf of Rapallo, with the opaque lavender hills following the coast south to Tuscany. The right hand edge of the harbour curves right round to the far promentary – a huge olive, yew and sea pine-covered rock rising 400 feet to the ramparts of the Castello San Giorgio. A steep flight of steps leads up to the pathway above the town, but it's too wet and depressing to explore today, so we have a delicious *tagliatelle marinara* in one of the restaurants and wander back to the car, hoping for a better day tomorrow with which to explore this stunning place.

Back in Santa Margherita we wander round the shops, picking up a few essentials, and I buy a Panama in the vain hope that I'll need it. It is from Equador of all places, with a thin green and leather hatband and rather rakish brim. Won't make me look any less of a Brit though. In the *farmacia* I am secretly delighted to find in their small book section an English copy of the latest Tom Clancy. Embarrassed to be seen buying it, instead of the Sartre or the Dante, I pile a load of condoms and Preparation H on top of it and ask for a female assistant and a brown paper bag.

The rain continues, so we have a long late siesta in our room, the salty mist of the receding storm wafting in through the French windows. I start a watercolour of Portofino, but then the comforting adventures of President Jack Ryan draw me in. Tosh, to be sure, but first class tosh.

DAY SIXTY | FRIDAY 29TH MAY

Portofino Peninsula

Still rather overcast this morning, but the storm has abated, and the sun begins to elbow its way through the scudding clouds by lunchtime. I have once again picked up my brush, and renew my daubish efforts at capturing some of the colours of Portofino. It actually turns out to be not too horrendous – at least you can tell it's a house.

In the afternoon we drive back into a much brighter Portofino. Like a Muscovy duck shaking off the raindrops, the colours of the village reappear, and they're even hanging out strings of bunting and fairy lights in honour of our arrival – Italy has almost as many fiestas as Spain. Time to explore the church and the castle.

There are two ways up to the saddle, or col, that sits in a dip between the two tree-covered peaks that separate the town from the open sea. Base Camp One is in the main piazza, and a very narrow cobbled path, just wide enough for a small *camionetto* delivery van, snakes its way up behind the waterfront houses. Tiny art galleries and vegetable shops line the cobbles, green leafy produce and gaudy canvases jostling for the tourist's eye. Soon the houses fade away and the path steepens. To the left, through the tumbling bougainvillea, the whole town begins to open out below, becoming more model-like as you climb. Then you reach Base Camp Two – the top of hundreds of very steep steps that you could have climbed up from the harbour, but we lacked the necessary crampons, and in my case stamina. And here is the church – perched implausibly 300 feet up on a narrow plateau of rock between the sheer cliffs that fall down to the sleepy harbour on one side and the still-agitated Med on the other. The bright yellow and white marble stone of the church shines newly-washed in the sun, and a very over-crowded cemetery clings darkly around the edge of the building. The ragged flag fluttering at the pole looks identical to the Royal Navy's White Ensign – I wonder what it really is? On the seaward side, a stone balcony hangs over the cliff, and you can walk out and look down at the magnificent cliffs – smooth rocks dropping sheer to foaming water at the base.

High as you are, this is only a staging post for the real summit goal – the Castello San Giorgio. A slightly less vertiginous path snakes on up, past some more houses – they must be fit – until you reach the castle entrance, an ordinary wrought-iron garden gate, edged with pretty flower borders. A few lire later, and you can walk through the dark rooms, with even darker furniture, towards the real reason for the climb – the high gardens. A thick low stone wall surrounds an unkempt area strewn with pine needles and tree roots, with one huge sea pine in the middle. You go over to the wall and there, as if you were in the basket of a balloon, is Portofino, 400 feet directly below. The open throat of the harbour contains the tiny fishing boats, and your eye is drawn up past the gaily-coloured houses, past the *campanile*, to the wooded bowl of hills above the town, dotted with private villas. If you time it right the sun is just dipping below the treeline ahead, and the twilight falls softly but firmly on the minature village beneath, like the gentle closing of a child's bedroom door.

And this is where – oh deary me, lawd help us – the Americans have got it wrong.

I'm afraid I have some disturbing news for you, with only a few globules of compensation. The above mentioned Americans, may their enthusiasm never dim, have a number of traits which one could, if charitable, classify under vaulting ambition, and if less kind, under colossal arrogance. They feel that there are many charming, 'right purdy', or even quaint, places in Europe, but the main problem is that you have to actually go to Europe to 'visit with them'. So they're starting to solve that minor inconvenience by re-building them in the good ol' USA. I believe they call it 'heritage recreation' or some such revolting newspeak.

Unfortunately this has manifested itself as follows: there is now a hotel in Florida that has been built expressly to satisfy Americans' demands to 'experience' Portofino without actually having to go there. It's called – and they insist on this – 'The Portofino Bay Hotel at Universal Orlando™ A Loews Hotel', and it's a scale model of the original village, so lovingly and wistfully described above. The bowel-wateringly worrying thing is that the scale is one-to-one. That's right, it's an *exact* copy, inch-for-inch, size-for-size.

The reason I know this and more about it, I blush to tell, is that I've stayed there. I can therefore relate a curious mixture of utter horror and offended European sensibilities, together with a very troubling conclusion – they've done it superbly well.

Standing in the piazza of 'The Portofino Bay Hotel at Universal Orlando™ A Loews Hotel' is a very strange experience if you've seen the original. The proportions are exactly right, the harbour and boats are faithfully recreated, cafés and shops line the piazza with parasols and Italian brand names, and I was served with the best freshly-made iced cappuccino I've ever had. One can't expect a hundredth of the atmosphere of course – the smells and sounds and dusty patina of the centuries – but it's a pity that across the lake, above the newly-planted saplings, you get a panoramic view of the world's biggest multi-storey car park (true), and that carried on the Florida breeze there's a never-ending background noise of screams and bangs and whooshes and the *Jaws* theme tune emanating from the Universal Studios fun park next door.

Of course they don't want you to *entirely* forget why you're there.

In Las Vegas – home to thirty-nine of the world's forty largest hotels –they have apparently gone one better. There they have recreated as hotels two entire cities – Venice and Paris – lessening even further the future burden on the US Passport Office. In 'Paris, Las Vegas' – as opposed to Paris, France – the staff are all trained to perfection in the art of 'heritage recreation'. To further foster the illusion that you are steeped in all things Parisienne, they use a double language. When passing a member of staff you will be greeted with a cheery "Bonjourgoodmorning!", and when thanking them for a service rendered, you will be merrily assured, "Jevousenprisyou'rewelcome!".

Merde alors!

With the sun gone the cicadas escorted us back down the path to a warm Mediterranean evening by the harbour wall, where we ate linguini and drank Pinot Grigio as the lanterns twinkled and danced on the surface of the water. The frapping of the masts on the yachts and the clink of glasses mingled effortlessly with the soft sound of American voices from all the surrounding tables.

DAY SIXTY-ONE | SATURDAY 30TH MAY

Portofino to Pisa to Florence

Today we travel south into Tuscany proper, and to meet up with my sister. Pisa airport has grown considerably in recent years, and is now the main port of entry for the area. Caroline has flown from the UK on Monarch, so we don't rush to make the scheduled arrival time, and sure enough she emerges, surrounded by shell suits and Duty Free, a couple of hours late. She's quite use to that, however, being somewhat of an amateur globetrotter. She works for a major UK charity, and seems to spend most of the modest amount they pay her on short breaks to all sorts of places. In the last two years alone she's been to Beijing, San Francisco, Munich, Toronto and Egypt, and that doesn't include weekend flits to places like Barcelona and Bruges. She goes with assorted friends and travelling companions, and when asked how she can afford it, she says "stay cheap, buy nothing and walk". She has, amazingly, never done Florence, so when we were planning the trip we suggested she join us for a few days. She might have to revisit her accommodation budget though. But first, Pisa, to which we have allotted half a day – probably not enough, but we are all keen to be in Florence for dinner.

We park in a dusty municipal car park not far from the centre, and walk through a gate in the city walls onto the Field of Miracles or Campo dei Miracoli. This is aptly named for two reasons – first, it's a miracle the Torre Pendente is still standing, and second it's a miracle if you get anywhere near it without being sold a plaster, plastic, porcelain, pewter or perfumed soap copy of it.

It is a stunning sight – a perfect emerald green swathe of grass sweeping across to the shining white marble of the Duomo church and the delicate columns of the Leaning Tower. The 'Keep Off The

Grass' signs are completely ignored by everyone, even if they understand Italian, but the field is so huge and the buildings so massive that it doesn't look too overcrowded. All down the right hand side of the area, backing on to the city houses, are 400 yards of enterprise – dozens and dozens of permanent stalls laden with Leaning Tower paraphanalia and trinkets. Models, of course, in every size and style, but also key rings, baseball caps, beach towels, doilies, lighters, clocks, pens, letter openers, boxes, books, sweets, bottles and T-shirts. Goodness knows what sort of Leaning Towers they've got under the counter for the more, er, discerning customer.

Pisa used to be a major Mediterranean power in its own right. Its fleet would plunder and trade, providing income for the construction of greatness like these buildings. Then nature took a hand by silting up the Arno and cutting Pisa off from the sea. Nature also left the city with a permanent Damoclean reminder by softening the clay and sand under the tower. The tower actually started to lean before they'd finished the third storey, but they continued building for another hundred years or so, and finished it, rather gingerly placing the last card on the house in 1350.

For nearly 700 years – nature is *sooo* patient – the tower continued to tilt, until it was nearly twenty feet out at the top of its 180 feet height. It really was very alarming to look at, and they had cleared a wide fall path for it – I suppose they did expect it to come down. Recently they have managed to arrest and partially rectify the tilt and the tower, leaning less but just as spectacular, is now open again.

After a disgusting lunch we take the smooth motorway up the Arno valley to Florence, where we are to stay six nights.

Not here, though. Oh, I don't think so.

The Palazzo Ricassoli had been billed as a beautiful Florentine palace with apartments and rooms of pleasing countenance. Possibly some of the rooms in the main old building were okay, but it turns out that this is a residence – sterile apartments let out on a student-type basis. Indeed the soulless sixties block we were led into looked as if it had been erected in a hurry during the long vac to house a minor polytechnic's new influx of undergrads. White plastic rooms with tiny single beds, formica kitchenettes and tatty throw rugs greeted us, and despite Caroline saying it was pretty luxurious compared to some of the places she's had to stay in, we (alright I) took the view that it wasn't close to being acceptable. So, having confirmed that we would

Towering over the Field of Miracles.

only stay one night, we resolved to venture into the twilight and find better accommodation, even if it meant not eating during our stay.

We wander through the city, catching tantalising glimpses of the Duomo, but wanting to get a place for our heads before we explore. Eventually, having tried several hotels of varying quality and expense, we cross the Arno to find an oasis of calm and refinement, the Hotel Lungarno. We are shown a room with a view that Lucy Honeychurch would have died for – a balcony over the river affords us the full sweep of the Ponte Vecchio, with the city rising over the opposite bank. Letting our plastic delay the financial shock, we book two rooms from tomorrow.

By now it is nearly ten, so we wander back through the city, having a pleasant wine-fuelled dinner in a little piazza, before we have to be back for lock down and lights out.

DAY SIXTY-TWO | SUNDAY 31ST MAY

Florence

Sore from spartan beds, we drive down to the new hotel, park in the underground car park, and are checked in and sorted in our (air-conditioned) rooms by eleven. The weather is cloudy with the occasional raindrop, but warm and sultry.

A quiet amble through the Florentine Sunday, up and around the incredible Duomo which we will explore more thoroughly tomorrow, then back down and across the Arno to the Boboli Gardens. You go through the huge courtyard of the Palazzo Pitti and out into the delightfully unkempt gardens which rise up the southern foothills of the city. We thought we might be able to get to the Belvedere for the classic vista, but the path leads up to a charming formal square rose garden which does have wonderful views, but south east, away from the city. It is a very peaceful spot, and we sit on the low wall for a while, drinking in the Tuscan air and watching a small family of wild cats who have made their home here.

It is now a very hot afternoon, so we wander back for a siesta, pausing only at a very strange building tucked away in the northern corner – the Grotto Grande. It's an odd folly, containing weird statuary and cavern-like stone carvings. Doesn't fit somehow.

After a cooling siesta and a glass of wine looking at our view, we all venture out for dinner in a little restaurant near the Uffizi. We have not yet managed to find any food which approaches the quality of even the most ordinary restaurant in France. The menus are very limited in their range and inventiveness, so your tastebuds are not very inspired. If you want a change from pizza and pasta, then trout in almonds or *escalope milanese* is about your only choice – and the La Scala restaurant in my home village has been doing those, and better, for thirty years.

The midnight air is still very warm. I think in an ideal world where matter transference was possible, I would spend my days in England and transport myself to the Med for the evenings, where you can eat in shirtsleeves and amble in warm pine-scented air. Just imagine it – "Okay, I've just got to get this last letter out and I'll see you at Giorgio's in the Piazza Navona in ten minutes. Mine's a grappa." Our route home takes us over the glorious Ponte Vecchio, with its honeyed stone arches and the dark wood of the jewellers' stalls. On the apex of the bridge a crowd has gathered to listen to live music. A couple of guitars and a saxophone are being played by wandering musos who've obviously just met, and are jamming whatever they can find of mutual pleasure; the crowd, where appropriate, are singing along. We perch on the centuries-old stone parapet above the dark Arno below and listen. Tracy Chapman's *Baby Can I Hold You*, Pink Floyd's *Wish You Were Here, Hotel California* (of course) and some Beatles songs waft over the water and rebound softly off the stone. Presently a girl is pushed forwards out of the audience by her friends and whispers to the players; they nod and she then launches into a very passable *Summertime*, her clear Australian voice carrying Gershwin's sultry melody into the still Florentine night.

DAY SIXTY-THREE | MONDAY 1ST JUNE

Florence

A clear blue sky greets us this morning – it's going to be a scorcher. Across the Ponte Vecchio again, passing the spot where Julius Caesar founded Florence in 1 BC. It took eleven centuries to really get going, but it was worth the wait. The bridge itself was built in 1345 and was the only one to survive the Second World War.

A cappuccino in the Piazza della Signoria while we drink in the political air of the city – this square was, and still is, the place where politics and gossip are rife. Statues surround the piazza, including the huge copy of David at the corner of the Palazzo Vecchio. This was where Michelangelo's original stood for 370 years until it was moved to the Accademia to protect it from the elements. We decide to go and see the real one a little later.

The Palazzo is huge and rather frightening. Sheer stone walls rise up to an overhanging ribbed upper storey with battlements above, and the massive tower of the *campanile* soaring up into the sky. Even in the friendly morning light it has a threatening look about it, perhaps because in my mind's eye I can see the twisting gutted body of *Commendatore* Pazzi swinging from Hannibal Lecter's noose.

Inside there are vast cavernous council chambers and gilded rooms to explore, topped with magnificent ceilings and minstrels' galleries. Gold *fleurs-de-lis*, the symbol of Florence, decorate everything, and in one high room the full glory of the Duomo can be seen to the north, framed in leaded glass.

We walk north towards the Accademia only to find that, like so many things in Europe, it's closed on a Monday, so we retrace our steps for the Duomo. The cathedral of Santa Maria del Fiore absolutely dominates the city, but rather like the Empire State Building it's difficult to gauge its sheer size from anywhere near it – you have to climb to Fort Belvedere to really appreciate its over-whelming presence. Still, it's pretty huge when you're standing next to it, and we walk around making appreciative noises at the sheer artistry of the ... scaffolding that has (of course) been erected around much of the eastern end.

In front of the western steps is the Baptistry, much older, with its world famous East Doors. They were commissioned in 1401 to celebrate Florence's avoidance of a plague, and a competition devised to choose the designer. Six giants of the renaissance, including Donatello and Brunelleschi, didn't make the cut, and Ghiberti was given the job. The doors are ten panels of beaten gold bas-relief, each representing a famous bible scene. When someone like Michelangelo dubs them 'The Gates of Paradise', you've got to consider it a job well done.

Inside the Duomo it is huge and quiet and still. And very sparse – there's not much in there except space, with the breathtaking vault of the dome soaring overhead. Brunelleschi got this gig, and set out to create the biggest dome in the world. It was technically mind-

From anywhere in the city, the Duomo dominates.

boggling, and he had to build two domes, one propped inside the other, to make it stay up. Again it was a competition that decided the builder, and in the Museo del Duomo you can see some original models submitted to the committee as competition entries. There are also original blocks and tackles, wheelbarrows and rope lifts used during the construction, which took fourteen years.

All the dust of the centuries has brought on my hay fever, and I'm sneezing so much I'm in danger of bringing the whole structure down, so I go back to the hotel to stick my head in the fridge, while Caroline climbs the Dome and Ali shops.

Another pleasant dinner under the stars – *Truita* with hazelnuts this time, who says variety is dead? – and then a grappa on our balcony listening to the echoed sounds of singing from the Ponte Vecchio.

DAY SIXTY-FOUR | TUESDAY 2ND JUNE

Florence and Siena

A day out to Siena today, so we drive south out of the city and forty kilometres down a concrete-edged racetrack *autostrada*, reputedly one of the most dangerous roads in Europe. Hah! What about the motorway outside Valencia?

The killer road expectorates us out into glorious Tuscan countryside and we wind up a hill into Siena. We park underground and emerge into a blisteringly hot, canyoned, terracotta hilltop town. Seven hills, as it happens, just like Rome. No street is level, and we switchback up and down until we reach the magnificent Piazza di Campo. Shaped like an open fan, nine sweeping cobbled segments spread out and up from the steps of the Palazzo Publico to an impressive semi-circle of high stone houses. All around the base of these are numerous cafes and restaurants, tables and linen shaded by coloured awnings. At the top of the centre fan section is the famous fountain of Gaia, a huge marble basin with elaborate reliefs. A copy, of course, but it and its original (now in a museum) have been fed by waters from the town's fifteen mile aquaduct for nearly 600 years.

Lunch, I think. And not at all bad, either – sautéed scallops and feather-light carbonara under a green awning, looking up at the unfeasibly tall bell tower, the Torre di Mangia, which at 330 feet is the second highest in Italy. Well *I* don't know what the tallest is – look it up.

Afterwards we wander up and down the streets and find our way to the Duomo, which is stunning even though they never finished it. You stand in the open piazza and realise the huge wall opposite the cathedral was intended to be the north wall of the nave. They wanted it to be the biggest church in Christendom, but they were practically all wiped out by Johnny Plague and it never happened. It still looks great though – the 700 year old western façade is a cascade of carvings and blinding gilt, all the way down to the, er, scaffolding-covered doors. The famous *campanile* rises imperiously above the piazza. From almost anywhere, in the hot sun, the striped marble of the tower looks black and white, but it's actually green and white, all locally quarried and worked.

Inside, the Duomo is a delight. The high vaults are midnight-blue studded with gold stars and *fleurs-de-lis*, the huge columns supporting the dome are black and white marble, and although much of it is covered for protection most of the year, the floor is of fabulous inlaid marble mosaics. At the western end was a roped off area inside which a group of people were sat on the floor surrounded by equipment and tiny arc lights. They looked like ordinary people under the direction of an expert or two, and they were, with great care and much joy, repairing and relaying a section of the ancient marble floor. They were chatty and happy – a veritable community of citizens looking after their heritage.

On the way back to the car we pass dozens of Siena's famous leather emporiums, so Caroline buys a superb leather briefcase for her new job, and we travel back in air-conditioned comfort to Firenze.

Tuscany's famous diaphanous light is now at its late afternoon loveliest, so we climb the southern hills to Fort Belvedere and the Piazza Michelangelo for The View. If there is a more richly satisfying vista of a city anywhere in Europe, I don't know it. Florence is laid out below like a medieval sepia etching – there lies the sleepy sinuous Arno, the high spiked tower of the Palazzo Vecchio, the long lines of the Uffizi, and dominating all, like a vast ocean liner among a flotilla of yachts and tugboats, is the Duomo. So huge is it, it seems to be not much smaller in the eye than when up close. It rises triumphantly from the chaotic rooftops, ever higher, until the Dome breaks the misty grey horizon of the northern hills.

The girls get cokes and an ice cream while I try a rather pedestrian pencil sketch to watercolour later. I then stand at the rail and do my infamous impression of Hannibal Lecter when Clarice first visits his cell and remarks on his drawings. "That is the Duomo seen from the Belvedere. Memories are what I have, Agent Starling, instead of a view."

Htszzzzztszzzz!

DAY SIXTY-FIVE | WEDNESDAY 3RD JUNE

Florence

Ahhh, Firenze! Glorious city of the Renaissance, jewel of art and culture, what shall we do this morning?

Get a haircut.

Ali has hers done supremely well – I've never seen it look so good – and I have mine trimmed attentively in a small *tonsore* under the southern arches of the Ponte Vecchio. Ten quid – one for the cut and nine for the search fee (©William Hague). Then we meet Caroline for David.

The Gallaria dell' Accademia is housed in an unprepossessing building a few blocks north of the Duomo, and the queues weren't too bad even though the season is now well started. You enter a long high hall, with streams of natural light coming in at the far end from a domed skylight positioned over David himself. You have no idea of his sheer size until you spot the tiny people clustered round his plinth.

He is absolutely stunning. The size, scale, detail, perspective and grace is breathtaking and one can't help wondering how this could a) be done by man, and b) be the work of just one? They've recently discovered that David's eyes are about twenty degrees askew, but only if you climb a thirty foot tower and look directly up his nose, which of course Mike never intended anyone to do. He did it so that from the proper viewing position his hero would look perfect. Which he does. So *stop meddling.*

Other sculptures are interesting, and there's one exam piece of the Madonna in a side room where the expression on her face is mesmerising, but David is in the retinas and cannot be approached.

There's a huge queue when we come out, and another has built up down at the Uffizi. Queuing and I have never been soulmates, and the day is now at its blisteringly hottest, so we agree to have lunch and a siesta and meet back when the punters and the heat have both died down a little.

At 6.30 the day is still warm, but we get into the Uffizi with ease. The oldest art gallery in the world, it was originally built as offices for the ruling Medici, who then spent contemporary millions, or even billions, on commissioning the finest work from all over Italy and beyond. Many of the galleries are closed for refurb (didn't I read somewhere that only about 20% of the world's art treasures held by public galleries are on display at any one time?) but we do see some spectacular stuff – Young Leonardo, Michelangelo, Giorgione, Titian, and of course Botticelli. The Venus is there – you know the one, naked girl standing in a scallop shell with a discreet hand and a wisp of long hair covering her bits. I can't help seeing Uma Thurman in that exact pose in *Baron Munchausen* (shot by Gilliam at trouser-melting expense down the road in Rome).

A final dinner in the Piazza della Signoria, under the sobering presence of the Pallazzo Vecchio with its wheeling bats, and then we say farewell to Caroline, who has to get up at sparrow's for her Monarch flight back to England. 100-8 she'll still be sitting in the departure lounge reading her Mary Wesley at lunchtime.

ROME AND AMALFI

Rome

In which we are chilled by the Colosseum, thrilled by the Trevi at 2am, stunned by the new improved Sistine ceiling, saddened by the world's largest scaffolding frontage, terrified by Roman driving and discover the 2-hectare plateau from which the whole world was ruled for a thousand years.

Pompeii

In which the incredible architecture and chilling mummies inside the site are surrounded on the outside by the most awful fly-blown tourist service buildings and food huts.

Positano and The Amalfi Coast

In which we have a vertiginous hotel room 1000 feet above the azure Med, discover a stunning town nestling in a steep valley and negotiate swooping, looping cliff edge roads.

Capri

In which we smell the money and sniff the bougainvillaea, while recovering from a rollercoaster hydrofoil crossing.

Torgiano

In which we stay in a lovely central Italian hotel for some R&R on our way north.

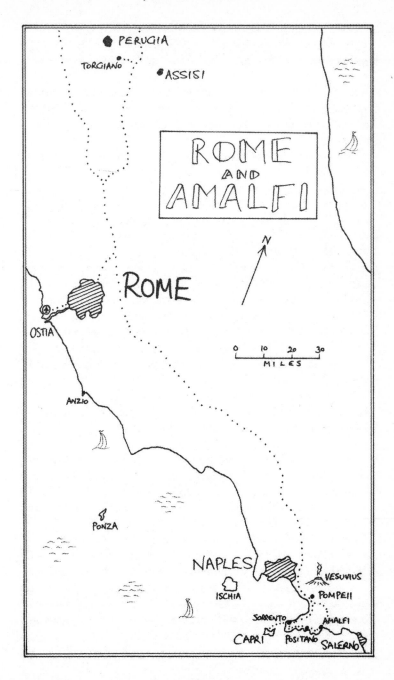

DAY SIXTY-SIX | THURSDAY 4TH JUNE

Florence to Ostia

Goodbye to the Hotel Lungarno (quietly excellent) and to Florence (sumptuously lovely) and we set off south towards Rome. Well, not Rome exactly, but its port town of Ostia, because we've got to go home.

When we planned this trip there was one fly in the ointment, one ant in the sugarbowl – I had to attend a work conference thing.

In Droitwich.

If you want to join us for the glories of Rome, skip forward to Monday the eighth, but I should be faithful to the diary and make an entry for each day. I suppose most occupations have an annual conference or get together affair, but mine has only recently started one because I do a very strange and sometimes quite solitary thing for a main living. I'm a voiceover. This might not mean much to you, nor should it, and it's hardly a glamourous occupation, but I can claim that if you live in the UK and you're over twenty five I *guarantee* you've heard my voice. You might have heard me say fairly ordinary things like "The Daily Telegraph – the A-Z of the General Election", or "Vidal Sassoon Wash & Go"; or your ears might have curled slightly at hearing me say, "Dear Anne, I'm writing to complain about this week's episode of 'Birds of a Feather' where Dorian removes her...."; you've almost certainly heard me say, "(such and such a programme)... tonight at 9.30 on BBC1"; if in business you might have heard me extoll knowingly about the wonders of computer accounting software, or blood testing machines, or Formula One Cars, (even, rather alarmingly, Karma Sutra instruction videos and roofing felt, although not as far as I know on the same tape); if you listen to your local commercial radio station you will, *ad nauseam,* have heard me exhort you to visit your friendly neighbourhood car dealer or supermarket or solicitor or restaurant or garden centre; and if you watch documentaries you will have heard me narrate the incredible images you are watching of sharks or polar bears or monster trucks or extreme sports or the Space Shuttle.

An odd sort of job, but most of the time I enjoy it hugely, especially the documentary stuff which is varied and interesting. I also write (your opinion may differ), and I produce radio and TV programmes, but voicing is my main gig. And this weekend's get together was a conference for those in the (mostly radio) voicing lark, called VOX.

"That is the Duomo, seen from the Belvedere". Okay, it's pretty awful, but it does look better in black and white.

The majority of my radio clients would be there (who by now might have forgotten I existed), as well as many of my co-gobbers, and I had to attend, even if it meant flying back half way through the trip.

We'd booked seats on BA's early flight to Heathrow on Friday morning, and we were due to stay at the Rome Airport Palace Hotel in order to be nearby. Sounds okay doesn't it? Except that it's nowhere near Rome, not very near the airport, is decidedly not a palace and its claim to be a hotel is on the shaky side.

Ostia is a place I know only from the BBC's wonderful adaptation of *I, Claudius*, where Derek Jacobi is always on his way there to visit harbour works or grain shipments, or on his way back to find his seventeen year old wife has shagged everything that moves in Rome and is about to declare herself Queen in his absence. The name in Latin means 'mouth' (of the Tiber in this case), and in its day was the main port of the Roman Empire, and as such hugely influential, with a population of 100,000. It's decline came with Rome's in the 4th century, when malaria wiped out the people and the Tiber's alluvial silt wiped out the city. It was only discovered again in 1909.

I wish I could say we went to the excavations and had interesting things to report, but we entered the new town on a dusty road towards bar-opening time, found the grey, hot apartment buildings so depressing, and the Rome Airport Palace Hotel nestling between them even more depressing, that we didn't have the heart to venture out further. Besides we had to pack, eat a revolting bowl of pasta and make admin phone calls first. It has not escaped our notice that we find it easier, and find ourselves feeling less guilty, booking ahead for nice hotels when we're staying in grotty ones. Odd that.

The hair-dryer temperature air wafts us to sleep, me dreaming of hot exhausts from turbine aircraft engines.

And what happens when they stop.

DAY SIXTY-SEVEN | FRIDAY 5TH JUNE

FCO to LHR

From the above description of today's journey (FCO-LHR) you might think I was a sad airport anorak who knew things like airport designation letters and could spot a 767-400 from a A340 at five miles. And you'd be right. I love everything about flying.

Except flying.

I stopped watching *Airport* after Jeremy Spake made me want to bite off a Jumbo's aileron and shove it up his arse, but for some reason I have always been fascinated by aircraft and airports, even though I am a nervous passenger. I don't know why – when I was a teenager taking my first flights I used to love it: the power in your back on take off, the amazing achievement of flying *per se* and the bustle and excitement and purpose of an airport. Then I went through a five or six year stretch of knowing, absolutely *knowing*, we were going to crash into the Staines Reservoir. Today I acknowledge that, okay we're probably not going to crash, but if I don't keep a strong upward pressure on the armrests, or if I stop my endless vigilance of the engine note, then we will, like Monty Python's sheep, not so much fly as plummet.

Anyway, we boarded our BA 737-300 at Leonardo da Vinci airport and shoehorned ourselves into the 'generous' seat pitch. Outside I could see the engine cowling with its warning messages and worn rivets, and the thin line where the thrust reversers would deploy on landing. Please, tell me there's a failsafe gizmo that means they absolutely can't deploy unless the undercarriage is bearing the full weight of the plane.

Yup, a little knowledge is a dangerous thing.

The flight was, as they all are really, uneventful, and we landed – conveniently missing the Staines Reservoir – at Heathrow on a mild but pleasant afternoon, picked up our hired Ford Mangrove, and drove home.

Weird. We've been away over two months, and yes the trees have blossomed and the skip's gone, but otherwise *nothing has changed at all.*

Surely several governments have fallen, the threatened by-pass has been built and next door's been demolished in a freak storm? No, all we got was, "Oh, you back then? Milk's up a penny. Nice weekend?"

Einstein *was* right – essentially, life moves at a totally different pace depending on your own perspective.

A few friends came over in the evening to catch up on all the gossip, and having sorely missed food from home we order a takeaway Ruby – tikka masala, peshwari naans and bags of poppadoms – mmm, so *English*.

DAYS SIXTY-EIGHT & NINE | 6TH & 7TH JUNE

Droitwich

From the chateaux of the Loire to the Chateau Impney. The non-profit VOX event, organised by a bunch of voiceovers, takes us up the M40 and down the M5 to Droitwich Spa, where a 19th century mill owner's huge French folly has been turned into a hotel and conference centre. It's all very English – rose pink wallpaper, melamine headboards, flock counterpanes, a Corby trouser press, strong Tetley tea in unbreakable cups, and if you ask for an orange juice you'll get served an orange squash.

I won't bore you with the details of the conference. Just because it's an unusual industry doesn't mean it isn't very similar to your own corporate jolly or works outing. The food and wine were uninspiring, but it was good to see everyone, the chat was lively, and there was even a fight!

Back home round the soon-to-be-not-missed-at-all M25, where late packing and last minute details occupy our evening. The half-time oranges have been eaten, the ref is looking at his watch, and it's time for the second leg.

DAY SEVENTY | MONDAY 8TH JUNE

Home to Rome

On an English summer morning it's pretty difficult to get up early enough for it to be not yet fully light, but we managed it, and dropped the car off before boarding our little plane back to Italy.

Our Merc is, amazingly, still where we left it in the car park of the Ostia Near-Airport Tenement Guest House, and even more amazingly still contains its contents. And so for Rome.

Let's say that once more with feeling: ROME!

Apart from love, I think Rome is the single most emotive four letter word in mankind's history. For billions of people across the centuries it has been the centre of their religion, Christ's Vicarage; for millions today it is a focal point of art, culture and politics; and for many more millions in far antiquity it was the heart of their existence – more than an Empire, an idea – and the rules, customs, gods, culture, discipline and civilisation that emanated from the Eternal City governed their lives utterly for a thousand years.

And the traffic hasn't got any better.

It's generally agreed among European motorists that Belgium is the most frightening country to drive in, but I think Rome is worse. The road surfaces are like driving over rockfalls, the signage is non-existant and the local drivers are all world-class sociopaths. Entering from the west we had to negotiate our way into and through the city centre, rattle our way over the cobbles along the banks of the Tiber, and then try to find a way to turn east off the Via Flaminia. But you can't. The central dual carriageway has two other lanes outside it, divided by concrete reservations, and there didn't seem to be a way to turn right. We had to go nearly two miles before we found a green filter light and a path back into the city. Finally we find our home for the next three nights, the Aldrovandi Palace Hotel. It's up beyond the Borghese Gardens and is certainly a palace but probably a mistake – we should have tried harder to find a *pensione* in the city centre.

We are slightly alarmed on the way to the room. The lift only goes to the sixth floor, and the bellboy then starts to walk us up some side stairs. Oh dear, I think, they've priced us up instantly and are sticking us in the attic. Indeed there is just one room up here, but it's fairly big, and the bonus is a large private roof terrace with loungers and tables and wide views across the northern part of the city.

The hotel itself seems overpriced and over-arrogant for its billing. It claims five star status but patently isn't. Surly staff, many touches missing in the room, a *charge* to use the swimming pool, and bemusement when you ask for a taxi. Still, our room should be a day's-end haven from the heat and bustle of the city. Following our early start and long day's travelling, we have a quiet dinner and Scrabble on our terrace as the sun sets over the pine and terracotta hills.

DAY SEVENTY-ONE | TUESDAY 9TH JUNE

Rome

Rome has held a mystical fascination for me ever since I made a model of the Parthenon for a school project. Yes, I know the Parthenon's in Athens, but the Pantheon – the other option – proved too hard. I mean it was fairly tricky for Agrippa. It bears his signature, but he didn't really build it. I steeped myself in Roman history – Romulus and Remus, Julius Caesar, the Emperors, the politics, the Colosseum – I loved the idea of what was essentially a group of civilized families and farmers getting together to bring order to their galaxy. Aquaducts, roads, underfloor heating, democracy (of sorts), nuances of language and behaviour, marble everywhere, silks and spices from all over the known world. Heady stuff, and conveniently ignoring the murder, torture, enslavement, occasional genocide and general utter barbarity required to achieve the above.

Then I discovered Robert Graves's remarkable *I, Claudius* and *Claudius The God*, and I was forever hooked. Fiction, yes, but I still think it's one of the most important historical documents about Ancient Rome. As the Sibyl prophesied:

'When he's dumb and no more here,
Nineteen hundred years or near,
Clau-Clau-Claudius shall speak clear'.

I think I've seen the BBC's superb 1976 TV adaptation, with Jack Pulman's dramatic script, about ten times all the way through, including (sad alert) one thirteen hour marathon on the big screen at the National Film Theatre.

But I'd never managed to *see* the place, to touch the very stones, to caress the marble, until the late eighties when I managed a short visit. I wandered round on foot for three days, carrying a copy of Georgina Masson's invaluable, if weighty, *Companion Guide to Rome*. Ms Masson's knowledge and love of the city is scholarly and Baedeker-accurate, but quite heavy going in its comprehensiveness. Persevere though, as there are golden nuggets for those who can sniff the centuries, and hear the hoof-beats.

The Forum. Unquestioned heart of the ancient city, political talking-shop, trading floor, home of the Senate, the orators, the union leaders and the money lenders. And it is they who provide our first chance to actually touch the past. Ms Masson begs the reader to walk across the marble flags of the Basilica Aemilia, where the traders and money-lenders set out their stalls two thousand years ago. Look down, she says, and you will see green flecks in the marble. And there they are, quite bright green, with perhaps a bronze-ish hue. I bend down, rather naughtily, and manage to scrape a tiny grain or two away with my fingernails. These green flecks, she says, are the melted remains of the money-lenders' copper coins that fell to the pavement and were fused into the stone by the heat of the wildfire that engulfed the city when the Goths sacked Rome in August 410.

Blimey. That's what I call history.

Ali and I also start our Roman adventure at the Forum. Having bored her silly with the above story (she was thinking Gucci and Versace), I was downhearted to discover that the Basilica, like so much under Italian antiquity management, had now been closed off. I suppose stupid tourists had been scratching away at the green-flecked marble for years. Gits.

It is stiflingly hot on the floor of the Forum, cradled as it is between three Roman hills and the racetrack road of the Via di Fori Imperiale. To the east rises the Capitoline Hill with the huge *conservatori*, and I fancy I can see the overhang of the actual Tarpeian Rock, from which traitors and other miscreants were ceremonially hurled to their deaths. Just to the north is the high square building known as the Curia, home of the Senate of Rome. You can't go in, but you can lean over the rail and look high through the gloom at the shaft of sun cutting down from the top windows onto the marble floor of republican democracy. This building dates from the 300s AD, long after the Senate had ceased to wield real influence on affairs, but it still has a strong atmosphere of power. The worn steps in front of the Curia are the *comitium*, or the earliest meeting place of Rome, dating right back to Romulus's founding of the city in 753 BC.

To the south is a veritable wall of pine and cypress trees running the whole length of the Forum and rising 200 feet off the floor – the Palatine Hill. You almost get the feeling you're in the largest arena ever built, and indeed the atmosphere is still palpable. You can imagine any citizen entering this marbled, columned valley and his senses heightening, his political antennae twitching, and watching his back. We wander round the ruins of temples, basilicas, rostra (orators' soapboxes) and then it's time to climb the steep path to the true epicentre of Roman imperial power.

The Palatine Hill rises a few hundred feet above the heat of the city. The plateau only covers a few hectares of ground, but the entire civilised world was ruled from this hilltop for a thousand years. The name itself is the root of every palace, and palaces there certainly were, together with temples, grand houses, pools and fountains, and sunken gardens. Now it's just ruins and greenery – marble column bases and half walls mingling with tall pine trees, shady olive groves and wild flowers. The noise of the traffic below is muted, and with bees buzzing and cicadas rubbing it feels like miles away from the metropolis.

It is thought that this is where Romulus first built a dwelling, after killing his brother and preventing us enjoying the glories of 'Reme'. That was not far short of 3,000 years ago, and ever since this hill was seen as *the* desirable neighbourhood to live in. The great familes had mansions here, high above the plebs and benefitting from gentle sea breezes and neighbours that wouldn't chuck their bin bags over your fence. Through the half a millennium of the first Republic, the noble families quietly went about their business, while the Senate ruled by committee down below in the Forum. Most of the families were heavily involved in the Senate of course, but ancient republican democracy held sway. The Emperors came later, and almost by mistake.

The idea of any one man holding power was anathema to the early Romans, and for centuries the Senate (selected from among the elite, granted) governed the Republic, headed by two Consuls who were elected for a yearly term. Then towards the end of the last millennium before Christ (not that His calendar meant anything to them) a character emerged who would be pivotal in Rome's history. A member of one of the noblest, but not richest, families of Rome, Caius Julius Caesar was prodigiously talented from an early age. With a razor-sharp political mind, good looks and brilliant military tactics, he became The First Man in Rome, an almost ethereal and semi-offical title (for a real sense of what life was like in the marble palaces and muddy battlefields of Rome, read Colleen McCullough's superb trilogy, starting with *The First Man in Rome)*. It was only later, after amazingly daring and accomplished land-grabs and Empire building (Britain being one of the most far-flung new colonies), that Rome turned to Caesar to save her from the squabbling morass of ineffectual old women that the Senate had become. Either that, or they were used to the idea of one strong man getting things done – Marius and Sulla had preceded Julius as First Men in Rome. Caesar, incidentally, was the generic name of a branch of the Julian family, and referred to the family's tendency to have a thick head of hair. Later Julian emperors took the name as a title, and Caesar came to mean 'absolute ruler'. I suppose that gave us Kaiser. King too, or is that pushing it? I wish I had the stamina or discipline of mind for Masson's or McCullough's detailed research, but hey, I'm just a punter doing a bit of ferreting and observing on your behalf. Amateur.

Anyway, to sum it up in an amateur's way: the Roman republic was waning and the people took to Julius Caesar – a patrician, a fixer, a multi-victorious general – as their dictator. When he was murdered his great nephew Gaius Octavius (Octavian) formed an uneasy ruling partnership with Mark Anthony. Anthony then went off and got into bed with Cleopatra, Octavian whipped them in a famous sea battle at Actium, nicked Egypt and proclaimed himself Dictator. A few years later he changed his name to Augustus and became the first Emperor of Rome, and probably its most influential.

And this is where he lived – the Domus Augustana on the Palatine Hill. Actually he was born here, on the twenty third of September 63 BC, and lived here for years as a private citizen. When he took over power he saw no reason to move, and so all the influence, together with it the marble, gilt and statuary, moved up the hill from the Forum, where it then remained for 400 years.

There's not a great deal left, but some walls and arches remain, and you can see where the rooms were, and walk out onto the huge terrace overlooking the Circus Maximus 200 feet below. Augustus built a massive double height collonaded Imperial Box from which to watch the Games and chariot racing with which he kept the populace entertained, and the whole of this hill was covered with palaces and marble.

One place I wanted to see was Livia's House. Livia was Augustus' wife, and by all accounts a twenty-four carat Queen Hellbitch. From a noble family herself, the Claudians, she was a famous beauty in her youth and had a mind like a steel trap. She spotted early on that Octavian was going to be the real power in the Empire, but she was inconveniently married to someone else. So she went through the rigorous Roman divorce procedure – you sent a slave to your spouse with a message saying 'I divorce you', and that was that – and threw her beauty and brains at Octavian. She took her two children Drusus and Tiberius with her, and set about making sure that her sons would succeed Augustus and continue the line of Emperors.

She was remarkably successful. Several other contenders stood in her way, including Augustus' grandsons by his previous marriages and his daughter Julia's subsequent marriages, but Livia had them all either murdered or banished. Her son Drusus was a Republican at heart, so she put him on the list (he was run over by a horse before she could get him) and then made sure that her surly son Tiberius was ready to succeed Augustus when she'd poisoned him. As I said, a real charmer.

She outlived them all, and after them her great-grandson Caligula, until she, to her ultimate chagrin, had to watch as her crippled and allegedly half-witted grandson Claudius was proclaimed Emperor. He didn't want to be – nobody wanted him to be except the Praetorian Guard whose jobs depended on having an Emperor – but he actually turned out to be an extremely able and fair administrator who would give Rome fifteen or so years of sanity between the excesses and ruin of Caligula and Nero.

What is claimed to be Livia's residence is slightly to the west of the main palaces, and is mostly underground and covered with a corrugated iron roof. It was rather dark when we went in, but the wall paintings were very fine, and the rooms surprisingly small for such a grand person. I expected to feel her monumental evil resonating down the centuries, but I didn't. My brother would have.

Down the hill now, past the great triumphal Arch of Titus and along the Via Sacra to the most famous structure in Rome, and the most infamous – the Colosseum. It post-dates the people we have been talking about above. Nero had finally gone, and his successor Vespasian, of the Flavian family (a generally good egg), started to build a great stadium for the people. His successors Titus and Domitian finished it, and it became known as the Flavian Amphitheatre, not changing its name to the Colosseum for at least 500 years. Better than Nero these later Emperors might have been, but they still allowed, and the people demanded, almost daily 'entertainment' of such a barbaric nature that the new arena became quite literally a cradle of blood. You might think of the Colosseum as a place of circuses and pageantry, but it was in effect a vast stage for the open display of ritual and systematic murder on a biblical scale. Just how many hundreds of thousands of men and animals perished on or beneath its sandy floor nobody knows, but the punters seemingly couldn't get enough of it – Masson estimates that Romans took a day off work every other day, and demanded entertainment.

Only about two thirds of the stone walls and tiers remain, which is fairly remarkable because until the nineteenth century the Colosseum was seen as a sort of open quarry for anyone to nick whatever stone and ironwork they needed. You enter up a steep stone tunnel and emerge on the middle tier, some seventy feet above the arena floor level. The floor is long gone, and exposed are the serried ranks of cells and animal cages below. The heat, stench and airlessness down there must have severely reduced the numbers of available performers:

> "Right, who's next?... oh, they're dead... so are they... mmm.
> You! Can you walk? Right, you're on after the Christians."

Above the arena rise the steep stone arch supports that held the tiers of seats, now gone. It's like a great open ribcage, flesh torn away to reveal a yawning chest cavity. If you close your eyes you can see the floor covered with sand; imagine the crowd, 50,000 colourful citizens baying for blood; you can hear the whinnied shrieks of the horses, the low snarls of the tigers and bears; then the slap of fists on breastplates as twenty gladiators stand before the Imperial Box and cry hoarsely, "*Morituri te salutant*" – "We who are about to die salute you". Your mind's eye rises to the purple-bordered royal box, where the fat Emperor Domitian flaps a lazy hand in return, and reaches for another quail's egg. Soon the chink and scrape of sword on sword, the *chunk* of sword in flesh and the screams of men with arms lopped off, arterial blood spurting onto the sand.

It can be no coincidence that the eighty exits from this chamber of horrors are called *vomitaria*.

Outside on the huge old cobbles of the Piazza di Colosseo we come across a wandering troupe of Roman soldiers and gladiators, resplendent in gleaming brass breastplates, leather battle shorts and red helmet feathers, performing mock fights for the punters. The Centurion grabs a willing female passer-by and she poses for her friend's camera with the soldier's sword at cut-throat. Meanwhile, one of the soldiers has broken ranks, and is sitting on the kerb talking rapid Italian into his mobile phone.

This is where Levin, or even Fry, would pull out a totally apt and witty Latin tag, and *not insult you by translating it.*

If we can stomach it it's lunchtime, so we take a taxi back into the city to the Piazza Navona. We sit at a pavement restaurant table under a huge canvas umbrella in this most beautiful of Rome's squares. It's actually a long thin rectangle, and was used by Domitian for games and athletic displays. In the centre stands Bernini's spectacular Fountain of the Four Rivers, with horses, men, palm trees and sea creatures intertwined with cascading water, bright in the sunlight.

The city's summer heat drives us to a well-earned siesta, and we venture out again at dusk for a walk through the streets to the Piazza di Rotonda, dominated by the columned might of the Pantheon. It's closed for the day now, so we have an al fresco supper as the moon rises over the honey and ochre stone of the buildings, and the lights come on in the high balconied windows of the square. Vespas buzz their way round the fountain, kids sit on the steps and gossip, laugh and snog, and the old beggar lady, stooped in black, offers tiny roses to diners at the café tables.

Ye gods, it's *Roman Holiday* in colour!

After dinner we meander through the chaotic canyons of the backstreets until we reach the Trevi. I'm always amazed at the scale of it. As you turn the corner you think, 'Oh look, here's a sweet little square and....*woah!* Suddenly, in your face, occupying fully two thirds of the piazza, is the most stunning fountain you've ever seen.

The effect reminds me of the film *Splash*, when Tom Hanks comes home to his tiny apartment in New York and finds a huge stone fountain taking up 70% of his home.

And the place is heaving. Every available step or rail is covered with people, the square is full too, everybody talking and laughing and just *being* with this marvel of marble gods and aquamarine waters. We nudge our way down to the edge of the pool and throw our traditional two coins in – one for a wish and one to return to Rome – I don't know what the third one in the song is for; to fall in love probably.

On to the Spanish Steps, again festooned with people, many of whom are cheering a just-married couple up them. The steps and the church at the top are bathed in floodlights and are impossibly romantic. A last drink at a laughter-filled bar and then back to our Borghese rooftop.

DAY SEVENTY-TWO | WEDNESDAY 10TH JUNE

Rome

Two evils: Getting up early. Queuing.

If you want to see something, particularly something everyone else wants to see, then it's one or the other I'm afraid, so I chose the lesser and hauled my arse out of bed long before a decent hour in order to avoid queuing to get into the world's smallest state.

The Vatican is only 109 acres large and it has a resident population of less than a 1,000 people, even if they are holier than thou. It has its own coins, postage stamps, flag and anthem, and until 1970 it had its own army. Now the Swiss Guard are all that remain, in their silly costumes, designed it is said by Michelangelo (well honestly, who *else* was it going to be?). You walk along the massive walls and turn left into the Viale del Vaticano, where the impressive entrance is just up on your left – the sweeping circular staircase inside carrying you up and up into what, so Georgina Masson says, is the largest collection of antique art in the world.

It is quite incredible, and cannot possibly be assimilated in a day, even by somebody who knows what they're looking at, which of course we don't. But even the meanest intelligence, and some of them do seem to be our co-wanderers, can see that here is the concentration, the *distillation*, of centuries of supreme artistry and talent. After all, if you're Pope you can commission the best. Who's going to turn you, or your devoted parishioners' tithed money, down? Botticelli, Raphael, Michelangelo – their names resound today and forever much louder than their patron Popes, but they were just artisans in their day, young men with talent to be sure, but needing work and praise and nurture. And food.

Obviously the Vatican City hasn't managed to be different enough from other cities to outlaw town planners. There's a one-way system. You *can* go straight to the Sistine Chapel (it's a quarter of a mile walk along the corridor), but you won't then be able to retrace your steps to the other galleries – it's out the exit, no refunds today. So you play along, and patiently shuffle forward with all the other sheep. The museum is housed in a stupendously large double level rectangular building many hundreds of yards long, inside which is a huge courtyard and gardens, so they send you down one leg and up the other, and then the same itinerary one level up with a break in the middle for the featured attractions, the Raphael Rooms and the Sistine Chapel.

Down the first corridor we go, and corridor is far too small and mundane a word for it – 500 yards of forty foot high vaulted ceilings, glistening in gold and aquamarine and cerise and jasmine; it's like being inside a very expensive kaleidoscope. To the left walls are hung with portraits and dotted with huge painted furniture, busts and sculpture at every turn and fabulous floors too. To the right enormous sash windows look out on the verdant gardens of the Vatican and, tantalisingly close, the back of St Peter's, the great cupola rising smoothly to the massive lantern. I leaned out of one of the open windows to take some pictures of the basilica, and it was a good thing I did as you will see later.

At length, and I mean length, the Raphael Rooms. Pope Julius II knew a good thing when he saw one, or more probably knew a good thing when he'd been told he'd seen one, and in 1508 hired the twenty-six year old Raffaello Sanzio to decorate his private apartments. My knowledge, or even appreciation of art, as you will have gleaned from these pages, is about as deep as paint on canvas, but what I most like about genius is that it cannot be denied by anyone. Surely the mark of greatness is that even to a person whose taste in art runs to 'Cat in a Wicker Basket' (no, not me – the bloke from Dusseldorf standing next to me) the unassailable superiority of a masterwork cannot be denied, even if it's not Mein Herr's sort of thing. I, and most of my fellow gawpers, am not qualified to comment on Raphael's genius as represented in these rooms.

But it was jolly nice to look at.

Meanwhile, back in 1508, while Raphael was daubing away in the Pope's bedroom, something even more remarkable was starting to happen next door. The Sistine Chapel, built twenty five years earlier for Sixtus IV – or was it Forthus VI? – was already beautifully decorated, with wall paintings by Botticelli and a ceiling of blue with gold stars. Julius had long been impressed with a couple of statues by a young man from Florence – the Pieta and the David – and commissioned the thirty year old Michelangelo to design his tomb. The artist set about buying the best marble and opening a studio in Rome but by the time he came to start chipping away Julius had changed his mind and wanted Mike to paint the ceiling of the Sistine Chapel. Our hero was a bit miffed because a) he was a marble sculptor at heart, and b) the Pope seemed to have shoved his huge invoice for the tomb's marble in a bottom drawer and forgotten about it. He returned to Tuscany in debt and a huff. The following year he was summoned to Rome, where Julius forgave him for the dreadful insult of asking for a bill to be paid, and commissioned him to... make a bronze statue of him for a church in Bologna. *Bronze, Holiness? But I... oh, never mind.* It took him a year and a half.

At last, in 1508, the famous commission came. He tried to wriggle out of it (he still had four tons of marble in his shed that needed carving), but the Pope was adamant, and soon Michelangelo stood on the inlaid floor of the Chapel, looking up – as he was to do for the next four years. Julius had only asked him to paint some apostles round the architrave, and a 'decorative' ceiling, but the artist decided to go for the full monty. Tradition led him to hire a few assistants for this mammoth job, but he soon realised that they weren't up to snuff and sacked them all. He locked the doors and started work.

When we were in Florence I said that it was hard to comprehend how the David could be the work of just one man, but he pales into insignificance next to the Herculean task of the Sistine Chapel. 10,000 square feet, painted to a standard never equalled, by one man lying on his back on rickety wooden scaffold boards a hundred feet up. Paint dripping in his eyes, stifling summer heat, and not easily able to step back and check the perspective.

No pictures, and certainly no description of mine, can begin to approach the seeing of it. You enter by the tiny west door, shuffling forward with the inevitable crowd, and in front of you are 300 noses pointed heavenwards. It's very quiet, just the rustle of clothes, a muted cough, and an imperceptible murmur of awe. When I first saw it, back in 1987, they were halfway through cleaning it, and a great wooden gantry bisected the ceiling widthways. The first half was wonderful – the familiar figures intertwining, the colours rich and textured. Then I walked under the half they'd cleaned. It was as if the whole ceiling had been placed on a lightbox – the figures shone with life, the colours leapt off the surface, bright and vibrant, the scenes seemed to be much closer, every detail of skin and sinew, cloth and cloud were as fresh and perfect as the day they were painted. The ceiling *sang*, as if released. Although a knowledge of the art and the meaning behind the work might add to one's appreciation, not even a total ignorance of the artist or the scale of the achievement can prevent the breath being knocked out of you.

Now they've finished cleaning it the full breadth can be seen, and we shuffled round, necks clicking, drinking it in. There are wooden pews at the side where you can rest and take in the atmosphere – or what the atmosphere must be like without 300 other punters there.

The east wall is entirely taken up with The Last Judgment, no less a masterpiece, but with a very different history. Twenty two years had passed between finishing the ceiling and being commissioned to start the east wall, and seven years since the dreadful sack of Rome (by the French, huh!) in 1527, with which died the golden years of the Renaissance and its high ideals of truth, beauty and classical art. It's a dark and difficult painting, full of the despair the artist must have felt at the new uncivilised world raging outside, and it took the ageing Michelangelo much longer to complete than the ceiling. Amazingly it survived several attempts to change it – the nudes were particularly frowned upon – and one Pope nearly succeeded in having it whitewashed.

On our way out we saw the iron stove where the ballot papers for the Papal elections are burned. Until a two thirds majority is reached the used papers are burned with wet straw to produce a black smoke that emerges out of the tiny chimney visible from St Peter's Square. When a Pope has been elected, dry straw produces the famous white smoke that heralds a new occupant of the Throne of St Peter.

Back out in the sunshine, we followed the crowds around the great Vatican walls towards the huge columned expanse of St Peter's Square. In front of us rose the most amazing structure I have ever seen. 400 feet wide and a 150 feet high, the man-made erection made ants of the people standing at its base, dwarfing the buildings around it and inspiring in the viewer a sense of wonder that such a creation could be possible, especially in such a golden city of creation. The scaffolding – surely the largest single expanse ever erected – completely covered the famous façade of St Peter's. I have written elsewhere of our jinx with scaffolding, but this did seem to take the Jewelled Biscuit. No impressive photos of the whole basilica would there be, no loving panning video shots across the majestic sweep of Bernini's piazza, so we went inside, confident that there weren't enough scaffolding tubes left in the whole of Italy for them to be working on the interior at the same time.

If the Duomo is large inside, St Peter's is preposterously enormous. The scale, sweep, vision and craftsmanship is quite awesome. You're immediately in no doubt that this is where the Big Guy lives, and respect is instinctively due. The other end is so far away it looks like it dips over the horizon. To the right is the chapel where the Pieta sits, rather small and forlorn behind her anti-crazed-idiot perspex. That her creator – yes, him again – is also responsible for much of the vast edifice in which she sits, is rather lost in the sheer immensity of it: you could fit almost any other church in the world into here, and it feels as if you could fit *every* other church.

I may get into trouble for saying this, but I personally get a rather pagan feel from the place. Everything is so huge that somehow the personal touch is missing – Bernini's baroque centrepiece with its sixty foot black and bronze twisted columns I find rather threatening. I know that it was built as the ultimate focus for the Almighty's grandeur and omnipotence, and was more intended as a place for Papal pomp, but it can be overwhelming. Perhaps that was part of the intention too. I would by no means describe myself as a religious person, but give me a simple English Saxon church that holds seventy people to feel closer to God.

Our busy and senses-saturating morning leads us back over the Tiber to a late lunch in front of the Pantheon. Above the perfect portico, supported on Corinthean columns of Egyptian marble, runs the

The biggest erection in the history of architecture.

inscription, in six foot letters carved in the stone, M. AGRIPPA (son of blah blah) FECIT. Marcus Agrippa, Augustus' old friend and famous Roman general, didn't 'fecit' at all. He might well have built a temple on the site, but it was the Emperor Hadrian, when he wasn't walling in the Scots, whose vision and will created this most pleasing of buildings. For 2,000 years the great dome was the largest in the world – six feet bigger than St Peter's and forty more than St Paul's – and it wasn't until 1960 that modern reinforced construction techniques could beat it. D'you know he actually poured the concrete? And the dome is much thicker at the base than at the apex, where the symmetrical vaults meet at the wonderful skylight – a hole to the heavens thirty feet wide. Inside the sense of proportion is very satisfying, and every hour the quality of the light changes as the sun streams in – a God-beam if ever there was one – or the rain pours in, through the *oculus*.

Hadrian, so Masson informs us, modestly never inscribed his own buildings, and re-created Agrippa's original self-dedication on the new, and mightily magnificent Pantheon – the Temple of all the Gods.

A final dinner in the balmy evening warmth of the Piazza Navona, and back to our roof terrace for a nightcap and Scrabble to the sound of cicadas.

Tell you what, let's play this one in Latin, then we could – *ouch!*

DAY SEVENTY-THREE | THURS 11 TH JUNE

Rome to Pompeii to Positano

Arrividerci Roma, pausing only to drag the manager of the Aldrovandi Palace out of his gilded office and gently let him know what we thought of his undeserved fifth star.

Getting out of Rome by road is almost as bad as getting in, and it takes us nearly an hour and a half to reach the autovia heading south towards Naples. Call me a hairdresser, call me a wuss, but all I know about Naples is that you see it and die, probably wearing an assortment of concrete garments or in a hail of lead in an ice cream parlour drive-by. No thanks. Besides we had a comfortable hotel room overlooking the azure Med to reach before drink time. Not so much an intrepid explorer, more like insipid. First though, whatever the risks, Pompeii.

Sweeping round Naples (wave to the assassins, darling), the motorway gives you about ten yards' warning of the Pompeii exit, and you hit the sliproad at seventy. At the bottom of the sliproad, and I mean right at the bottom, is the gateway to this tragic Roman ruin. The real tragedy hits us immediately – clustered around the gatehouse is a collection of buildings, car parks, dodgy pizzarias, gift shops and hot dog stalls of such depressing ugliness and danger that we almost drive straight up the ramp and keep going. We park in an attended car park, the attendants conveniently on hand to nick the car and all its contents, and venture out to find some acceptable food. The smartest restaurant in town had scuffed grey plastic tables with heavy ceramic Boddington's ashtrays as the centrepiece, and the only thing on the menu that didn't look like it would instantly kill us was pesto linguine, so we had two of those and two cans of coke. The gourmet tour continues.

It was threatening rain as we joined the queue of spectacularly fat and smelly punters, who wobbled their way up the steep cobbled ramp and through the western gate of the town, the Porta Marina. I knew a certain amount about what had happened to the town, but I hadn't been prepared for how large and well preserved it is. Half way through the first century Pompeii was a boom town. Many families from Rome had settled here, bringing trade and culture, order and prosperity. There were workshops and light industry, a port not far away on the Bay of Naples, water and warm sunshine, and rich fertile farmland all round. 25,000 people lived inside the city walls – working, trading, paying taxes, going to one of the town's two theatres and generally living the civilised life of a Roman satellite resort town.

In AD 62 an earthquake shook things up a little – part of the town was badly damaged, and a fair amount of rebuilding had to be undertaken, but disasters come and go, and life must go on. Then on a hot August afternoon in AD 79, the huge lowering mountain to the north of the town began to rumble and bubble and spit. Hot lava began to flow red over the crater's edge, brimstone missiles began to fly and a dust began to settle over a wide area. Concerned, the population wondered what to do. Flee? But to where? Anywhere out of the mountain's range was hours if not days travelling time. This couldn't last long could it? And it didn't seem too bad – after all mountain itself was a day's ride away – surely they would be safe? By the time the townspeople had decided that they probably *should* go and visit Aunty Julia in Rome, it was dusk and no travel was possible. They resolved to leave it till dawn and make up their minds then.

Vesuvius literally blew its top. The entire cone and top of the magma tube vaporised under the massive pressure of the earth's mantle. A billion tons of rock turned into cinders and fell, like a black duvet, on Pompeii. Within minutes the town had been almost completely buried by twenty five feet of ash.

Below this killing blanket the town, its people, animals, chariots, pots, pans and pennies were instantly entombed, and remained frozen in time for 1,700 years. The first excavators found bodies preserved in their original shapes, arms raised to ward off the toxic fumes and deadly dust. Many buildings remained almost intact, shops with goods displayed, inns with the day's takings in the till, animals in pens and on the streets. There's still a fair amount of the town yet to be properly uncovered, but the main parts are there to see, and are fascinating. Walking along the main thoroughfares, huge cobbles underfoot and high pavements either side, you get a real feeling of what it must have looked like. Every fifty feet or so you come across a pedestrian crossing – large stepping stones providing a bridge across the street, the gaps just made to fit the cartwheels. The Great Theatre is almost whole, and one can talk on the stage and every word can be heard by the gods (oddly every word from the gods can also be heard on the stage, such as "Oh *do* shut up, you old tart!"). The Forum is a wide space with semi columns surrounding it – the market place and centre of justice for the town. Today, eerily, over the ruins of the Temple of Apollo, the dark shape of Vesuvius can be seen, shrouded in mist and cloud, hunched and patient. Oh, how patient.

Sobered and fascinated we say hail and farewell to the Roman Empire and her memories, and head back to the Med. The sweep of *autostrada* carries us thirty feet above the concrete jungle of the Bay of Naples and eventually, just short of Sorrento, we turn left and climb over the pass to the Amalfi coast. Emerging onto a sinuous corniche road 1,000 feet above the sea, the view is instantly transformed from tenement Neapolitan satellites to breathtaking cliffs tumbling into aquamarine waters. Clinging to the rockface we drive slowly along the road, new views at every corner, fully expecting to meet 007 in his Aston coming one way and a large oil tanker coming the other.

The Amalfi coast is Italy's finest, and until less than a century ago was all but isolated from travellers, as the mountain passes were, well, impassable. The main town was the centre of its own maritime empire in the 11th century, and the tiny ports along the coast were the only channels to and from the precarious dwellings, churches, mills and trading houses that occupied every nook and inlet where you could build something without it falling into the sea during your lunch break.

Our destination is the glorious fishing village, now favoured resort, of Positano – a rambling, cascading, brightly coloured collection of houses wedged into a steep V-shape ravine. The main road curves round above the town and everything is below it, rushing headlong for the thin beach. When you say "I'm just popping down to the shops" here, you really mean it.

The hotel Le Agavi is signposted as you come round the last bend towards Positano, and you have to trust them and drive straight over the edge. A narrow cobbled lane leads down to a tiny plateau where the cars seem to have been parked by touch. Thankfully, you can simply abandon the car and let them sort it out. The hotel is clean and welcoming, and built into the cliff on several levels below. Our room is on Floor -6. Floor -8 brings you out at the swimming pool level, where the cliff beneath falls 800 feet straight into the sea ("if you want your ball back little Tommy, you'll just have to go and get it yourself"). We have a small balcony and simply spectacular views over the bay, the town and the endless rugged coastline to the east.

Just as we are sitting down for dinner and realising we are as far away from our tiny Surrey village as we are going to get on this trip, two other residents of walk in and sit at the next table – Tony Hart and his wife. This hugely talented and delightfully affable artist, who has taught generations of children to paint and draw, apparently comes here on a regular basis.

It must be the light.

DAY SEVENTY-FOUR | FRIDAY 12TH JUNE

Positano

A very lazy day. The weather changes more often than the Italian government, so we alternate between lazing in the sun and sitting in the pool bar as a scudding black cloud passes by to water the bougainvillea. I do a few minature watercolours of some of our experiences (less paint, less to offend the eye), and Ali aims for a smooth transfer from teak to mahogany.

Stunning, but a long way down for a dip.

DAY SEVENTY-FIVE | SATURDAY 13TH JUNE

Positano

Up smartly to explore Positano. The walk down didn't look too bad, but I knew the walk back up would be at the least tiresome, so we drove down into the town and left the car with a young lad who whisked it away into a cave. From this height, about half way down, it's car-free, so we point our toes beachwards and follow the cobbled main street towards the sea.

There's the usual collection of shops and cafés, but also some quite smart names too, and dozens of emporia devoted to the lemon – soaps, essences, perfumes, oils, lotions and unguents, paintings, ceramics, glass sculptures, teatowels, mugs and T-shirts, juices and additives by the hundred, and baskets and baskets of the humble fruit itself. The path emerges by a small church and then gives onto the cobbled piazza by the beach. The sand is grey volcanic and not very inviting, but the serried ranks of bright fishing boats add colour, and a few bathers are braving the increasingly choppy seas. We stand on the breakwater and I try to take a photograph of Ali with a wave smashing up the wall behind her – a hanging backcloth of spray. A roll and a half of film later we have a couple of capuccinos at a café below the balcony of the restaurant where they shot a rather sweet romcom movie called *Only You* with Robert Downey Jnr and the delectable Marisa Tomei, and I did an appallingly bad pencil sketch of Ali. Perhaps if I tried drawing her upside down?

Despite the increasing choppiness of the seas, we thought we'd try and make Capri for lunch, so we drove back round the high corniche to Sorrento to see if we could get the hydrofoil.

Sorrento is the largest town on the peninsula, and is busy and colourful with tourists for much of the season. The high cliffs above the harbour are lined with the posh, rather Victorian hotels, grandly overlooking the Bay of Naples. We just manage to find the last space in the car park and run for the boat, me asking Ali once again if she's up for this, as I know she's not the greatest seafarer. Yes, yes, come on, she yells, and we make the ferry with seconds to spare.

The sun was shining and the water inside the harbour hadn't looked too bad, so it isn't until we round the breakwater and hit the open sea that we realise quite how dodgy this is going to be.

Lift, turn, corkscrew, smash... lift, turn, corkscrew, smash! I though hydrofoils raised you out of the water on stilts or something – this is really quite hairy. Ali has gripped the gunwale with all her strength and is grimly faced for'ard. I look around at the crew – always the first sign of trouble – but they don't seem to have a problem, and so we begin to batter our way to the island of Capri.

The Island of Dreams it's been called, and it's certainly a major destination for the glitterati and the beautiful people. After disembarking from our sea-borne cement mixer, rather gingerly and with much relief, the smells rose up from the island – fuel oil, fish, bougainvillea and what's that? Oh yes, money. Marina Grande, where you land, is a charming fishing village with colourful houses and restaurants along the harbourside. We lunched on linguine marinara and a local wine. I didn't see the label, but I would have called it *nitromorsia*. Then it was time to explore the main town, high up in the saddle of the island, which you reach by modern funicular. The little train, on its permanent 40° tilt, hums up the mountainside through lemon groves and palm trees and arrives just below the main piazzetta – the central point of island life. Cafés and restaurants surround the square, tables and parasols cover the edges and everywhere is Armani, Versace, D&G and docksiders – millionaire dress. A wander through the gorgeous cobbled streets (no cars allowed, only porters dragging cartfuls of Louis Vuitton luggage) brings us to a succession of hugely flash hotels that would make some of our posher accommodation blush with shame. Our rather rushed visit, and wish to get back across the bay before the storm maroons us, only allows us a short walk round, and prevents a visit to a place I really wanted to see – Tiberius' villa.

I didn't mention Tiberius a great deal in my Rome ramblings (oh God, but you're going to now, aren't you?) as he didn't figure greatly in the history of the Palatine Hill, merely being custodian of Augustus' empire. Capri, however, was his domain for twenty or so years, and his influence is everywhere.

Having finally fallen out with his despotic mother Livia, who still thought she ruled through him, Tiberius left Rome in his sixties, never to return. He had built several large villas on the island, high on the clifftops, and ruled the Roman Empire from there. Or rather he allowed his Machiavellian lieutenant Sejanus to rule it for him, while he indulged in his favourite pastimes of seducing young girls and boys, composing silly poetry and throwing lots of people he didn't like off his sunlit terraces into the sea. A very nasty piece of work, Tiberius, even by Caligula's standards – he was plain mad, I think, whereas his uncle was rotten to the very core of his being. His mother's fault, of course. Anyway, we didn't have a chance to go and look round the ruins. Strange, we seemed to have some time for shopping though.

The return voyage to Sorrento was not quite as bone-jarring and gut-churning as the outward, and we collected the car and headed back over the pass to Positano.

A high hot-buttered moon, as Bernie Taupin describes it, hangs over our bay, turning the sea to antique silver and washing the lemon grove slopes of the mountains with an opaque luminescence.

Gosh that wine was awful.

DAY SEVENTY-SIX | SUNDAY 14TH JUNE

Positano to Torgiano

Two long days driving up the spine and east coast of Italy towards Venice are next on our itinerary, so we set off early, pausing for coffee in Ravello. This stunning village is perched high in the hills above Amalfi, and there are wide satisfying views in all directions. The huge church in the square emits the lilting sounds of a choir – practising for a wedding, we're told.

Over the pass and down towards the slopes of Vesuvius, looking much friendlier in the Sunday morning sunshine than it did a few days ago, but still with an ominous collar of steam (alright, cloud probably) around its murderous neck. The motorway whisks us north, past Rome and then up into the Perugia region, near Assisi. It's now nearly five, so we are grateful to find the tiny town of Torgiano, and our hotel, Le Tre Vaselle.

It's an impressive establishment, constructed inside a dozen or more rambling but connected town houses – cool, smart, expansive and expensive. Our room is a huge split level apartment, with a mezzanine for the bedroom, and cedar shutters opening to a rooftop view of the town. We've been told that, apart from the restaurant, the pool is the chief glory of the place, so Ali is ready to swim within a picosecond of arrival. Yes, but where is it? To reach it, you walk down a long stone underground corridor, under the houses and the road and emerge on a plateau below the town. You are greeted by a magnificent vista of rolling Umbrian countryside and set into the lawns before you is a huge blue swimming pool, with loungers and parasols. And nobody else around, except for the barman. Oh, alright then woman, even *I'll* have a swim in this pool, oh, and just one olive in the martini, Fabrizzio, if you'd be so kind. *Grazie.*

The sun finally dips below the yellow fields of Perugia, and we go inside for our best dinner since France. In the cool stone dining room we have seared scallops, perfect beef in a balsamic grape jus and mouthwatering chocolate terrine. Then to bed, where they spoil an excellent record by turning off the hotel's air conditioning between midnight and six.

VENICE

San Marino

In which the road just keeps going up, but when it gets there all you can see is how spectacular it must once have been. Now it's horrid.

Ferrera

In which we stay inside Barbara Cartland's Barbie Doll's House – everything is shellac pink and ruched – oooh, yuk! And they charged us £15 to bring us breakfast.

Venice

In which we lose ourselves in La Serenissima. We walk, we gondola, we dance in Piazza San Marco at midnight. It was all completely perfect, and we met an amazing sculptor who looked like Dali and took us home for tea (once he'd sold us two grand's worth of art, of course).

Sirmione

In which we discover a superb hotel protected by a medieval town thrusting out into the lake. Lazy days and perfect dinners under the stars.

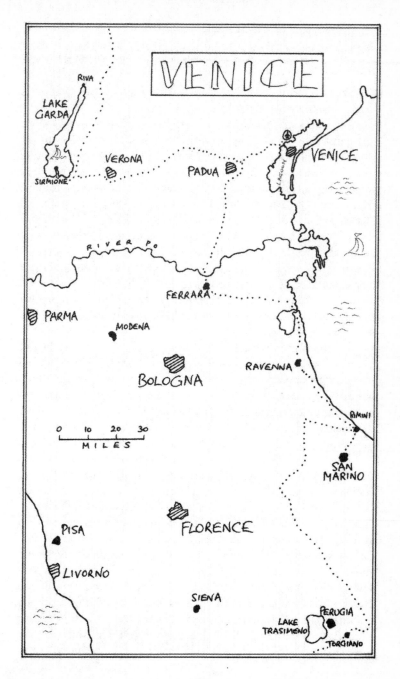

DAY SEVENTY-SEVEN | MONDAY 15TH JUNE

Torgiano to San Marino to Ferrara

Another long drive today, but with a lunchtime detour to another country – our sixth.

The Republic of San Marino is pretty small, just twenty three square miles, so it's made up for it by being high. It stands on top of a huge sandstone ridge just inland from Rimini, and you wind round a looping road that climbs to the top. Somewhat reminiscent of Rocamadour in the Dordogne, the castle walls and narrow cobbled streets occupy the summit of the mountain, and the centre of town is car-free. Leaving the Merc in the 'Park And Walk' down the hill, we amble up to the main streets. Oh dear. Again. Almost every shop seems to be owned by the cousins of the shopkeepers in Carcassonne. Perhaps when they can't shift this year's collection of faux antique swords and daggers they swap stock and see if the others' punters will buy it. What they also buy is copious amounts of San Marino's own stamps and coins, and probably cardboard copies of San Marino policeman's helmets.

Up to the topmost lookout, where the plain must be 2,000 feet below, and the Adriatic glimmers greyly in the distance. They say you can see right across to Yugoslavia on a clear day, but perhaps today, like many sad days over there, it's obscured by mortar smoke. An indifferent lunch overlooking a spectacular view and then back to the car, pausing only to buy a huge jewelled battle sword. No, not really, but I suppose I could have used it to hack my way back to the car.

On ever northwards, via the coast road past Ravenna, to Ferrara, where we'd booked a hotel for the night so as to be close to Venice for the morning. This was the Duchessa Isabella, another Relais & Chateau, but what a dreadful place! An imposing frontage, bedecked with flags to show how important it was, led to an interior that was a clashing riot of gilded furniture, paisley carpeting, lime green walls, smoked mirrors and baroque *objets*. Our room was pink. No it wasn't, it was PINK! Everything was ruched – the curtains, bedcovers, loo roll holder, tablecloths – the throw rugs looked like pink fluffy slippers and there were odd regency-type frescos on the walls. It was like living inside Barbara Cartland's head. Practically everything white had the hotel's name stencilled on it (with Relais accreditation proudly displayed) and to cap it all the bed was nothing but a metal tubular barracks put-u-up. With those cross-mesh flat springs. And a deep blush pink cableknit counterpane. Yuk.

The restaurant, which might have been their saving grace, is closed tonight (but of course), so I venture forth to see if there's anywhere, or anything, to eat. The town seems to be devoid of restaurants, so I find a small supermarket and buy a simple carpet picnic to take back to the room. Well, I suppose it will save us a few lire that we will need – oh, how we'll need them – in Venice.

DAY SEVENTY-EIGHT | TUESDAY 16TH JUNE

Ferrara to Venice

We leave the Hotel Duchessa – or should that be Ruchessa? – after breakfast, which was not only extra, but they charged us nearly £15 *to bring it up one flight of stairs*. When questioned, the Signora (whose taste had undoubtedly decorated around us) was not too bothered. She obviously has enough proper Relais customers to fill her beloved creation. You know, *naice* people, who compliment her flawless des*aign* sense and don't complain about anything.

And so north to the crown jewel of the Adriatic – or anywhere really – Venezia. We'd made a few phone calls the previous week to Hertz, persuading them that we would graciously deign to allow them to service their precious Mercedes while we were staying in Venice, and that we would be prepared to collect it from Venice airport two days later. Amazingly, they bought it, and we had somewhere to park the car for forty eight hours. Result.

Having dumped the car we wheeled our luggage round to the pier, where various ferries and boats awaited passengers for Venice. A small number of jetties were reserved for the posher hotels' private launches, and there on its own, with a highly polished sleek teak launch riding gently on its mooring rope, was the smartest – the Gritti's. Tell you what, let's stay there!

Well alright, we had booked, which is one of the reasons we'd camped outside the city walls last night, and why we were only staying two nights – the Gritti Palace is the best hotel in Venice and is eye-wateringly expensive. Of course it went stratospherically outside our daily budget, but we hadn't got long, and Venice is Venice, and... well... buggerit.

The launch captain, in pristine white ducks, loads our bags with a smile and backs out into the channel for the three or four mile trip across the lagoon. The ancient piles that mark the navigation lanes stretch into the distance ahead of the bow wave and gradually, through the morning mist, the magical mirage begins to appear – La Serenissima.

It is quite possible that I am the least qualified person to write about the glories of Venice. There are probably Uzbeki herdsmen or Chilean fishermen or even *Daily Mail* columnists who could do a better job, even if nothing had ever been written about it. But of course everything that can be written about the city has been, so if you want to know about Venice read Goethe or Byron or Baedeker or Morris or Michelin. If you want to follow us round gawping, read on.

As we approach the city, the wall of terracotta looming ever closer, we pass the Isola di San Michele on our left. It's basically the Venetian's cemetery, and everyone who was anyone is buried there, along with lots of the world's greatest artists, writers and composers who came to Venice to die and be interred near their beloved muse. I was once told that the place is so stuffed with stiffs that there's a rental agreement – if you don't keep paying great-grandpa's ground rent, up he comes.

Suddenly we have ducked right, and into the most astonishing maze on earth. These tiny stone canyons, with a sliver of black water at the bottom, connect and interconnect with each other in a baffling shambles of creeks and inlets and pontoons and bridges. In the smaller ones, barely a boat width wide, it grows eerily quiet and all that can be heard is the echo of a gondolier's voice round the next corner and the scrape of the boat against the stonework, down by the waterline where the sun never reaches. Equally as suddenly we have emerged onto the Grand Canal and all is chaos, or appears to be. At second glance the hundreds of boats and gondolas and vaporetti seem to be following a relaxed pattern of movement, an operational ebb and flow that speaks of centuries of practice. We putter peacefully under the Accademia bridge and gently bump the private landing stage of the Gritti Palace Hotel. Uniformed flunkeys whisk our bags off, our launch swings away to another assignment, and we wander through to reception. We're much too early to check in so we leave the luggage with the flunkeys and set out for lunch at Florian's.

Napoleon described the Piazza San Marco as the finest drawing room in Europe. So he nicked it. Then the Austrians nicked it in the latest round of divisions of the European pie. Finally, fifty years later, the Venetians voted to become part of a re-unified Italy. You may remember when we talked about Nice that the plebiscite had thrown out the Austrians with a vote of 99%. In Venice's case the YES vote was 99.99%. Only sixty nine people out of well over half a million decided they liked Austrian imperialism. D'you think there was any sort of pattern beginning to emerge here?

Through all the warring and posturing of its many masters St Mark's Square has remained its own dignified and perfect self. The piazza teems with life today as it did six centuries ago – traders, restaurateurs, artists, musicians, thousands of visitors and tens of thousands of pigeons. We enter by the southwest corner and the graceful cloisters of the square flow away from us towards the magnificent domed basilica. Piercing the view, soaring up 300 feet to its golden apex is the Campanile, brand new by comparision to its neighbours (it was built last century) but utterly in place.

Half way along the south cloister is the Caffe Florian, the oldest on the square, and along with Quadri's in the opposite cloister, *the* place to sit, sip and gossip in Venice. So we do, very contentedly. The sun is hot and the Florian orchestra is just warming up for its lunchtime recital – a pleasing combo of grand piano, violins, cellos and an accordian player who looks exactly like Tom Conti. From our table the Campanile almost completely obscures the frontage of the Doge's Palace, which is a mercy as – here we go again – it's covered with scaffolding. The difference between this and the ugly erection across St Peter's in Rome is that here they've commissioned a huge dropcloth, painted like the frontage, to cover the bare pipework. The effect is not bad – 'sorry about the disturbance folks, but this is what it will look like when we've done it'.

After a long lunch and a leisurely stroll around the piazza we go back to the Gritti to check in. It is a stunning building, the palace of a former Doge, and everything is old gilt and shot marble. It's nice to stay in a really superb hotel just once in a while, but in some of the grander ones, including this one, there's always an air of "And you are…?" I bet Papa Hemingway didn't get this sort of treatment when he used to stay here. Mind you, he could write a bit.

The *signore* at reception looks over his *pince-nez* at us and gives us the attic room at the back. I wouldn't mind being treated like a refugee if the place was full of film stars and royalty, but it's not – in the bar later, the *dross* that wandered in, were loudly rude to waiters and each other. Rich Americans, I'm sorry to report, not knowing how to behave. The room itself is softly beautiful – an opulent blend of oak panelling and gilt-edged mirrors – but you have to press your nose to the window to see any sky, and if you lean out and stand on tiptoe you can just see a few slates on the dome of La Salute.

When you go to Venice, particularly for the first time, you have to go in a gondola. I mean, you simply have to, don't you? And the gondoliers know this. Alessandro floated up to the Gritti's pontoon, tanned and splendid in his white shirt, black trousers and straw boater with red ribbon, and we set off for our hour's early evening bob. He speaks excellent English and told us he's twenty-four, lives with his wife in her mother's house in the city, and trained for four years to become a gondolier. He dreams of one day owning his own gondola, but since they cost 60,000,000 lire he thinks it will be a long time coming.

I reflect on the similarities between gondolas and London taxis: they're both black and shiny and convey passengers for money; their drivers have to know every backwater of their city; many of the drivers don't own their vehicle but rent it from a co-operative; both vehicles can turn round in their own length; an hour's journey costs a similar amount (about £35); they cost almost exactly the same to buy (about £25,000); and the gondola is constructed from 600 pieces of wood – I have no idea how many pieces of metal a London cab is made of, but I wouldn't be at all surprised if it's about 600. The London cab can get you to your destination slightly quicker, but the gondola is 600 years old and has never belched carbon monoxide at you or run over your foot.

And Ali says not many London cabbies look like Alessandro.

We float peacefully along the tiny canals, brushing against other gondolas and damp stone. We ask Alessandro if he sings. He says he can, but he doesn't usually as there are better singers, who are hired, with their accordians, to join a gondola's party and serenade the passengers. We can hear one approaching now, the music echoing off the walls ahead.

Out onto the Grand Canal now – rather choppier and unstable, but the glorious breadth and sweep of this amazing street occupies the eye constantly. Magnificent palazzos in ancient colours – ochre, umber, jasmine, terracotta, mulberry, royal blue and shining gold; jetties and pontoons anchored by barber's-pole piles in twisting stripes; service barges carrying everything from fruit to wine to breeze blocks to garbage; here and there a glimpse of a tiny garden or courtyard; busy *vaporetti* criss-crossing the canal from bus stop to bus stop; a line of gondolas perfectly framed by the Rialto bridge; canal-side cafés with bright umbrellas; and everywhere the hum of a busy modern city but placed in a huge and perfect Renaissance film set.

Talking of movies, I think I've caught out the mighty Michelin on a fact! In the copy of their Venice guide that never leaves my side it mentions a number of films that have been shot against Venice's ultra-photogenic backdrop. It says that the second James Bond film *From Russia With Love* was shot here, when Sean Connery goes to Murano in search of a particular glassmaker, and that special effects include an amphibian gondola scattering pigeons in St Mark's Square. But surely that was Roger Moore in *Moonraker*? Wasn't it? I think we should be told.

Our charming *gondoliere* delivers us back to the Gritti's pier as the sun begins to be replaced by some ominous cloud. We decide to explore the Rialto region for dinner, and negotiate our way through the maze of paths and bridges back to the most famous bridge of all. Until the 19th century the only way across the Grand Canal by foot was over the Ponte di Rialto, which had stood in various guises for 800 years. Similar in many respects to the Ponte Vecchio, the shops and stalls line the bridge, although the Venetians sell more clothing and leather goods than jewellery. We cross over to find a canal-side restaurant just down from the bridge, where we have a simple soup and spag supper. It's now nearly eight, and the last of the sun is shining on the white stone of the bridge, which is cast into sharp relief, behind it and moving this way, the blackest cloudbank I've ever seen. It's rather like a horror movie, where bad weather comes on suspiciously fast – passers-by start to huddle down and quicken their step, waiters start to hover over outside diners, gondoliers and boatmen start strapping green tarpaulins over their craft and umbrellas and awnings start to ruffle and snap in the rising wind.

Suddenly the sky flashes with sheet lightning, and hailstones the size of marbles make depth charge plumes in the Grand Canal. We shelter, blitz-like, under the restaurant's awning (all the inside tables are full) until we can risk a dash for the Vaporetto station. We can see it, tantalisingly close down the canal, but as with most places in Venice you can't just walk along the bank to it, you have to go inland and through a maze of back streets to find the one little alley that leads to the pontoon. A gap in the hail, and we're off, slipping on slick cobbles, until we arrive under the *stazione's* perspex shelter. The vap comes quickly and we criss-cross our way to Santa Maria di Giglio. Again, the mad dash round the streets and alleys to the Gritti, and as we approach we can hear the new cloudburst of hailstones *chase* us down the street. Amazingly we don't get pummelled to death, and are soon ensconced in the bar with a *grappa*, listening to the heavens spit, crack and roar outside.

We play a couple of games of Scrabble and can't help overhearing assorted conversations floating across from nearby tables and sofas: ... *"well of course we come here at least twice a year, the Upper East Side can so tiresome in June"* .... *"Ja, I seenk two hundred sousand units iss possible, I will hav to consult Hamburg"* .... *"Have you seen the Picasso at the Grassi? You know Harry met him once, and"* .... *"Do not worry Padrino, Mario sleeps with the fishes...."*

Alright I made that last one up, but it was a very satisfying hour or so of people-watching, and then we retired to our upper room, the sky still flashing with lightning but the worst of the storm gradually fading away south into the Adriatic.

DAY SEVENTY-NINE | WEDNESDAY 17TH JUNE

Venice

There can be few more pleasurable experiences than breakfast on the terrace of the Gritti Palace. The day has dawned bright and blue, everything washed (or scoured) clean by the storm, and once again the Grand Canal sparkles in the sunlight. We are given a large table by the water's edge and have a sublime breakfast of smoked salmon and scrambled eggs, freshly-squeezed juice, croissants and *pain au chocolat* and the world's best coffee. For goodness sake don't spoil it all by look-ing at the bill.

Afterwards, Ali gets her book out and has more coffee, and I attempt a watercolour of the view. The Basino di San Marco opens up in front of us and although we can't see the square from here, the view extends across the smooth waters to the gorgeous church of San Giorgio Maggiore. But filling the eye and the senses, directly opposite us, is the Venetians' favourite church, Santa Maria della Salute.

Santa Maria della Salute – a tribute for an answered prayer.

In 1630 a terrible plague fell on the city, and Venetians pledged to build a magnificent basilica if the epidemic subsided. Their prayers were answered, so they built this impossibly lovely monument as promised. The great steps sweep up from the water to the baroque columned portico while above, the larger of the two domes rises to the ornate lantern. It's at times like this you start to think about what Venice stands on. Elsewhere you see a big building and you don't think about its colossal weight – you just assume that it's sitting on solid ground, no problem. But here everything sits on wooden piles, some of them centuries old, that have been driven down through the silt and mud to the clay bedrock. Yes, but a huge church? What on earth does that weigh? How many piles would you need to keep your worshippers dry? Michelin, once again, provides the answer – 1,106,657. Wow.

My sketch of the wide view is a little pedestrian, so I abandon it for later watercolouring, and try an ink and pencil drawing of the church. It's actually not too bad for a rank amateur, if a little stark and cold, and a fellow guest comes over and confirms this view by saying, "Oh, are you an architect?" Huh!

A mid-morning stroll into St Mark's Square, and its own wonderful basilica. The frontage is incredibly ornate with great gilded arches and ormolu scrollwork and finials above. The roof has five 13th century Byzantine domes, and the whole effect is very eastern, almost mosque-like. Inside is quite awesome – not in size but in richness of colour and depth of atmosphere. Everything seems to be suffused in a soft light of old gold and silver, and I get an image of being inside Aladdin's lamp. The marble floor is beautifully decorated and edged, like stone bokhara rugs, and it undulates alarmingly – one can almost picture the great supporting piles pushing up underneath. We join the queues making their slow way up the stairs to the balcony overlooking the square, where the famous Bronze Horses prance and flick their massive heads over the crowds below. Opinions about their age and provenance vary wildly – 1,600 year old Roman or 2,400 year old Greek – but they were so prized that Napoleon nicked them for a few years, taking them to Paris. Amazingly he sent them back.

We walk down to the water, past the Doge's Palace and the whole lagoon opens up in front of us. Giudecca over to the right, La Salute on the far right, San Giorgio directly ahead and behind it the Lido and the open sea. We wander along past the Bridge of Sighs and the Danieli to catch a vaporetto for a tour of some of the above. The best place for panoramic pictures is from the clocktower of the San Giorgio Maggiore basilica – the whole city is laid out beneath you and on a clear day it's one of the most breathtaking sights on earth. We used up most of a film and hopped the vap over to Giudecca, ambled along the sea wall and caught another ferry back across to Zattere. I was amazed to find piazzas with trees in this part of town. Time for capuccino, so we found a small café in the shadow of the Accademia bridge to watch the world go by, and it did – I think I counted nine different languages being spoken by passers-by in the twenty minutes we sat there.

And now for Picasso. We cross over the bridge and turn left for the magnificent Palazzo Grassi, the last great Venetian palace to be built before the fall of the republic. Massive sweeping staircases take us up to the galleries and the visiting Picasso exhibition – concentrating on his French and Italian periods from 1917-21. Some stunning works, but not as captivating as Barcelona. I once bought a small watercolour by an unknown artist at the Royal Academy's Summer Exhibition, but otherwise neither of us had really invested in art. That was about to change.

Just outside the Grassi Ali spots a small shop in a tiny piazza. The only things in the window are three balloons and a large paintbrush. The paintbrush is a couple of feet long and hand carved out of wood, and the balloons are hand blown from glass. Interested, we go in, and discover the magical world of Livio de Marchi.

Around the modest showroom are some stunning pieces – coats hanging from racks, a trilby hat, a pair of riding boots, an armchair, a round table covered with drooping cloth and laid for breakfast. Every detail, every fold of material, every nap of cloth, every natural crease is perfect – and every single item is hand carved out of wood. It was simply a joy to see, and to touch. In the corner was a huge terracotta pot, at least four feet high, with seven or eight paintbrushes upended in it, the bright colours of the paint still on their flexing bristles and the shafts covered with the spatter patterns of long and loved use. The brushes were six feet high, and again, everything hand carved in wood. We wandered round entranced, and blusteringly tried to ask questions of the lady behind the counter. She smiled and asked us to wait a moment, and then, from his workshop in the back, the artist himself appeared.

Livio de Marchi is a gentle, charming and laughing Venetian who's been creating wonders in wood for twenty years, and he looks exactly like Salvador Dali. The lady turned out to be his wife, whose English was much better than our Italian or Livio's English, so between us we managed to communicate a little. He explained the various works on show and showed us book after book of other things he's done in wood, from tiny coffee cups to entire houses built of wood carved into huge books. We spent a delighted half hour discussing the pieces, and he showed us his workshop where he was currently carving a lifesize trenchcoat out of lime.

It was obvious to both of us that we loved this stuff, so we thanked the de Marchis and said we'd come back after lunch, if that was alright. Shaking a little with anticipation, we went round into the Campo San Stefano for lunch. Were we really going to do this? Nothing beautifully hand made is going to be cheap, but ... well we simply adored them, and we wanted them. We would have to find the money from somewhere and look on them as investments in art.

Back we went after lunch, and spent a while choosing what we thought we could afford. Two six foot paintbrushes; a paintpot chair (the base is a paintpot with drips of multicoloured paint down the sides, a flat wooden seat, and five paintbrushes upended in an arc to make the chairback); a small terracotta pot about a foot high, with twenty eighteen-inch paintbrushes loose inside, like a flower arrangement; the Trilby hat, carved out of mahogany; and two four foot long pencils, with coloured leads and erasers on the ends – everything carved by Livio in various woods. A wonderful small collection, modest by de Marchi's usual customer's standards no doubt, but we were delighted. He said that as it was a slow day, would we like to come round to his house for coffee, and see some other pieces? Since he knew we'd already overspent, it was a purely friendly gesture, and we accepted with interest. He only lives around the corner, and his house is full of his creations, small and large. We had coffee on his *altana* – the typical Venetian roof terrace – and he told us about his car. It's entirely carved in wood, full size, it has a petrol engine and it floats. Yes, he's even driven it up the Grand Canal. He showed us a video of it in action, and there he was, hat tilted rakishly and moustache twitching, driving this wooden boat-car between gondolas and *vaporetti* with St Mark's Square in the background. Amazing.

Finalising arrangements for shipping our new art back home, we shook the hand that had carved them and floated, elated, back to the hotel. We decided to celebrate with a drink at Quadri's, so we changed and ventured once more into Europe's finest drawing room. The Quadri orchestra were in full swing – a similar combo to Florian's, and indeed they seemed to take it in turns to do sets, so as not to clash too much. After a couple of glasses of champagne we wandered back to have dinner on the Gritti's terrace – sublime food, quite the best we've had in Italy, and a genuine 15th century russet and gold sunset over the gently lapping waters of the Venetian lagoon. Bliss.

Around eleven we strolled back through the warm evening to a St Mark's Square lit by ancient lamplight and a bright moon. We had coffee and aperitifs at Quadri's and danced to *La Vie en Rose* under San Marco's ceiling of stars. A magical two days in a magical city.

Yes of course, every café, restaurant and hotel bill in Venice is like being mugged; but boy, they're entitled.

Portrait of the artist on his paintbrush chair. It now sits in our front hall.

DAY EIGHTY | THURSDAY 18TH JUNE

Venice to Sirmione

A final *vap* trip up the Grand Canal and a walk round the Rialto area. We bought a couple of classic Venetian painted masks and Ali bought a very cool leather bag by someone called Kara Van Petrol (what, as opposed to Kara Van Diesel, the more economical leather designer?). A last kir at Florian's and then the Gritti's sleek launch back across the lagoon to Marco Polo airport to collect our freshly-serviced car. Thank you Hertz.

Our destination today is Sirmione, a narrow spit of land stretching out into the waters of Lago di Garda, Italy's largest lake. A simple drive past Verona brings us to the southern shores of the lake, and we drive up the peninsula to the gates of the tiny medieval town at its tip. There you are stopped and not allowed to proceed unless you have a reservation in one of the town's hotels – cars are frowned upon. Luckily we have booked rooms at the Palace Hotel Villa Cortine, and they let us through. Very narrow cobbled streets lined with tourist shops and tourists take us through the town, and when we stop at traffic lights to cross over the single lane drawbridge of the castle, we are instructed to switch off our engine so as not to pollute the air. Quite right.

The hotel is in the most enviable position, high up in cypress and pine-treed gardens on the rocky outcrop of the peninsula. The 'villa' bit is a palladian-portico'd classic mansion, but the main part has been stuck on the back and is modern. It's actually not too bad, and the main rooms are large and welcoming. Our room is huge, with a balcony overlooking the gardens and the lake, and has a big marble bathroom.

The grounds are extensive and private, with winding paths and plenty of statuary, palm trees and fountains. The main area in front of the hotel is massive – a large pool, a wide terrace overlooking the lake for al fresco dining, and a lovely open stone loggia whose columns and lintels are covered with ivy. Apparently they have their own secluded beach restaurant and private jetty too. We'll investigate that tomorrow, but first a relaxing swim and a drink before dinner.

As we towel off the sun is setting and waiters are adding the finishing touches to the linen-covered tables on the terrace. The lamps are lit, and we return, dressed, to have a lovely dinner under the stars, with the lights of the lakeshore winking below, and cicadas chorusing in the bushes.

Now we've started moving north on our way back home, I find I'm going to miss these warm wine-fumed Mediterranean evenings. Can't imagine why.

DAY EIGHT-ONE | FRIDAY 19TH JUNE

Sirmione

A blissful day of hedonism.

I had suggested at breakfast, as the sun was pre-warming the day and the waiters were asking us what fresh catch we'd like to have caught for our lunch on the beach, that we might go and look at Catullus's villa. This went down like a kipper yogurt: "Haven't we seen enough bloody ancient Romans?", she yelped, "Here's a newsflash – they're all dead!"

That'll be a no, then.

Hardly had the croissants cooled before Ali was stretched out by the pool in the smaller of her two bikinis, fully intending to stay there till lunch. I went and got my paints and established myself under the vine in the loggia at the edge of the terrace, where, Casson-like, I attempted to watercolour my sketch of Venice. Not very successful really – the perspective is alright, but the colours are much too heavy and the result looks like it should be on a child's bedroom wall.

For lunch we wandered down to the hotel's beach, where the clay oven was producing piscine delights and the waiters were mixing cocktails at the tables. More poolsiding and painting in the afternoon and then another delightful dinner on the terrace, Ali looking stunning in a cream linen suit. The pianist had a go at *La Vie en Rose*, and we tottered round to much amusement. From us, not our fellow diners, who must have hoped that idiot Brits had stopped with Byron and Shelley.

SALZBURG

Salzburg

In which we stay in a charming and efficient small hotel (the Hotel Mozart, of course) where the owner speaks seven languages; discover this lovely city, with its celebration of Amadeus, risk our little all in a magnificent casino, and laugh for four hours on 'The Most Unique Sound Of Music Tour', which doesn't actually let us see anything like the Von Trapp house (opposite) except the inside of the guide's brother's souvenir shop.

The Eagle's Nest at Berchtesgaden

In which we are chilled by Hitler's cloud-brushing retreat.

Dachau

In which we are chilled to the bone.

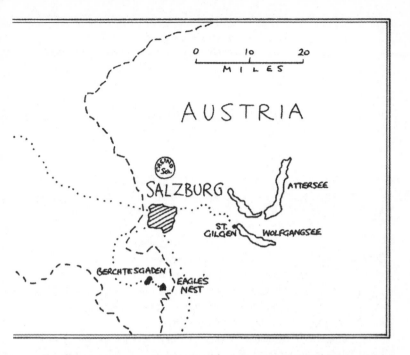

As close as we were taken to the Von Trapp story.

Austria

"The Hills are alive..."

DAY EIGHTY-TWO | SATURDAY 20TH JUNE

Sirmione to Salzburg

Our last morning in Italy, and we say a reluctant *ciao* to the Villa Cortine, promising to return. An easy drive up the eastern shore of Lake Garda, heading for the main invasion route of old – from Goths to Napolean – the Brenner Pass. A wide toll station has been built at the apex of the road, and we stop to buy some schillings and a coffee before entering our seventh country, Austria.

I've mentioned Austria a couple of times, neither in a very complimentary way I'm afraid. I'm not sure quite why I have a problem with it – Hitler, obviously; Waldheim's reign of power said as much about him as it did about the populace that elected him; Austrian imperialism over the last 700 years; this new politician bloke who says Nazism was quite cuddly really; and veal. Oh yes, and the fact that the most frightening people in Europe live in it's prettiest country.

The trouble with this is that the Austrians we came across, as you will see, were universally charming. Damn, now *I* feel guilty.

We had decided, with our now diminishing schedule, to spurn Innsbruck, delightful though it may be, in favour of Salzburg. Good directions lead us easily to the Hotel Mozart (what on earth made them choose that name?) on Franz Josef Straße, where we are welcomed by Marius and family. A modest establishment, but clean and efficient, and our room is large and well windowed. There's no air-con against this sultry weather and most surfaces are covered in woodette effectette Formica, but it will suit us admirably.

The sun blazes out of a blue evening sky as we amble down the pedestrianised Linderstrasse, through a buzzing festival. Quite what this festival is celebrating is not clear, but there are craft stalls and street theatre, tressle tables laden with beer, and the same guy you see at every fair, fête or market everywhere in the world – he's wearing a threadbare camouflage jacket and standing behind racks and racks of every album and CD you never bought. Because they were crap.

The street kinks left and suddenly we're on the north bank of the Salzach river looking up at the towering ramparts of the Hohensalzburg, 400 feet above the old town. We walk across the bridge and look down at the shallow swift-flowing river, scurrying between beautifully kept banks of mown grass. It's a good place to stand and do a 360, to take in the sweep of the town between the high hills of the Monchsberg and the Kapuzinerberg. It really is very attractive with its ornate green church and lantern roofs, and pale yellow house frontages. The most famous of all is right in front of us, just across the bridge – the Mozartgeburthaus, which we will explore tomorrow. Now it's time for a glass of wine at a café in a cobbled strasse, followed by dinner at ... a Chinese restaurant. It may seem surprising, but after all this cuisine, both *haute* and *bas*, we both suddenly said we could just do a Chinese. It was very good too, but like all chinese food, not nearly as cheap as you think it's going to be (half an hour later you can't afford another one).

A final coffee on the terrace of the Oesterreicher Hotel, looking back across the river to the floodlit gables and cupolas of Salzburg.

DAY EIGHTY-THREE | SUNDAY 21ST JUNE

Salzburg

Rather like with Venice, I am the least qualified person to try to explain Wolfgang Amadeus Mozart, but that's alright because unlike Venice nobody *can* explain him. He rises head, shoulders and powdered wig above every other tunesmith in history. Milling around in the pantheon of stratospheric talent are Handel, Bach, Puccini, Strauss and others; most might elevate Beethoven to a higher level of genius; but then up, up through the rarified air we go to see little Wolfie, bathed in golden light sitting on entirely his own unique cloud.

He was born here in Flat 3, Getreidegasse 9 , Salzburg SW1, on the twenty seventh of January 1756. It's an imposing five storeyed town house with attractive sash windows, overlooking a little *platz* and beyond across the river. We wander round the atmospheric interior, where some of his pianos, spinnets and violins are displayed, together with many assorted manuscripts in glass cases. An enthusiastic guide, who I think was the deputy director of the museum, is explaining animatedly to a group of American tourists how much he had disliked Schaffer's play and Foreman's film of *Amadeus*.

"Eet was not good," he says, "Saglieri was not being an evil man, no no, he just was…er…jealousness. And Mozart was not this buffoon who all the time giggles – he was… a… *genius!*"

A coffee in the *platz* and then some window shopping – in Ali's case, pre-shopping, as she has seen some amazing painted eggs – and then back to the hotel to await collection by our Tour bus for this afternoon's excursion. In all our travels we have not allowed ourselves to be guided or escorted around an attraction, preferring to make our own mistakes and draw our own conclusions, but for once we have made an exception and booked tickets for The Original Sound of Music Tour.

No, I'm not kidding.

We knew it would be pretty awful, but that's probably part of the reason we signed up, and anyway they'd know all the best sights and how to get close to them. Wouldn't they? The bus was waiting not far down the street and we got on to find it was packed – about fifty people across all age ranges and nationalities, from grandparents to backpackers. After a short wait a good-looking man in a sports jacket bounced on board, tapped the driver on the shoulder and off we went. As we turned the first corner the man leant over and pushed a tape into the cassette player.

"Let's start at the very beginning… "

Oh God.

As Julie's crystal voice floated across the seatbacks, and people began to variously sing, giggle or squirm with embarrassment, our man picked up the microphone.

"Hello everyone!", he began, cheerily, "My name iss Andi and I am originally from Trieste which as you know is in Yugoslavia but used to belong to Austria so I am happy now to be living here in Salzburg. I would like welcome you on board The Original Sound of Music Tour which you must know is the very best of all the Sound of Music Tours in Salzburg. I speak four languages so if you are needing to ask me anythings I will be pleased to help. Bonjour tout le monde! Je m'appelle Andi et… ".

And off he went, demonstrating his language skills. The girl in front of us was a twenty year old American who had joined the bus with several others from a nearby youth hostel. Quite what trendy young things were doing on an ultimate saddo tour like this was beyond me, but she was obviously impressed with Andi from Trieste and was telling her seat neighbour that she'd spent four years at the American School in Switzerland but "hadn't learned a word of Swiss." By now, Andi had switched back to English and was pumping us up for the delights and sights for which we were in store.

"As our coach drives out of the city you will be able to be seeing the magnificent Hohensalzburg fortress that dominates the skyline. This featured many times in the movie. We will not be going there to visit on this tour, but if you look quickly to your left as we pass between these two buildings ... now, *there!* ... you can just see the ramparts. Good. Now we are heading for our first exciting stop on the tour – the house of Captain Von Trapp! (murmers of excitement). Yes, we will see the actual house used in the film although it was not the actual house of the Von Trapp family. Now, while we drive there, who would like to sing a song from the movie? (murmers of fear) Yes, yes, everybody plis ... *how do you solve a problem like Maria, how do you....*"

I was frantically searching the seat pocket in front of me for the paper bag they must surely feel necessary to supply on this bus, when mercifully we pulled to a stop by the side of the road, and Andi bade us disembark and follow him, crocodile-like, down a public footpath by a lake. About 200 yards further we emerged onto a grassy picnic area by the water, complete with bench, snogging couple and overflowing litter bin.

"There!", he said proudly, indicating the far side of the lake. And there it indeed was, the imposing Georg-ian frontage of Georg's house from the film – picturesque, even though it was quite some considerable distance away. Cameras were raised and zoom lenses fully extended. I assumed he wanted to show us the establishing wide shot before moving inside for the interiors. "If you are looking carefully you can just see the terrace where Maria and Captain von Trapp were standing for many scenes. Unfortunately we cannot go closer because the house belongs to an American company so we cannot see the beautiful gardens where the summer house from the movie is, so plis, everybody back on the bus!"

Back we filed and piled in, the whole thing reminding me of Marty Feldman's hilarious 1960s film about a works outing where the passengers are herded at great speed past sights and the whole day out becomes an unsatisfying blur.

"Now we are going to see the famous lake where the opening shots of the movie were filmed, but coming up right now a treat for you! Yes, in a moment I will be wanting you to look to your left where you will see the actual Abbey where Maria von Trapp was being a nun...as the road is busy we cannot stop so be quick....between those trees, up on the hill....*there!*...did you see it? Oh, sorry."

So on we went, driving on roads that sometimes went fairly near places that had featured in the film. On the road winding down to the blue waters of the St Wolfgangsee, Andi gave us a whole eight seconds' glimpse through the trees of the church spire that you see in the opening credit sequence, and then we arrived in St Gilgen on the shores of the lake, where we were once again allowed to get off.

"So, mein damen und herren, here we have thirty minutes to explore the town. It has nothing to do with the movie, but you will find Mozart's mother's birthplace and a very good souvenir shop opposite. I know that it is good because it is owned by my cousin."

We wander round a peaceful little lakeside village, buying an ice cream and several assorted knick-knacks from every *other* souvenir shop in town. Exactly twenty-eight minutes later (*'Raus!'*) we get back to the bus to see that this little town appears to be a favoured, or organised, stop for other tours as well. Next to our coach is a brightly painted bus with its title emblazoned all the way down the side – The Most Unique Sound Of Music Tour. Darn it, we had obviously picked a slightly less unique tour. Fools.

Onward! We are told that soon we will actually be allowed to not just see a featured place, but *go inside a building* that was in the movie! "But first, messieurdames, I see from my watch that we have a little time in hand, so who would like a very special treat? Would you? Okay then, we go!" He signalled to the driver, who was obviously going to turn left here anyway. "This iss a very special bonus, signores y signoras – we are going to the summer Cresta Run!" Apparently we were going to be given a rare opportunity to spend more money – this time on sliding down a coal chute that had been glued to a hillside. Only forty schillings extra, come on everyone don't be scaredy-cats, don't be weaklings, don't on any account be seen to be different. While Ali and I sat on the grass verge, we watched most of the others get winched up the hill on their doormats and then slide down the chute. *Wheeee!*, went the tobogganists. *Ker-ching!*, went Andi.

Nearly time for our promised holy grail, but first – look! Over there beyond those trees, as we drive past without stopping, you can see the von Trapps' house from the front! You remember, when they pushed the car out and got caught by the Gauleiter? And here, let's stop and look at the summer house – yes, the one where Maria and the Baron fell in love, and where Lisl skipped round the benches singing about being sixteen. There it is! It's a copy of course and you can't go inside, so everybody back on the bus – *schnell!* And finally, we arrived in a town that contained the church where the wedding was filmed – and we were going to be allowed in!

"Ja," said Andi, "The wedding scene was shot here, but only the outside. Inside was too small for the cameras, so they used another church that we won't be visiting today. But please feel free to walk round this very pleasant town for the next forty-two minutes, and you might want some refreshment. Luckily this town has the best apfelstrudel in all Austria, so don't forget to stop and have an espresso and a slice of apfelstrudel at Café Braun in the main square.

Did I mention that my surname was Braun?"

You're now thinking I made all the above up. Nope, all true – except for the souvenir shop and the café being owned by Andi's relatives. I mean, he didn't *tell* us they were owned by his relatives. But I bet they were.

As the bus hissed to a stop back in Salzburg, Andi thanked us for our company for the last three hours, reminded us that our hotel would bill us eighteen quid, and further reminded us that it was traditional in Austria to show our appreciation for our guide.

If, no doubt, we knew what was good for us.

Alright then, let's do our *own* Sound Of Music Tour – then it will be the Most Uniquely Unique. We start in the Mirabell Gardens (just across from the bus stop, for goodness' sake) where we walk round the fountain that Maria and the children danced round in the Do Re Mi sequence. Then we climb the steps up to the wrought iron gates and look back. There on the horizon is the Hohensalzburg castle, with the Mirabell gardens in the foreground, and we can picture the final chorus of the song, where Maria climbs the steps, arm upraised for the big finish, as the children hop up the steps in sequence beside her. And we're standing on the exact square foot where Robert Wise must have put the camera.

Just to impress Ali I take over from Andi: "Und here iss a couple of facts about the movie that they can't tell you on the official tour. At the beginning of the Do Re Mi song they're dancing through a market, and you can clearly see a box of oranges on the fruit stall. Stencilled on it in large letters is 'Product of Israel' which of course didn't exist until nearly ten years after the film was set. And the opening 'hills are alive' shot, of Maria twirling on the mountain, nearly never happened. It was the last morning of an already overrunning shoot, and Wise wanted this complicated swooping helicopter shot. The weather had been too bad for three days, the crew's meters were running, and the studio was about to pull the plug. With an hour to spare before the wrap, the clouds cleared and Julie could spin round and 'sing once more'.

There you are, fascinating stuff. There seem to be seven or eight SOM Tours in Salzburg, surely there's room for one more; five quid all in, no tip, and I won't make you slide down a bloody pipe.

For dinner we take a lift up inside a mountain – the Monschsberg. This great monolith surrounds the old town of Salzburg on three sides, crowding it against the river. On the south east promontary is the Hohensalzburg fortress and on the other is a famous lookout with a famous eaterie – the Café Winkler. We sit on the terrace 400 feet above the city and have a very pleasant dinner, served with great charm by an Indian waiter. Beyond the huge fortress to the south rises the massive Untersberg mountain, a 6,000 foot escarpment the other side of which nestles a pretty Bavarian village that was once, for a few years, a cradle of evil. But that's for tomorrow, and tonight we watch as the sun goes down and the huge searchlight on the lighthouse above us stabs a sweeping beam across the valley.

Later, in Mozartplatz, a café spreads its tables and chairs across the cobbles and a quartet plays music to the late night drinkers. The violinist walks between the tables, bends down to a very frail-looking biddy sitting on her own, and plays her request – obviously an old favourite, as the crowd softly joins in. The song, a lilting ballad, finishes with her eyes full of tears and her voice, wobbly with age and emotion, carrying across the quiet square. Warm applause rises from all the tables, and the violinist whips a single rose out of nowhere and presents it to her with a deep bow. Tart.

DAY EIGHTY-FOUR | MONDAY 22ND JUNE

Salzburg

The weather has broken overnight, with rain and thunder this morning – rather appropriate for our trip to Berchtesgaden.

In our shallow but broad study of Europe we've touched on art, wine, ancient history, palaces, coasts, music, language, sport and of course scaffolding, but I don't think you can appreciate today's Europe until you've examined, however briefly, one of the continent's most tiresomely frequent features – war.

On a fairly regular basis I thank whomsoever it may concern that, unlike my father's, grandfather's and great-grandfather's generation, I have not so far had to go to war. Most, although sadly not all, of Europe has been war-free for half a century now, and I hope that my children will never have to be caught up in one. What I'm damned sure about is that I'm going to teach them the lessons of history so that they and their governments will not be condemned to repeat it. Lest we forget....

Anyway, I had long felt it was important to visit some of the sites and museums that have been preserved precisely so that new generations do not forget, so Ali and I had planned to see some on this last leg of the tour, which happened to coincide with a fault-line and time-line of slaughter – from the Bavarian Alps, up the Rhine and up the Somme to Agincourt.

Berchtesgaden is not the site of a great battle or great massacre, but is a sleepy little alpine town that for nearly fifteen years lay at the throat of The Valley of the Nazis. It lies only about a dozen miles from Salzburg, just inside a pocket of Germany that slips into and under Austria, so is in fact due south of Salzburg. The town was not the central concentration of megalomania and fear – that was up the valley at the smaller Obersalzburg – but Berchtesgaden was the main settlement in the valley, so the name became synonymous with the Nazi High Command activity in southern Germany.

Adolf Hitler came to the valley in the early twenties and returned often, mostly to hide out when he'd tried a failed *putsch*. Later he rented a house in Obersalzburg and liked it and its view of the Untersberg so much he bought it off the owners in 1932. He actually paid cash money for it – 40,000 gold marks – probably the last time he paid for anything instead of nicking it. Gradually the lair of the wolf became so attractive to other Party members and Reich officials that every house in the village was bought by Nazis. Bormann, Speer, Goering – all had residences here, and over a billion marks was spent on construction of buildings, stormtrooper barracks and tunnels. To start with Hitler himself paid for much of it (he was hugely rich – *Mein Kampf* was a compulsory purchase in the Reich, and he charged royalties for being on the stamps) but soon either the state paid or the owners were sent letters that contained the word Dachau. By the beginning of the war not a single house in Obersaltzburg was still occupied by its original owners, and by the end of the war practically none remained standing – the R.A.F. bombed the shit out of the village on the twenty fifth of April 1945.

Hitler's Berghof, the mountain chalet he'd hugely extended from the house he'd bought, was nearly destroyed, and was finally blown up and razed in 1952. It was at the Berghof that he'd lived in baronial splendour, playing despotic host to world leaders, including the sadly deluded Chamberlain in 1938, and all were impressed with the Fuhrer's new valley which could be seen laid out below his gigantic picture window, his beloved Untersberg mountain in the background.

We didn't go to Obersalzburg because there's nothing to see – all the official buildings and Nazi chalets have gone, so too the network of tunnels and arsenals built into the mountain. It would have become a shrine to nasties, so it was wiped clean. What we had come to see was the Eagle's Nest – Hitler's eyrie perched unfeasibly atop the Kehlstein alp, 6,000 feet up above the village. It sounds, as it was no doubt meant to, rather romantic – the lonely great leader ruling the world from his Wagnerian mountain fortress, impregnable and omnipotent – but the reality, as always, is somewhat less theatrical. Assorted Nazi *obergruppentoadies* decided to built a fiftieth birthday present for their Fuhrer on top of the alp – it would prove the might of German engineering and willpower, labour was cheap and expendable, and it would get them a billion brownie points. The result *was* a triumph of engineering and deadline-beating (not more than a hundred workers died during construction) but Hitler hardly ever went there – he was afraid of heights.

What the building was for is the subject of some debate. It is generally known as the Teehaus (as in tea), but apparently was supposed to be the D-Haus (as in diplomatic), where Hitler or high Nazis could take visitors to impress the hell out of them. Which it did. The French Ambassador visited the Eagle's Nest in 1938 and was awed by its position and the obvious marvel of German engineering that had put it there.

You can't drive up to it – the single lane road is spectacularly narrow and vertiginous – so you gather at a car park and bus terminal half way up the mountain, and catch a shuttle. It's worth the trip just for the bus ride up the hill. It's difficult to believe how it could have been built sixty years ago, and impossible to believe it could be built today. Several miles long, there's not a straight bit longer than twenty yards. Clinging to the cliff face, ducking in and out of tunnels, twisting and turning like a snake, the road is quite the hairiest I've ever been on. Eventually it arrives at a small plateau at about 5,500 feet, where you get off. So as to preserve the outline of the mountain top, and no doubt for added security, they blasted straight into the rock and put in a lift – the only way up. You pass through a stone arch (with 1938 engraved into the keystone) and immediately pass into movieland – *The Guns of Navarone, Where Eagles Dare, Indiana Jones*, take your pick. The long stone-lined and marble-floored corridor is damp with condensation and lit with small yellow bulbs in brass housings. It slopes gently upwards to a circular domed ante-chamber where there are a pair of huge bronze doors – the lift. Inside it's the original lift, with brass and mahogany fittings and mirrors. This is getting very creepy indeed – what have *these* walls heard? 400 feet higher, the doors open into the stone building, and you are instantly hit by the smell of warm cabbage and roast something in gravy. Yes, it's a restaurant. Well you've got to cater for the masses who've made the schlep – sorry pilgrimage – up the alp.

The original building still stands, but every corner of it smells of cabbage so we go outside onto the stone terraces. Wow. I mean whoa! This really is very high indeed. On three sides the cliffs simply disappear beneath you and all you can see is the valley floor 4,000 feet below. To the west is the beautiful Konigsee lake and to the north the Untersberg, the summit of which you are now level with, and beyond is the smudge of Salzburg on the horizon. You can climb up a path on the forth side, further up the mountain, and turn to look back at the Eagle's Nest framed against its impossibly breathtaking 270° view. There's a large wooden cross and a cairn of stones at the top of the path. It would be nice to think it had some small meaning in this unearthly place, but it's a memorial for the Alpine Climbing Association or some group of that ilk. I suppose a cross large enough to address the bigger issue would have to be as tall as the sky.

We have a basic lunch out on the terrace, and just before we go I notice a covered stone balcony or terrace to the left, one wall completely open and looking out westwards. A few steps lead down into it, and it's obviously not meant for punters because there are steel beer kegs, white plastic stacking chairs, Coca Cola umbrellas and crates of 7-UP lying all over the place. There's nobody there so I quietly walk along, looking out to my left at the amazing view. I suddenly stop cold and open my copy of the brochure I'd bought at the shop and flicked through during lunch. There on page nineteen was a black and white picture of the Fuhrer with the French Ambassador. It was grainy, but it was quite clear that I was now standing on the exact same spot, on the same unchanged and undamaged flagstone as Adolf Hitler had stood on exactly sixty years ago.

Time to go, I think.

This evening, after some R&R and more hotel bookings by phone and fax, we head for our next casino. It's quite a way out of town, and we are surprised to see that it's housed in the very impressive Klessheim Castle – a huge mansion, along the lines of Blenheim, where Hitler occasionally took visiting dignitaries. We have dinner in a rather cold dining room, and then head for the tables. The gaming room is huge and ostentatious, with vaulting ceilings and glittering chandeliers. In one corner is a bar, where England are losing to Romania, so I am deputised to get the drinks while Ali cases the joint. She starts her roulette crusade and I saunter into the other *loozenmonizimmer* for a few hands of blackjack. Amazingly I manage forty five minutes and come out even, to find Ali is a 150 quid up. She keeps winning, albeit small amounts compared to the slabs of ivory being placed around her, so I have a go and start losing. Eventually, after two or three hours, her winnings are fifty quid up on my heavy losses, so we retire happy and return to the homely comforts of the hotel for our last night in Salzburg. The city is charming and friendly, and has managed to erase from its memory, and visitors' perception, its shameful association with the Third Reich, while glorifying its association with Mozart and the family Von Trapp. We will return.

DAY EIGHTY-FIVE | TUESDAY 23RD JUNE

Salzburg to Moos

We are bound for the Swiss-German border this afternoon, which necessitates a drive into Germany and around Munich towards the Bodensee.

A few years ago I was in Munich for a weekend to visit a friend. Travelling on the Underground to meet them I found myself on a station looking, as you do, at a map to check which stop I should get off at. Suddenly I involuntarily took a sharp intake of breath and two steps backwards – the station at the end of my line was Dachau.

I looked around, feeling a little foolish at such a physical and visceral reaction to a simple word on a poster. I also felt a little naïve at my ignorance – I should have known where Dachau was, I should know much more about it. No part of me is Jewish or German and I know no family who was remotely involved, but isn't that all the more reason to acquire knowledge and make sure it is passed on? Again, lest we forget....

This was of course many years before *Schindler's List*, and we had been taught only surface facts in school, but on that platform I resolved that one day I would visit at least one camp, and know in advance what I might expect to see and learn. Until Spielberg's masterful version of Keneally's book about Oskar the flawed hero, huge swathes of non-Jews had no idea what had really gone on in those few short years. Naturally they could not ever begin to *know*, but the facts and lessons should be drummed into all of us. I remember seeing the film in London the week of its release, and as the end credits started to roll not a person in the huge cinema moved or uttered a sound. Not until the last credit had finished and the screen went black, some six minutes later, did people slowly start to rise, collect their coats and file out. My own fingers had to be prised from the dents they had made in the armrest of my seat, so full of anger was I.

If one can describe any of the camps as 'not the worst', you could probably include Dachau, if only in terms of numbers of deaths. In ten years 32,000 prisoners died, and 6,000 Russians soldiers were gunned down on a nearby SS field. Auchwitz, Buchenwald, Belsen – all killed hundreds of thousands more, but is weight of numbers the benchmark for horror? Surely if just one soul is tortured, starved or gassed the outrage is no less.

The pretty satellite town of Dachau lies a dozen or so miles northwest of Munich, and the tree-lined approach gives no indication of what lies there. They have not attempted to hide it, but it is a very small sign (KZ-Gedenkstatte) that takes you off the main road and half a mile to the car park. It's a cloudy Tuesday morning but there are several hundred cars in the car park, and six or seven coaches. We park and walk round to the gate, and there's a guard tower – black, wooden and exactly what you're expecting to see, but it still stops your heart. This is real.

The site itself is simply vast, dozens of acres of ground once covered by row after row of prefab huts. Now only two remain, and they are copies. The wide dusty expanse of the *Appelplatz*, or roll-call square, is about the size of four football pitches, and all along one length is the main building and processing centre, fully 200 yards long with wings at each end, hunched and menacing. I have never seen a more depressing structure – it could not possibly be mistaken, even in the worst photo, as anything other than what it is. The sun has come out now, which somehow makes it worse – one always imagines the worst horrors happening in brutal weather, but for ten sky-blue summers the same abominations were happening here as during the snow-covered winters.

We go into one of the prisoner huts, which have been recreated as they were originally constructed. At first it just seems like a series of classrooms at a boys prep school, but of course it's all untouched and untainted wood and metal – none of the physical scars, stains, smells or secrets have etched themselves into the grain. You have to imagine. Which you can't.

In the main block, all is busy. Busloads of schoolchildren jostle with day trippers, and you collect your brochure and start the walking tour and photographic exhibition. Within seconds the schoolchildren have gone quiet, and the normal giggling, shoving and name-calling of a school outing has ceased. It is not just the material on show, but the whole atmosphere of the place that would silence a scalded cat. The children probably don't know quite why they have been so affected, but we do – huge black and white photographs have been hung floor to ceiling, many depicting scenes or aftermaths of bestial brutality, but also photos of documents, lists of processed people, SS orders and so on, which are just as terrifying to see. Here and there are glass cases with yellow-starred striped camp clothes, shoes, armbands and memorabilia, all faded by time. About half way through Ali can't take any more and, her eyes brimming with tears, she flees back out into the sunshine. I continue grimly, my teeth grinding, and find, on joining her outside, that I have scrunched my brochure beyond repair.

We don't speak on the way back to the car. We have seen only a tiny fraction of what lies behind the terrible curtain, and that was dulled by time and safety, but there is nothing to say that has not already been said. It can only be hoped that young ears will still listen.

Westwards on slow, roadworked roads to Lake Constance – or as we are still in Germany, the Bodensee. Bernard Levin's enchanting book *To the End of the Rhine* mentions his love of the remarkable church at Birnau on the northern shore of the lake, so we take a small detour to see it. The outside is not much to write home about, except its superb position high above the lake, but inside is quite captivating. Rococo, baroque, iced wedding cake – I don't quite know how to describe it – everything is carved, gilded, sculpted, painted or marbled. Designed by the wonderfully-named Peter Thumb in the mid 1700s, it seems to let in and amplify twice as much light as the windows should allow. With neither the majesty of St Peter's nor the serenity of Montserrat, it nevertheless seems to glow with the pure joy of religious celebration. I was very pleased we'd made the effort to see it. And thank you, Sir Bernard.

Around the western end of the lake we go, to the tiny village of Moos, where we have booked a room in the Hotel Gottfried. It is small, modern and clean, with an oddly large and very overheated indoor pool, as if that was all the owner had ever really wanted. We were welcomed charmingly and given a superb gastronomic dinner in the pretty garden. Ali was shocked when I asked for the English menu – something I never do. But I simply didn't understand a word of the German menu, and couldn't begin to guarantee that Ali would receive no meat on her plate (quite difficult to ensure at the best of times in Germany – non-meat eaters are rare and very few dishes do not contain some sort of *fleisch*). They didn't have an English menu, so we took a chance on Wels, a *bodenseefisch* which I'm sure I've never had before. Delicious white flesh, but encased in a worryingly thick layer of fat or blubber. Most odd.

Late Scrabble and schnapps under the apple trees in the very warm evening air. A lovely end to a sobering day.

THE RHINE

Schaffhausen Falls
In which we climb the siren's rock between the raging torrents of the Rhine's biggest waterfall.

Baden -Baden
In which we stay in what many say is Europe's finest hotel. Yes, it's stunning, but we still think the Arts beats it. Relax in water-fed gardens,

swim in best hotel pool ever, dine on marble terraces and drop a packet in the Casino.

Luxembourg
In which we wander around the rather boring city, look into the quite interesting ravine that bisects it, and retire to our plastic, and boringly expensive, hotel.

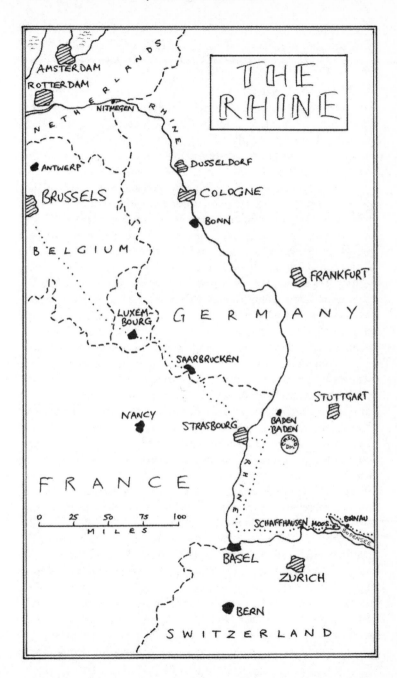

DAY EIGHTY-SIX | WEDNESDAY 24TH JUNE

Moos to Baden-Baden

I could have hit Switzerland with a well flung croissant at breakfast this morning, so we head off down the Rhine as it flows out of the Bodensee on its stately journey to the North Sea. Shortly afterwards its journey brings it to a big hurdle, the Schaffhausen Falls.

You can hear the great cascade and feel the moisture in the air long before you reach them, and on the Swiss side that is via a castle perched right on the falls. You go in, buy a ticket (this is Switzerland) and make your way down a wide stone path which stops at terraces and balconies every so often, so you can look out at the falls. And touch them – one terrace has a little rabbit cave leading off it where you can tunnel round a corner and actually stand under one of the side races to stick your hand in the flow.

Damper, we emerge at lower river level, where there's a boat landing stage and a wider view of the falls. They are impressive, by European standards – nearly seventy feet high, a couple of hundred yards wide and pushing 600 cubic meters of water over the rocks every second.

Although Europe leads the world in many wonders of civilisation, when it comes to nature's most spectacular wonders you have to travel further afield. I've been lucky enough to see the Iguazu Falls on the Brazil/Argentina border, which is five times the height of Schaffhausen and, in the wet season, can push ten times the flow over its huge abyss. This is where David Puttnam filmed *The Mission*, when Irons and DeNiro had to climb the falls to reach their new parish. Eleanor Roosevelt, on seeing Iguazu, said, "Oh gee, poor Niagara!"

Schaffhausen is however one of Europe's biggest waterfalls, and they are impressive – just how impressive you can discover up close and personal. A shallow launch, not unlike a small landing craft, takes you up river to the base of the falls, the noise now thunderous, the mist drenching, and the power quite awesome. Right in the centre of this liquid onslaught is a huge rock which you can climb up. A tiny landing slip has been constructed at the base of the rock, and some very fancy tiller-work by the driver, involving a slip-shimmy-and-rev-*NOW* manoeuvre, deposits you on the hard. Steep steps have been carved into the rock which is, I suppose, eighty or ninety feet high. You emerge on the tiny railed viewing platform and the whole Rhine is rushing at you. There's a distinct Leo & Kate feeling about it, as they leant over the bow of the steaming Titanic, the water rushing beneath and to either side of them.

A precarious journey back down the narrow slippery steps, back on the boat, and over to the German side for lunch on the downstream viewing terrace. The standard of food is no better, I'm sorry to say, than at a similar type of venue in England; why is it that at attractions or theme parks anywhere, despite a massive throughput of punters with varied tastes, the food is always *awful*? Does it say more about the organisers, the caterers or the punters who accept/prefer it? The only exception is Disney, where it is possible to eat superbly in at least two of their parks (q.v.: Eurodisney).

We say goodbye to Switzerland after only half a day – hardly adequate or fair, but schedules mean priorities – and head north into the fatly comfortable southwest plains of Germany.

Baden-Baden doesn't do anything so crass as *market* itself, but if it did I'm sure it would bill itself as a luxurious German health resort, catering to every Teutonic whim of the well-heeled. Think Harrogate for the waters, think Bath for the Royal Crescent, think Edinburgh for gravitas – but then none of those places has the Brenner's Park.

I've said that Bernard Levin once posited the theory that the Brenner's Park Hotel and Spa is the best hotel in Europe; we may end up disagreeing, but not by much. I'm sure Mr Levin receives a level of sophistication, refinement and service that meets his needs and *Enthusiasms*, but then he is a vastly more cultured and discerning person than me (as the standard of English in this sentence will testify), and no doubt fits right into the rarified atmosphere, whereas I don't think we do quite. However we are only in Baden-Baden because of him, so here goes.

We enter the leafy outskirts of the town and almost immediately are swept underground, as if roads and traffic would disturb the quiet peace of the town centre – which they would. The whole central road system has been tucked discretely under the carpet of green that occupies much of the resort, and they've even rebuilt the river so that it flows serenely along a precise path through the park. We pop up a few hundred yards from the hotel, and are confronted with more Royces than I've ever seen. Hundreds of them, all lined up on the tree-lined avenue the other side of the river. Guest car park, I wonder? Do you think we'll be let off because at least our car is German?

The hotel is vast and elegant, rather like an imposing Victorian railway hotel, but set in shady parkland grounds with immaculate pathways and wide terraces. Our room is exquisite, but has no air conditioning – I suppose the weather is usually more temperate than this sultry heat we're having. And I suppose I'm a whingey old git. We have a view of the approach road, but that's probably because we're not only the least important people in the hotel, but also the youngest – Ali says I should make the most of it, as it doesn't happen very often. I do feel a bit of a fraud here though; I'm not saying we haven't been welcomed genuinely, we have, but I get this feeling they've worked very hard to create a huge fluffy bath towel of exclusive luxury, and *arrivistes* – temporary ones at that – could spoil the ambiance. I'm probably being a little unfair, but there's a slight *membership* air to the place, and not only do I not qualify but the application form's in German.

The swimming pool, however, in the spa complex attached to the hotel, is simply stunning – vast and silky, the water stretches away under a Romanesque roof towards the completely open far end, beyond which the trees and gardens spread out towards the river. We have a relaxing swim and take a walk along the manicured banks of the Oos. It flows prettily through the park, arrow-straight, taking little genteel waterfall steps every dozen yards or so. We amble over to the line of magnificent Royces and discover that they're in town for the Rolls Royce Enthusiasts Club annual convention; perhaps gathering would be a more acceptable term – no chrome chairs and overhead projectors for these chaps. There are cars from all over the world, and all manner of models from 1930s Silver Ghosts to the latest sleekest Mulsanne Turbos.

A drink on the terrace before dinner, and as the last of the sun dips below the treetops there's a sudden whirring sound, seemingly from all around us. We look up and see that every single green and white striped awning that has been extended over each bedroom window is slowly reeling itself in. They all reach their backstops at the same time, and silence is restored. It's as though the hotel has spent a sleepy day in the sun, eyelids half closed against the glare, and has now fully opened its eyes, closed its beach novel and is ready for its first cocktail of the evening. What cocktail would a big hotel like this order, I wonder? A Manhattan? An Old Fashioned?

Dinner on the terrace is delicious, and they've wheeled out the Bechstein and a singer to serenade us all. But nothing later than Gershwin, *bitte*.

DAY EIGHTY-SEVEN | THURSDAY 25TH JUNE

Baden-Baden

Ali spends the morning in the pool, or stretched out on a lounger on the emerald lawn outside. I sit under a tree like Lytton Strachy and paint. Occasionally waiters bring us things. Heaven.

For lunch we stroll along the Lichentaler Allee – the Royces have moved on – walking in the footsteps of Queen Victoria, Naploeon and the King of Prussia, who survived an assassination attempt in these gardens. Other lesser mortals who have survived a long life can come and live in the huge mansion next door to the Brenner's Park, the poshest retirement home I've ever seen. On the left the trees part to reveal the Grand Casino and Spa – it looks very smart and expensive, with reputedly the finest gaming rooms in Europe. We shall see. The town itself is sleepy and prosperous, with very expensive shops, but lunch in Leopoldsplatz is excellent and good value.

A lazy afternoon and then, dolled up for the tables, we return to the town for dinner in a cheery outside place called Le Bistro. The food is fine, but sitting near us is a middle-aged English couple, very prim, who are complaining of this and that in a pursed-lip sort of way. A little dog, belonging to some youngsters on the far side of the terrace, had been sniffing round the tables, as dogs do. This English woman proceeds to kick it quite hard in the ribs, and it yelps away. I was gobsmacked and ashamed, and wanted to go and kick *her*, but Ali contented herself with quietly shopping this anal old witch to the dog's owners as we were leaving. If you have no conception of how to cope with 'abroad', then bloody well stay in Esher.

The Grand Casino of Baden-Baden has very sumptuous *salles des jeux*, golden baroque rooms and dozens of tables. The place is packed, as I gather it is most nights – people come from all over Europe to gamble here – but nothing compares to a casino I once went to in Sydney. It was a brand new aircraft hangar in Darling Harbour and there must have been 4,000 people in there, eyes glazed and wallets shrinking. Anyway, here in much grander surroundings we played roulette and blackjack for rather less time than we would have liked, and came out having lost our stake, but not breaking our golden rule of dipping beyond it. It's a very attractive and grand place, but has a cold edge to it and not the right atmosphere – I mean they won't even let you drink at the table! They're taking it all much too seriously.

DAY EIGHTY-EIGHT | THURSDAY 26TH JUNE

Baden-Baden to Luxembourg

I'm not saying Luxembourg is small but you could probably get somebody to quote you for carpeting it. I'm not saying it's uninteresting but Insight Guides' 468-page *Continental Europe* guidebook awards it one paragraph. A whole country gets one small paragraph of one column width. I'd say poor Luxembourg, except it isn't – many international banks have headquarters here, the taxes are very low, and the 300,000 population seem prosperous and cheerful. I should have bought a dedicated guide book to the place but it would probably have blown away in a gust of wind.

We'd country-hopped on our way here – out of Germany into France near Strasbourg, back into Germany briefly to empty the ashtray, then along the border into Luxembourg. A few traffic and navigation problems and we arrived at our hotel, Le Royal. This is another member of *The Leading Hotels of the World*®, but I'm afraid I would hazard a guess that it's only a member so that that large organisation can have a positive answer ready for a valued customer's question: "I have to go to Luxembourg, do you have a member hotel there?"

It's large and clean, but is patently a conference hotel first and a luxury hotel third. Our room is large but antiseptic, with very few touches of refinement, but it does have air-conditioning. Hang on, I'm beginning to see a pattern here....

We venture out into the city, which is peaceful and pleasant to walk through. At length we come to the cathedral, quite recently rebuilt, which is peaceful and pleasant inside. A tree-lined square nearby is peaceful and the glass of wine consumed in it is pleasant. My, we are one for patterns today. I wish I could enthuse about Luxembourg, but there was nothing in any way offensive, nor in any way spectacular – except the ravine, some 300 or 400 feet deep, that cuts through the city centre like an axe's bite out of a log. That really was quite mildly interesting.

Dinner was excellent – but we'd bought the ingredients ourselves from a supermarket and had a carpet picnic in our room.

Required reading for the criminally uninformed.

THE FATAL AVENUE

Waterloo

In which we climb the Lion's Monument and try and visualise the carnage; and pay a quiet and drizzly visit to the Hougoumont Farm, where the battle turned on the closing of two wooden gates. They're still there.

The Somme

In which we fulfil a long-felt feeling that we should go, lest we forget. Visits to many graveyards and monuments, and the superb Great War museum in Pérrone, where we are the only visitors. Also, on the eve of the anniversary, cars with English plates gather to spruce up

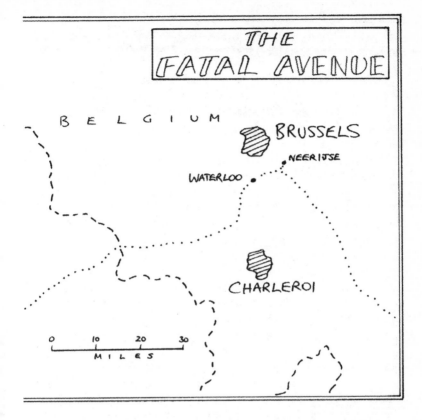

a memorial for tomorrow's remembrance service. We stay in a chateau that used to belong to Laura Ashley.

Crécy and Agincourt
In which we visit, in much the same rain-sodden conditions as they were fought, the sites of two of England's

greatest victories. Cannot begin to imagine the slaughter.

Le Touquet
In which we begin to wind down for our journey home, walk on the wide windy beach, and lose the last of our money in the Casino.

DAY EIGHTY-NINE | SATURDAY 27TH JUNE

Luxembourg to Waterloo

"The location of the cassle tempts on to take a walk or a bicycle ride in the surroundings with their beautiful nature." Well how could you resist that? The Kasteel van Neerijse is about twenty minutes east of Brussels and was another good find out of the excellent *Relais du Silence* book.

Having taken the E411 north west out of Luxembourg, we wound our way through little brick villages, many with their Christmas lights still (or already) up. Nope, no idea. A small lane leads off to the right, and the *kasteel* is at the end of a rural drive either side of which deer and horses gambol. The chateau is in a brick regency style with a French blue slate gabled roof, and attractive in a slightly run down sort of way. We are greeted charmingly, given an early lunch of smoked salmon and a glass of wine on the terrace, and shown to our room. I have a sneaking feeling, by the size of the lift and the layout of the corridors, that this has not always been a hotel – there is a whiff of nursing home about it – but I could be wrong. It doesn't matter, as the room is fine, the welcome is warm, the menu for tonight looks good, and the room rate (self-booked) is very reasonable. We dump our bags and go straight out again for our first battlefield.

A few years ago there was a six part series on BBC2 called *War Walks*. It was written and presented by a military historian called Professor Richard Holmes, who basically took us for a walk over some famous battlefields, as they are now – grass, fields, car parks etc. You might not think that this would be electrifying TV, nor might the Prof. classify himself as an experienced Autocue presenter with perfect teeth and television hair (he looks and sounds exactly like what he is – a teacher), but it was gripping stuff.

Holmes obviously loves his subject (so much so that on the side he is Britain's senior serving reserve officer) and knows every fact that's relevant, but more importantly he can make us hear the hoofbeats, muskets, arrows, cannon, whinnies and screams; smell the mud and the fear; taste the acrid smoke and revolting tea; and see the field as it must have been on that crisp July morning or dark October afternoon. His book accompanying the series is written in the same style, aimed no doubt at someone like me – absolutely no knowledge of military history or tactics, but an interest both in the fateful days that shaped Europe and in the human face of those of our ancestors unlucky enough to have been there. His book was in my hand as we approached the first of our war walks, Waterloo.

Holmes says that one of the first things you notice about Waterloo as you walk around the site and its gift shops is that you might be mistaken in your belief that Wellington had won. He's right – Naploeon's image is everywhere – on poster, dishcloth, commemorative medal, postcard and plaster bust. Perhaps the French, geographically closest to the site, reckon that Boney only *just* lost (0-0 at full time, lost on penalties), and is still a hero. He certainly was in 1815 – having rampaged round Russia a few years earlier (to the music of Tchaikovsky), he was defeated at Leipzig and packed off to Elba, while Louis XVIII was put back on the throne. But the French really had had enough of monarchy by then, and when Boney hopped a boat to the Cote d'Azur and started marching north, he gathered almost everyone back to his team. The Allies (practically all of Europe except France) said "here we go again" and sent Wellington at the head of a multi-nation force to explain to Boney that no means no. They met on these rolling fields just a few miles south east of Brussels on the eighteenth of June.

Napoleon should have won, and very nearly did. Various historians, and the combatants themselves, have had several theories, but there are two I like in particular. At the height of the battle in the late afternoon, Marshall Ney galloped up and begged Napoleon for more troops for a last push. The Emperor snapped at Ney, "Where do you expect me to get more troops from? Do you want me to *make* them?" History doesn't relate whether the great man then said "Fut!", but I bet he did; nor does history relate what Ney's reply was, but he might have said, "But look, mate, Your Excellency, my general, there behind you! Several thousand of your Imperial Guardsmen haven't even got their knees dirty yet. Can I have those?" "Non!" was the answer, and it is claimed that if those guardsmen had been committed at that moment then the battle would have been won.

In the other goalmouth Wellington was fighting a rearguard action, the famous British squares receiving a dreadful onslaught and horrendous casualties. To one side of the battlefield was the Hougoumont Farm, around which a fierce battle had been raging all day. The French had been attacking in waves, and several times breached the walls and attacked the two great wooden gates of the farmhouse. The British garrison held out – just. At one crucial stage the gates had been breached and fire was raging through some of the buildings. A few incredibly brave men managed to close the gates again, and the heat of the French attack was finally spent. Later Wellington gave it as his opinion that the entire battle of Waterloo had turned on re-closing the gates of Hougoumont Farm.

And they're still there.

The farm is a private house and going concern now, but you can park on the verge at the bottom of the track and walk up and around it. On the southern side the stone buildings look almost the same as they did that summer day, and the great arch with its wooden gates is still there. To the right is the orchard where the British made their stand, and to the left the small trees from which the French army made their attacks. We stood utterly alone on the edge of the yard and listened to the birdsong and the humming of insects.

10,000 men died on this small patch of ground that afternoon.

From the farm where we stood, and from many miles around, you can see the huge memorial erected in 1823 to mark the site of the battle of Waterloo – the Lion Monument. 42,000 cubic yards of earth were piled into a conical mound, and a stone plinth built to carry the massive lion statue at the crown. There's a wide viewing terrace around it, reached by climbing the steep and narrow 226 steps from the base. Ali didn't fancy the angle of the steps, and elected to stay at the bottom, while I gamely made the ascent. The wind snapped at my coat as I looked out at the amazing view. There below is the wide sweep of plain where Napoleon's main forces advanced towards the Allied lines; to the left the strategically vital farm of La Haie Sainte; to the right the trees and rooftops of the Hougoumont Farm.

It's difficult to imagine what it must have looked like on that June day nearly 200 years ago, but at the base of the mound is an odd round building which tries to help. Within is a mural – a panoramic 360° view of the battle, painted many years ago in fine detail. A wooden rail separates you from the wall by about six feet, and the space between is filled with grass and earth and waxwork models of fallen horses and soldiers. A tape plays the sounds of battle. It's very old-fashioned by today's standards of computer technology and flash graphics, but I found it extremely evocative and it helped me to understand just a small fraction of what it must have been like to be in the terrible heat of the battle.

None of the 50,000 or so Englishmen that fought that day had the luxury of driving back to a nice hotel, eating a delicious dinner and discussing their upcoming wedding arrangements.

France

*"There's some corner of a foreign field
that is for ever England"*

DAY NINETY | SUNDAY 28TH JUNE

Waterloo to The Somme

And so, for the final time, back into France. Ali has found a fantastic base for our Somme visits – Laura Ashley's chateau. Well not anymore of course, the estate sold it when she died, but she and her husband had restored it to its former glory and lived there for many years. It's now owned and lived in by a couple – he South African, she American – who run it as a bespoke hotel, not unlike the lovely Chateau LaMothe near Bordeaux.

The Chateau de Remaisnil is quite exquisite. Built in 1760, it's perfectly proportioned in the classic French rococo design – three storeys, the third being dormer windows set in the sloping blue slate roof – and set in rolling parkland with horses and sheep. And a long scrunchy drive, of course. Once again we have probably aimed too high, because while we like the room we've been shown very much, we quietly agree that, based on three months experience, it's not really worth what we're being asked to pay for it. On asking if we can see the rooms in the coach house, we are shown a room that's just as nice, but not being in the chateau itself is a third less money. Perfect.

Cocktails with our hosts and fellow guests – a very chatty mother and daughter from Calgary who are here to follow the wartime footsteps of their father/grandfather and his Canadian buddies. We chat about Calgary and the eastern Rockies, where I had been the year before, and then our host Adrian offers us some advice about our Somme pilgrimage tomorrow. He is very knowledgable and enthusiastic, and produces a map with his own suggested places on it. I tell him about Richard Holmes' *War Walks*, and he is keen to buy a copy.

Laura Ashley's chateau at Remaisnil.

Dinner is taken in the sumptuously elegant *La Salle a Manger Louis XVI*, which probably accounted for it being fairly overpriced, while the family ate in their own dining room next door.

DAY NINETY-ONE | MONDAY 29TH JUNE

The Somme

We have been so very lucky. We have had a once-in-a-lifetime opportunity to travel all over the most richly varied and fascinating continent on earth, stay at gorgeous places and see wonderful things. The sunlight has streamed through our windows, and soon we will be going home to begin a new life together that, barring extremely unlikely circumstances, will not include war and violent death. It seems only right to spend at least one day remembering the men and boys, many only half my age, who died in this valley fighting for the peace that took another generation to achieve. This 'fatal avenue', as De Gaulle called it, is only a hour's drive from Calais, and I felt somewhat guilty at not having visited before.

The oddest things stick in your mind when you're a child. For most of my schooldays important history facts like dates, place names, kings and Prime Ministers tended to fall through the (wide) cracks in my mind, but one image about the First World War remained from the day I heard it. Our teacher was trying to get across to our unruly class of fourteen year olds the unfathomable futility of the Great War, and said, "The Somme lasted over four months, over 1,000,000 men died, and the amount of ground won and lost stretched only from this classroom to School Chapel" (about 1,000 yards away). We were suitably awed by this, and even though it's not strictly accurate, it would have rung true for many of the trench-tied soldiers – of both sides – who had to take, lose and re-take the same hilltop or hamlet in the muddy countryside of Picardy.

If, for whatever reason, you are familiar with the Somme and what happened, please forgive the generalisations and opinions I give below; I make them for those who, like me, had little or no idea what went on, and who should know. Once again, lest we forget...

The first day of the Battle of the Somme was from every angle one of the worst days of war in Britain's history, and perhaps of any war anywhere. Ali and I stood on a quiet verge near the infamous Sunken Road and, leaning heavily on Prof. Holmes again, I explained to her what happened.

On a crisp, blue sky morning, on the first of July 1916, a hundred thousand British soldiers were ordered to clamber out of the trenches in this valley and walk very slowly towards the German front line – in some cases only a few dozen yards ahead. By nightfall 60,000 of them lay dead, or dying. That's more men than fought for Wellington at Waterloo; more men than fought on either side at Agincourt; and over half the total number of serving men in the current British Army. In one day the army lost more men than the Americans lost in *ten years* of Vietnam. It was, in my opinion, an act of criminal military folly, the lessons from which our glorious leaders, including the dreadful Haig, significantly failed to learn.

There are far too many and complicated answers to Ali's question "why?", none of which I am qualified to address, but one of the simple ones was that the top brass thought the British big guns would have killed all the enemy in their flimsy trenches and that the men could simply walk over, bayonet a couple of survivors and take the objectives. Unfortunately the German trenches were like Fort Knox, so all the enemy had to do when the barrage stopped was brush a light coating of dust off their uniforms, step outside into the dawn air, and shoot the shit out of our boys as they walked across No Man's Land.

There were lots of appalling mistakes made in that battle, and throughout the war, on both sides – the most appalling of all was totally misjudging the balance of power in Europe and having the war in the first place. I can't put it better than Richard Curtis and Ben Elton in their sublime *Blackadder Goes Forth*, when Edmund is explaining to Baldrick and George that the big nobs' idea was that with two great opposing military powers there could never be a war. But there was one tiny flaw in their plan – it was bollocks.

The whole Somme valley and the swathe of former battle lines are now dotted with perfect white cemeteries, some only a few yards square, some containing thousands of fallen men. I was amazed to see so many, and pleased to see them so well tended. We stopped at a few and read the headstones. Far too many ages beginning with 1.

We had been advised to visit the Newfoundland Memorial Park just east of Beaumont-Hamel, as it contains a number of important features in one relatively small area. We are the only car in the wide driveway, and there is a watery sunshine as we walk quietly in through the gate. A young man of perhaps twenty walks up and introduces himself. He is a Canadian student over here to take his turn as a host for the park – the Newfoundland state government and the Canadian government fund a programme to maintain and staff the park. This provides students with knowledge and experience, and the visitor, whether curious or related, with courteous guidance if required. I was very impressed.

We elect to take a leaflet and wander around by ourselves. A neat gravel path winds through mature pines to the crest of the rise, where the battlefield opens out before us. To our left, looking out over the trenches and calling to its countrymen, is a huge bronze caribou on a high rock plinth, its antlers seeming to spread in sympathy with the branches of the pines. Below, etched in the bronze tablet, are the names of the fallen. On that summer morning at 7.30am the 1st Newfoundland Regiment climbed out of their trenches like all their comrades for miles either side, and were instantly silhouetted against the dawn sky. They advanced as ordered, and within a hundred yards and less than half an hour three quarters of the regiment were dead. 715 officers and men, in less than half an hour. No other regiment lost more men, although many came close.

The trenches are very emotional to walk along. Rounded and grassed over now, they would have been angular and brown then –

sandbags piled high, duckboards underfoot slick with mud. It is but a few hundred yards to the German trenches near Y Ravine – the ones High Command thought would be flattened by the artillery, but turned out to be so deep, sophisticated and safe that an Allied battalion was quartered there later in the war. From there you can just see the village of Beaumont-Hamel. The Allies were expected to take it on the first of July; it finally fell on the thirteenth of November. As we walked around the park we saw a few people moving between the trees or bending to read a headstone, but the most moving sight for me was the flock of sheep in the very centre of the battlefield, contentedly chomping the short grass. *'Where sheep may safely graze…'*

From many places along the line you can see on its distant hilltop the Thiepval Memorial to the Missing. You think by the scale as you approach it that it's going to be big, but when you park up and walk round to the lawned and gravelled approach, it's gigantic. Designed by Lutyens, it bears the names of 73,412 British and South African men missing on the Somme. If a tiny roadside cemetery, with its manicured grass and few dozen white stones, brings home the personal tragedy, then this massive monolith stamps the enormity of it on you like an anvil. Apart from an unfortunate resemblance to Guildford Cathedral, I found it imposing and sobering.

False sense of security though the British artillery barrage instilled, they also decided to deal with some of the German strongholds with mines. Incredibly brave sappers were sent to tunnel hundreds of yards under No Man's Land and plant thousands of pounds of high explosive under the most feared positions. At 7.28 am on the first of July these mines were detonated, in what was then the loudest man-made sound in history. Some of the huge craters these left are still in existence, but many were filled in by French farmers and ploughed over. We went to see one – *La Grande Mine* the signs say, but the Lochnagar Crater is how it's known to those who come every year to visit and remember. After months of tunnelling, 60,000 pounds of ammonal blew thousands of tons of earth over a mile into the sky, leaving a crater 90 feet deep and a sixth of a mile round. The crater was under threat of being expunged when it was bought in 1978 by an Englishman, Richard Dunning, who lives in Surrey. Now, together with Dunning, there is a large 'Friends' organisation who maintain it as a permanent memorial to the fallen, organising trips, information and gatherings.

We park at the side of the road and walk across the grass. The crater looks like a moon crashed into it – the leaflet says it is still the largest hole made by man in anger – and we walk awestruck around the perimeter. There is a war memorial with a large cross, and as we walk over we see a number of cars with British plates. Nearby a group of men are unpacking some tools and unscrewing thermos tops for a pre-work cup of tea. I wander across to ask about Richard Dunning and how I could find out more about the Friends. One of the men comes forward, puts out his hand and says, "I'm Richard Dunning, welcome. How can I help?"

He and some Friends had driven over, as they do every year, to do some tidying and maintenance on the site to prepare for the dawn remembrance service that they hold every year on July the first. He was very friendly and gave me some literature on the history of the crater. We had a very interesting few minutes chat, at the end of which he invited us to come to the service in two days' time, but unfortunately our itinerary didn't allow it, much as I would have liked to have been there. I make a donation to the organisation by way of apology, and because I think they're great, and we go on our way.

The small town of Péronne has a fairly new museum called the Historial de la Grande Guerre, housed behind an old fort in the centre of town. It is late afternoon and we are the only people in there. It is superbly laid out and contains hundreds of artefacts, weapons, uniforms and pictures, together with dozens of small TV screens showing archive footage and newsreel reports. It would repay a much longer visit, but it is nearly closing so we go into a small cinema where the friendly attendant shows us a tribute film to Harry Fellowes an ordinary soldier of the Northumberland Fusiliers. It is incredibly moving, and we leave sobered and much better informed.

We wind our way back down the Somme valley, the waving corn coming up to the verges and dotted with bright poppies, and eventually find our way to Amiens, capital of Picardy and home to Jules Verne and St Martin, the patron saint of France. On the banks of the river we find a row of fish restaurants, and have superb *moules frites* and a bottle of Pouilly Fumé, while overlooking the monstrous Gothic cathedral that dominates the city – it's the largest in France apparently. Back to the chateau and a late and rather unsteady game of snooker in the coach house's billiard room before bed.

As I drift off to sleep I replay in my head the final moments of the last episode of *Blackadder Goes Forth* – the finest half hour of comedy ever made by the BBC. You would have thought that the First World

Y Ravine. There are hundreds like this... lest we forget.

War was about the last subject that could be made funny, but Curtis and Elton made us roar with laughter all the way through, using their razor sharp pens to underline some of the ridiculousness of the war. We laughed because the jokes were funny, but also because if we had looked too deep, looked at the essential truths behind the jokes, we would have cried.

With a few minutes running time left, the mood alters dramatically. Tim McInnery's Captain Darling, who has spent most of the war at GHQ, "right behind our boys" (Edmund: "Yes, about thirty five miles behind."), is at the last minute sent to the front line for the Big Push, and suddenly realises it's all real and he's almost certainly going to get cut to ribbons in the first ten seconds.

"Rather hoped I'd get through the whole show", he says, resignedly, "Go back to work at Pratt & Sons, keep wicket for the Croydon Gentlemen... marry Doris. Made a note in my diary on the way here. Simply says: .... 'Bugger'."

Then our chums go 'over the top' in sepia'd slow motion – bullets, earth, shrapnel and limbs flying. The mournful theme tune begins, played *andante* on a single piano, as the scene crossfades into the aftermath – broken bodies, barbed wire and drifting gunsmoke. Slowly the image mixes to the cornfields of today's Somme, red poppies waving bright in the sun, birdsong and bees replacing the music. No credits have rolled – just at the end a small and simple "
BBC MCMLXXXIX.

Masterful.

The Somme to Crécy to Agincourt to Le Touquet

We paid the bill at the Chateau. Adrian was a very friendly host who obviously enjoyed his *seigneur*ship, but I got the impression his wife had lost her appetite for having guests in her magnificent house.

And now for our final battles, turning the clock back 600 years. Even back then this north east corner of France was the blood-soaked fighting ground of Europe. Agincourt is our main destination, but Crécy is on our way, so we stop off briefly to survey the field.

Edward III was jammed between two enemies – France and Scotland – and because many areas of France belonged to England, or were English influenced, he decided to have a crack at the French. He cut a murderous swathe across northern France and was finally made to stand still and fight at Crécy in 1346. The French made a furious attack but were effectively levelled by the English secret weapon – the longbow. By the end of the day 1,500 French knights and 10,000 soldiers lay dead.

There is a small car park and a wooden observation tower that overlooks the battlefield. It was a grey and damp day, and we climbed up to read the carved map on the balustrade. Only one other person was there, a Frenchman from Lyons. After reading the description of the battle and looking out at the fields, I apologised to him for Edward's greed. He smiled sadly and said, "Merci monsieur, mais c'est la guerre."

On we drove, the weather still drizzly, towards the town of Hesdin where we hoped to find some lunch. The main square didn't look too promising, but down a side street we found a charming little creperie called La Belle Epoche. I'm not saying all conversation stopped abruptly as we opened the door, but certainly the place was full of citizenry having a quiet lunch – always a good sign if the locals eat there. The décor was Victorian funeral parlour but the food was delicous. As we ate I reflected on one of the most famous battles in history.

Most people's, and certainly most Englishmen's, views of Agincourt are inevitably coloured and textured by Shakespeare:

Thus should the warlike Harry, like himself,
Assume the port of Mars; and at his heels,
Leash'd in like hounds, should famine, sword and fire
Crouch for employment.

Heady stuff, and that's only the prologue to a sweeping tale of the arrogant effette Froggies, with their weak King and posturing Dauphin, having their arses whopped by a much smaller army of brave Brits led by a young King whose cause was just. Even today you'll hear rugby fans responding to French *rosbif* taunts by ticking off on their fingers, 'Crécy, Poitiers, Agincourt, Waterloo, Parc du Princes, Stade de France…'.

Well of course it wasn't like that in reality. The English had been trying to nick France for nearly a century, fired by greed and religious fervour. Edward III and his son the Black Prince had inflicted terrible losses at Crécy and Poitiers in 1356, where they managed to capture the French king John II. This was almost as worthwhile as capturing huge amounts of land, as the French paid a ransom of £500,000 for him. This was a staggering amount of money, and if we take Richard Holmes' sreckoning that a minor English gentleman or merchant could live on an income of around £17 a year, and equate that to £40,000 today, we arrive at a contemporary figure for John's ransom of well over a billion pounds. As Holmes says, it cemented English royal finances for a generation.

When Henry V came to the throne at the age of twenty five in 1413, he inherited a nervous kingdom and quickly set about trying to unite it behind his claim for the Throne of France. Having learned the lessons taught his predecessor Edward II by the Scots, who had kicked serious English butt at Bannockburn exactly a century before, Harry gathered together a medium-sized but well-coordinated force of knights and archers – carrying the deadly longbow. For the full story of the campaign that began with the seige of Harfleur, I urge you to read Holmes' *War Walks*, but let us jump to the day before Agincourt, where Henry and his much depleted host arrived on twenty fourth October 1415 – cold, wet, exhausted, fed up with war, and most suffering from the serious trots. Henry had realised that his blitzkreig path through France had not been very successful, and all he wanted to do was take the remains of his army back to English-held Calais, and then home – returning to fight again another day. Just let us through, he told the French, and we'll sod off home and leave you alone – if not we'll deck you. Bill wrote it snappier:

We would not seek a battle, as we are;
Nor, as we are, we say we will not shun it.

The French though, were pretty cocky. They'd danced around Henry's army for months, letting him dash himself against the cliff of Harfleur, and were waiting for the moment to face him down. They had five times as many men, all fresh, and besides, their horses were better groomed and plaitted, and their nobles' silken surcoats were much more *chic*. Chatting and drinking till the early hours in their gilded tents, they thought they had him.

It is now two o'clock: but, let me see, by ten
We shall have each a hundred Englishmen.

Meanwhile, 2,000 yards away, *the poor condemned English,*

Like sacrifices, by their watchful fires
Sit patiently and inly ruminate
The morning's danger

The twenty fifth of October dawns damp and miserable. Henry's army emerges from the trees and lines up, mounted knights and men-at-arms in the centre, archers on the flanks. They would have kept their bowstrings dry in pouches, and only now loop them to the yew and stick arrows in the ground next to them for rapid fire. Leather tabs protect their drawing fingers – the same two fingers that are to this day stuck up in the offensive 'V' sign: Holmes tells us that captured archers were likely to have their two firing fingers hacked off by the French to end their military careers, so if intact, archers would gesture to the enemy with their bow fingers to indicate they were in full arrow-ready condition. Shakespeare has Harry's nobles bemoaning their lack of numbers, and indeed it must have seemed a desperate situation – the French had 60,000 men to their 12,000, and they'd been marching and fighting for over two months and were knackered. From out of the dawn mist, the French Herald comes for the last time to offer the English safe passage in return for their king, and Harry tells him to bugger off. Then the king mounts a carriage and delivers the pre-match speech – one of the most stirring peptalks ever written:

He that outlives this day, and comes safe home,
Will stand a tip-toe when this day is named....
...For he today who sheds his blood with me
Shall be my brother; be he ne'er so vile
This day shall gentle his condition:
And gentlemen in England now a-bed
Shall think themselves accursed they were not here.

In reality of course, no more than a couple of hundred men could have heard the king's words, whatever they might have been, but the sight of his bright silk surcoat and golden crown standing at the head of his army, ready to lead them personally into battle, would have set the blood coursing and the adrenalin bubbling. That, and being scared completely shitless.

A sudden deep rumble reaches their ears – the French cavalry charge. "Ready!" cries go up from each company of longbowman; the creak of bowstrings being drawn ripples along the lines; behind gritted teeth each archer whispers to himself, "wait for it, *waaait fooorr it....*".

The battlefield of Agincourt is one of the few that look fairly similar today as they did to the combatants. It's a long north-south rectangle, perhaps a mile and a half long by 1,000 yards wide. The tiny hamlet of Maisoncelle is due south, where Henry's army billeted on the eve of the battle, and the village of Azincourt is about two thirds of the way up the edge of the western side. The field is bisected by a road almost exactly where the two armies met, and when we were there the 'English' field was ploughed earth and the 'French' one waving corn with poppies at the roadside. The only indication of history is a few cardboard cutout archers nailed to the telegraph poles. They're facing the wrong way.

We stopped for a few minutes, and then drove into Azincourt, where there is a tiny museum. Run enthusiastically by a little old lady, it's a very amateur but still interesting collection, which unlike Waterloo doesn't try to pretend the French won. Our hostess bid us enter *'le cinema'* where we were shown the worst video ever made for public eyes – well intentioned, but truly dreadful. I felt they needed a donation, so I made one and we returned to the killing field, to stand by the side of that lonely road and imagine.

At the signal for the archers to release, the sky instantly became shredded with zinging death. Holmes estimates up to 80,000 arrows a minute were punching down into the French army – some barbed, some bullet-tipped, all murderously efficient. Armour was punctured, visors and helmets penetrated, flesh speared, horses stabbed and felled. Utter carnage. Still they came, the French, courageously, more and more men and horses surging forward to try to join in hand to hand combat. Still the sharpened death rained down, decimating knight and crossbowman, horse and foot-soldier – the sinewy Welsh bowmen were simply too accurate and too quickfire for any effective defence or retaliation.

At length, sheer weight of numbers drove the French army far enough forward to clash with sword and mace. There then ensued a butcher's frenzy on a scale unimaginable to us. Not for these men the 'tidy' death of a musket ball or bullet, nor even the instant death of a mortar or shellblast: here limbs were hacked off, faces slashed open to the jaw, heads stoved in, torsos unseamed and guts let loose, throats severed – and each wound would produce a spray of arterial blood so that within seconds the slick mud of the churned up field would have turned as scarlet as the slaughter-house floor. We cannot begin to know what it was like, even from the few contemporary reports we have – stories of piles of bodies as high as a man, thousands of unattached limbs and heads all over the field, rivers of blood and mud and internal organs.

Huge numbers of French were captured, disarmed and moved to the back. Shakespeare has an unforgiveable act perpetrated by the French – the killing of the young lads looking after the supplies in the English camp – but Henry committed a gross violation of the conduct of war: possibly thinking that he was being attacked from the rear, and fearful that the large numbers of French prisoners might be released to pick up abandoned weapons and resume the fight, he ordered that all of them be killed. To kill a knight or nobleman who had surrendered was bad enough, but each of them also represented big ransom money. But then perhaps, with hot blood spinning in his eyes from all directions, he wasn't thinking too coolly.

The third wave of French, seeing the day was lost, turned and fled. It's impossible to count the dead from this distance, but an average of estimates would put the French losses at at least 10,000, with another 1,500 captured alive for ransom. The English lost few men of rank and perhaps a few hundred archers – no one knows – but certainly the blizzard of Welsh arrows had simply destroyed the French army, as it had at Crécy and Poitiers. One French historian has calculated that the monarchy lost a full third of its supporters. Henry married Catherine of France and arranged that he would succeed the throne after her father's death, but less than eight years after Agincourt, at the age of thirty five, he died of dysentry six weeks before Charles VI: he never became King of France.

Enough of war. We came, we saw, we remembered.

Rather like Cannes, Le Touquet is an English invention – at the beginning of the twentieth century a British syndicate began building exclusive villas in a swathe of pine forest near the wide sand beaches. Within a decade or so it had become so fashionable among the English and Parisian elite, that it adopted the rather poncey, and frankly optimistic, name of Le Touquet-Paris-Plage. Today it is still the Cannes of the north, with posh shops, gambling, racing, golf and quiet, expensive villas you never get to see.

For the last two nights of our tour we have booked in to the Westminster, an imposing building that inside looks like a Poirot set and outside looks like a glue factory. Our room is large and comfortable, with a thirties-style black and white bathroom. I half expected to find a special jar of wax for my 'leetle moustaches'.

A pleasant walk down to the sea, the shops getting less posh as we approach the bucket and spade area of town, but Ali spots a branch of Blanc Bleu and we are diverted. It's now early evening, and after a glass of wine in a bar, we decide to have a last night on the town tomorrow night, while tonight we'll have a hedonistic night in: room service, decent wine, the new Bond film on the movie channel, and England v. Argentina live from St Etienne. The food was delicious, the film was good and England was robbed – after a nail-biting game, including that stormer of a goal by the boy Owen, they deserved to win. But they didn't, of course.

C'est la guerre.

DAY NINETY-THREE | WEDNESDAY 1ST JULY

Le Touquet

It's the last day, and Ali wants to go to a theme park. No, really, she does. It's called *Bagatelle*, and its gaudy brochures are to be found everywhere – in shops, hotel foyers and, rather ominously, under car windscreen wipers. Against every fibre of instinct I agree to give it a go, so we drive a few miles south. On the journey she reads out the attractions and my heart sinks even further, and when we arrive and pay fifty francs to park in a muddy car park among the pines I finally bottle. We can see the park on the other side of the road, and it's got that faded pink look to it – you know, huge coloured fibreglass 'characters' that you've never heard of, grinning inanely and peeling where the salty air has leached and bleached them. I know she won't really like it after Disney, and I know I'll utterly hate it, so I beg a break from sight-seeing and tempt her with a walk on the beach and a last blowout French lunch; reluctantly (although as we drive away she has the brochure in her hand and is starting to look relieved) she agrees.

The beach at the amusingly named town of Berck is wide and almost deserted. We walk a mile or so on the golden sands, the odd dog or owner passing by, and the breakers themselves many hundreds of yards away at low tide. You can't quite see England from here, but on the highest dune with a pair of Luftwaffe fieldglasses, Goering could. Luckily he was a fat git who made the wrong decision.

On the Montreuil road we found a restaurant called Au Bon Acceuil, the same name as my former favourite restaurant in London, sadly now closed down after thirty years. We find it full of locals, and the genial patron greets us pleasantly. Like its London namesake, the food is quite superb. We start with *moules en pot* (its powerful garlic infusion came through the kitchen door ahead of the waiter and knocked over a small potplant), and then Ali had steamed brill and I had steak tartare. Being a fishetarian she hadn't come across this carnivore's delight before – "I don't believe you can even *look* at that, let alone eat it! *Raw* meat, with a *raw* egg on top? Eyuuuh!" She made me prop the menu between us, so *she* didn't have to look at it. Of course, it was quite heavenly and I devoured every morsel, deliberately licking my chops loudly like Clement Freud's bloodhound.

This still being France, we didn't rise from the table much before five, and made our satisfied way back to Le Touquet. Some last minute shopping was needed (apparently) and then after a bath and change we ventured out for our last evening. There's a famous fish restaurant in Le Touquet, half of which is a shopfront for their home-made bouillibases and bisques, boxed and ready for the punter to take back on the ferry. We chose to have some on the premises, followed by a lobster each – it's alright, it was nearly nine by now, and our lunch had moved over to make room. And it was a long bath. Then it was time for the final throw of the dice, the last spin of the wheel, the endgame.

I wish I could report that the casino in Le Touquet is gilded and grand, the baize greener, the croupiers prettier and the stakes higher. And that we won. But it isn't and we didn't. Never mind, we reckoned we had come out only slightly down on our gambling tour, which for lowest-rolling amateurs isn't bad. We wandered contentedly back through the ornamental gardens to the hotel, and slept the sleep of the only slightly guilty.

DAY NINETY-FOUR | THURSDAY 2ND JULY

Le Touquet to Home

And then to Calais; and to England then;
Where ne'er from France arrived more happy men.

The rail of a ship is a good place for contemplation. White water hisses by below and gulls wheel overhead. We had deposited the trusty Merc back at Hertz after its long and mostly trouble-free nine country drive, and caught the lunchtime sailing from Calais. Perhaps the town centre is attractive – we didn't go there – but the rest of the town and the docks area is quite depressingly awful.

We stood and stared out at the calm Channel, Britain's moat, that has divided and protected us from Europe for a thousand years. I'm pleased it has provided an effective barrier when required, but I'm also pleased that the ease of crossing it, over and under, has increased – everyone should have the oportunity of discovering this most beautiful, diverse, interesting, cultured, infuriating, multi-lingual, history-rich and complex of continents – instead of going to Magaluf or Alicante or Rimini, which are just Sheffield with sunshine. It needn't cost anything like what we spent – there are thousands of incredibly good value hotels, B&Bs and campsites, and hundreds of books and guides which list them and how to book them – not, repeat not, underline not, italicise *not* via a tour operator. Please.

In our suitcases are clay pots and ceramic candlesticks, painted eggs and wooden boxes, Italian vellum and French clothes, fine wine and Venetian masks. And of course drugs, a couple of handguns and a rabid rat. But in our heads are the experiences and images that will become lasting memories. The idea of such a huge trip was that it would last us for years and cure us of the travelling bug so we could settle down and lead an ordinary, dutiful life. Neither of us has told the other, but of course it's only made it worse.

As the ferry slides into Folkestone harbour, just managing to avoid dinking the breakwater, I can't help thinking there's something we've forgotten….

"Oh yes, darling, I know what it is. We're getting married in three weeks – shouldn't you start thinking about a dress?"

Ali & Jonathan's European Hotel Guide

Our ratings system is of course highly subjective, but we've tried to be fair, and rate against expectations, price levels and the hotel's own publicity. We scored each hotel in ten categories, listed below, giving a final total out of a hundred. The following three pages provide a description summary of the hotels in order of merit, by country, and then there is a table listing individual scores in each category. Where there is a figure in brackets (6), it indicates that this item was not offered and so cannot be rated; we've given it 6/10 assuming it would have been average standard if offered. Naturally we didn't examine any rooms other than our own, nor necessarily use all the facilities on offer. Any of these hotels may be under different management since we stayed, so this can only be our personal opinion from one visit.

Location: Either usefully located or pretty, or both
Reception: Genuinely welcoming / low snot level
Room: Clean, decent bed, big enough bathroom, little touches (i.e. window)
Porterage: Anywhere from 'holding out key without lifting eyes from newspaper' to 'bags in room and on stool before you get up there.'
Mini Bar: Usual selection; we were looking for dry white wine and lots of cashews
Food: Hotel's own restaurant and/or Room Service
Service: Of staff in general, restaurant staff, and concierge if applicable
Value: Was it worth the dosh we paid?
Facilities: Pool, laundry, games/sports, bar etc
Feel: Comfortable, friendly, staff attitude, atmosphere, sminess etc

The Martini Awards

A key question is would you return to a hotel? We've devised our own star system, based on the following number of martinis:

♍♍♍♍ To stay in this hotel would be a major, or even main reason for a journey.

♍♍♍ If in the area again, we would definitely stay in this hotel, and would recommend it to you.

♍♍ If in the area again, we might choose to stay in this hotel.

♍ If in the area again, we would AVOID staying in this hotel.

1. The Arts, Barcelona 87.5 **2.** Brenner's Park, Baden-Baden 83 **3=** Villa Cortine, Sirmione & Chateau LaMothe, Bordeaux 81 **5=** Hostellerie Bellecroix, Chagny & Gritti Palace, Venice 80

SPAIN

Barcelona | Hotel Arts ♈♈♈♈

Simply the best. Ultra-modern and chic. Room superb, with loads of mod-con buttons to press; stunning bathroom; service, especially the concierge, flawless; food excellent. On beach and next to casino, but a fair walk from the city centre. We have been back to Barcelona since – simply to stay here.

Madrid | Palace Hotel ♈♈♈

Stunning domed bar and dining area, superb all-you-can-eat buffet. Room very clean with top-notch marble bathroom. Opposite Prado and Thyssen museums.

Toledo | Parador ♈♈♈

Superb hilltop location overlooking the whole of Toledo, with breathtaking dining terrace. Large room with balcony. Good value.

Vejer de la Frontera
17, Plaza de Espana ♈♈♈

As close as you'll get to staying in a Spanish home. Lovely location in old plaza of traditional hilltop town. Half a dozen rooms, on several levels, all done in trad Andalucian style – not luxury, but achingly genuine. Town is fascinating, with steep cobbled streets and loads of tavernas. Tapas heaven!

Puçol, near Valencia
Hotel Casino Monte Picayo ♈♈

Astonishing Bavarian décor, like the Schloss Adler in Where Eagles Dare. Huge room with balcony, pools, casino down the road, bars. Very friendly and helpful after 'the incident'.

Cordoba | Hotel Alfaros ♈♈

Large and marbled, within tiled townhouses. Small but comfortable room. Pool and nice bar. Cool in the heat.

Aigua Blava | Parador ♈♈

Amazing clifftop location (state owned), rather boxy but spacious hotel. Big bland room with balcony, not much atmosphere. Very pretty beach down steep path.

Tordesillas | Parador ♈♈

Former Castillian mansion, rather cold atmosphere. Extensive grounds.

Granada | Hotel Saray ♈

Huge and impersonal conference hotel. Food very low standard. Service perfunctory. If you can afford it, stay at the Parador in the Alhambra.

Gijon | Parador ♈♈

Lovely old building with duck park, but next to football stadium. Great food.

Puerto Banus
Hotel Rincon Andaluz ♈♈

Posh Butlins; two-storey villas round themed pool. Huge apartment with huge bathroom, but otherwise disappointing. Food very average, service surly.

FRANCE

Near Bordeaux
Chateau LaMothe ♈♈♈♈

The most beautiful private house I've ever seen. 12th century moated castle, family owned. Very welcoming, drinks with family. Five vast, sumptuous and elegant suites (we saw them). Excellent restaurants not far. Breakfast on terrace. Very good value.

Chagny, near Beaune
Hostellerie de Bellecroix ♈♈♈♈

Old chateau in lovely grounds with big pool. Huge medieval stone room with round tower bathroom. Outstanding restaurant – the best dinner we had.

Cannes | Hotel Martinez ♈♈♈♈

Superb location with private beach. Cooler than the Carlton. Good room and balcony overlooking spectacular bay. Very expensive during Film Festival, but never cheap. We have been back twice for special treats.

La Motte en Provence
Villa Pays en Ribas 🍷🍷🍷🍷

Wonderful small villa high in the hills, sleeps six, massive master bedroom with sunken bath. Not overlooked at all, very peaceful, good pool.

Chablis | Hostellerie de Clos 🍷🍷🍷

A three-winged house and barn, converted with modern rooms, in centre of town. Rooms are basic standard and very good value so you can sleep off the world-class food.

Talloires | Le Cottage 🍷🍷🍷

Superb location on edge of chocolate-box lake village. Stunning views of water and mountains. Room fine, with lake-view balcony. Lovely dining terrace, good food.

Doullens, Picardy
Chateau Remaisnil 🍷🍷

Breathtaking classic French chateau, formerly owned and restored by Laura Ashley. Rooms grand and ornate. Family owned and hosted. Sweeping grounds, pool. A little overpriced though, and difficult to relax – it's their home.

Rocamadour | Hotel Beau Site 🍷🍷🍷

Best location, in centre of village. Suite overlooking valley. Astonishing value.

Le Touquet | Hotel Westminster 🍷🍷

Huge and redbrick conference/seaside town hotel. Very 20s inside – our room is large and comfortable with B&W bathroom. Good bar/room service.

The Loire | Chateau de Chissay 🍷🍷

Grand old chateau, billed as 4★ but not quite. First room poor, second room huge and delightful. Poor services and facilities. Excellent, if pricey, restaurant.

Near Chartres
Le Manoir Pres de Roy 🍷🍷🍷

Rambling farmhouse hotel in quiet setting. Room large but faded. Garden and tennis court. Superb rustic restaurant.

Valbonne, Cote D'Azur
Hotel Opio Golf 🍷🍷

For golf enthusiasts, excellent. Good mezzanine'd room, with terrace next to 5th tee. Restaurant overlooks course and is very good.

Sarlat | Hotel de Selves 🍷🍷

Not bad for a budget hotel. Travelodge standard, enclosed pool and small garden. Two minutes walk to lovely town centre.

Carcassonne | Hotel Montsegur 🍷

Run down old French hotel. Room tiny, bathroom ridiculous. Owner friendly but everything musty and funereal. Restaurant nearby, owned by them, excellent.

Cognac | Domaine de Breuil 🍷

Very faded mansion-type hotel, with rooms split by hardboard partitions into horrid DSS-type accommodation. Restaurant surprisingly good. Unless you're a Cognac-sseur, no particularly good reason to visit the town.

ITALY

Sirmione, Lake Garda
Palace Hotel Villa Cortine 🍷🍷🍷🍷

Expansive and comfortable hotel in enviable setting. Excellent room with balcony. Romantic terrace dining, good pool, private beach with lunch/bar. Great for a week's pampering.

Venice | Gritti Palace 🍷🍷

What can you say? One of the best hotels in the world. Our room is a poem, but up the back, of course, because we're nobodies. Location unequalled, and breakfast on the terrace is a religious experience. Huge money, but unique.

Florence | Hotel Lungarno   ♀♀♀

A Room With A View – our balcony overlooked the Ponte Vecchio. Superbly comfortable small hotel on the Arno. Quietly excellent.

Torgiano | Le Tre Vaselle   ♀♀♀

Luxurious hotel converted from several Umbrian townhouses. Huge suite. Fantastic pool area with views and bar. Excellent restaurant. Torgiano is remote.

Positano | Hotel Le Agavi   ♀♀♀

Luxurious hotel clinging to cliffs above the Amalfi coast – one of the best views in the world. Room small but good, with balcony. Good public rooms and restaurant. Pool and bar on lower level.

Santa Margherita Ligure Hotel Continentale   ♀♀

Grand old hotel in attractive Italian Riviera town. Room okay, with balcony, but faded. Restaurant a bit stuffy and short hours. Good public areas. Pool and rocks.

Rome | Aldrovandi Palace Hotel   ♀

Quiet and imposingly grand position in the Borghese, but standards not quite up to the five star rating. Unusual room with large roof terrace. Charge for pool!

Ostia | Rome Airport Palace Hotel   ♀

Name is a bit misleading, as none of the four words seem to be entirely accurate. Conferences/aircrew hotel only. Room good size but hot. Not a nice place, but they did let us keep the car there over the weekend.

Ferrara | Hotel Duchessa Isabella   ♀

Ridiculously puffed and ruche'd pink palace. Room huge but PINK. Restaurant closed, and charged £15 to bring our breakfast. An experience.

Florence | Palazzo Ricassoli   ♀

Actually a residence, not really a hotel, as we discovered too late. We were put in red-brick student-level accommodation, all white melamine and throws. Not a success – went looking for another hotel before we'd even checked in.

AUSTRIA & GERMANY

Salzburg | Hotel Mozart   ♀♀♀

Fairly central and family run hotel. Room large and slightly faded. Friendly and multi-lingual reception. Not much character, but very good value.

Baden-Baden | Brenner's Park Hotel and Spa   ♀♀♀♀

World-class luxury hotel in stunning parkland location in quiet city centre. Rooms very good, food delicious, grounds lovely. Pool quite stunning. Expensive and grand – and knows it.

Moos | Hotel Gottfried   ♀♀

Quiet village location, hotel modern and quirky. Room large but rather spartan. Delightful garden for dining. Food excellent. Overpriced.

LUXEMBOURG

Luxembourg | Hotel Le Royal   ♀

Featureless conference hotel not worth anything like its five stars. Room large but sub-Hilton standard.

BELGIUM

Near Brussels/Waterloo Kasteel van Neerijse   ♀♀♀

Grand old redbrick chateau, rather faded. Lovely large grounds with lake and deer. Friendly, with big, old fashioned room. Food very good.

THE MARTINI AWARDS (Winners in bold)

	Location	Reception	Room	Porterage	Mini Bar	Food	Service	Value	Facilities	Feel	TOTAL
SPAIN											
Hotel Arts	**8.5**	**8**	**10**	**8**	**8**	**9**	**10**	**8**	**9**	**9**	**87.5**
Palace Hotel	9	8	8	8	8	9	7	7	7	8	79
Toledo Parador	9.5	8	8	9	7	6	7	8	6	8	76.5
17, Plaza de Espana	9	8	7	(6)	(6)	(6)	8	8	(6)	10	75
Hotel Casino Monte Picayo	6	8	8	8	7	7	8	8	8	6	74
Hotel Alfaros	7	7	7	8	7	6	7	7	8	7	71
Aigua Blava Parador	9	7	7	(6)	7	6	6	8	7	7	70
Tordesillas Parador	6	7	6	6	7	7	7	6	6	6	64
Hotel Saray	6	7	6	8	7	5	5	6	7	6	63
Gijon Parador	7	6	7	3	6	8	6	6	4	6	59
Hotel Rincon Andaluz	7	5	8	7	4	5	4	6	7	5.5	58.5
FRANCE											
Chateau LaMothe	**10**	**9**	**10**	**(6)**	**(6)**	**(6)**	**8**	**9**	**7**	**10**	**81**
Hostellerie de Bellecroix	**8**	**7**	**8**	**10**	**7**	**9**	**8**	**7**	**8**	**8**	**80**
Hotel Martinez	9	7	8	8	8	8	8	6	9	8	79
Villa Pays Ribas	9	8	9	(6)	(6)	(6)	8	8	8	10	78
Hostellerie de Clos	8	8	7	7	7	9	8	9	6	8	77
Le Cottage	9	7	7	7	(6)	7	7	7	8	8	75
Chateau Remaisnil	10	7	8	(6)	7	8	7	6	8	7	74
Hotel Beau Site	9	8	8	(6)	(6)	(6)	8	9	6	7	73
Hotel Westminster	8	7	8	7	7	7	7	7	8	6	72
Chateau de Chissay	7	7	8	(6)	(6)	8	6	6	7	7	68

	Location	Reception	Room	Porterage	Mini Bar	Food	Service	Value	Facilities	Feel	TOTAL
Le Manoir Pres de Roy	7	6	6	(6)	6	8	7	8	6	7	67
Hotel Opio Golf	7	7	8	(6)	5	7	7	7	6	6	66
Hotel de Selves	8	7	6	(6)	7	4	7	7	7	6	65
Hotel Montsegur	6	7	4	(6)	(6)	8	6	5	3	5	56
Domaine de Breuil	6	5	3	(6)	(6)	8	4	5	4	5	52

ITALY

	Location	Reception	Room	Porterage	Mini Bar	Food	Service	Value	Facilities	Feel	TOTAL
Palace Hotel Villa Cortine	**9**	**8**	**9**	**7**	**7**	**8**	**8**	**7**	**9**	**9**	**81**
Gritti Palace	**10**	**7**	**8**	**8**	**8**	**9**	**8**	**7**	**7**	**8**	**80**
Hotel Lungarno	9	8	8	8	8	8	8	7	7	8	79
Le Tre Vaselle	8	7	9	7	7	9	8	7	9	7	78
Hotel Le Agavi	8	8	7	8	8	8	7	7	8	8	77
Hotel Continentale	8	7	6	8	8	6	7	7	7	7	71
Aldrovandi Palace Hotel	8	7	8	7	7	7	7	5	6	6	68
Rome Airport Palace Hotel	5	7	6	8	7	7	6	6	6	3	61
Hotel Duchessa Isabella	6	6	6	6	6	(6)	6	5	5	5	57
Palazzo Ricassoli	6	6	4	(6)	(6)	(6)	6	5	5	5	55

AUSTRIA & GERMANY

	Location	Reception	Room	Porterage	Mini Bar	Food	Service	Value	Facilities	Feel	TOTAL
Hotel Mozart	8	9	8	6	7	(6)	7	8	6	6	71
Brenner's Park Hotel	**9**	**8**	**8**	**8**	**8**	**8**	**9**	**8**	**8**	**9**	**83**
Hotel Gottfried	7	7	8	7	7	8	7	5	7	6	69

LUXEMBOURG

	Location	Reception	Room	Porterage	Mini Bar	Food	Service	Value	Facilities	Feel	TOTAL
Hotel Le Royal	8	7	7	8	7	7	6	5	6	5	66

BELGIUM

	Location	Reception	Room	Porterage	Mini Bar	Food	Service	Value	Facilities	Feel	TOTAL
Kasteel van Neerijse	7	8	7	6	7	8	8	8	6	7	72

BIBLIOGRAPHY

There are hundreds of published Guides about Europe and its countries, and no doubt many new ones since we travelled, but we happened to use these:

Michelin Green Guides, published by Michelin Tyre plc in Watford.
(we used at least ten of them – the pink stripe indicates the English version)

Eyewitness Travel Guides, published by Dorling Kindersley.
Richly illustrated and annotated.

Continental Europe, published by APA Insight Guides.
All Europe in one book, well distilled.

Again, there are hundreds of hotel guides, some independent, some representing member hotels. These were the ones we used:

The Good Hotel Guide, Continental Europe edition. Ebury Press.

Alastair Sawday's Special Places to Stay: French Bed & Breakfast. ASP.

Bed and Breakfasts of Character and Charm in France. Fodor's / Rivages.

Relais du Silence – Silencehotels. Over 300 medium-priced members.

Chateaux et Hotels Independants. Nearly 500 members, across the range.

Best Western France. Franchise Chain. Everything from budget to four star.

Concorde Hotels. Membership. Some of the larger and grander city hotels.

The Leading Hotels of the World. Membership. Exclusive and expensive.

These are the books I refer to in the text:

To the End of the Rhine and **Enthusiasms,** Bernard Levin. Sceptre.

I Claudius, Robert Graves. Penguin.

The Companion Guide to Rome, Georgina Masson. Collins.

War Walks, Richard Holmes. BBC Books.

Made in America, Bill Bryson. Minerva.

The First Man in Rome, Colleen McCullough. Arrow.

TravellersEye Books

Jungle Janes | Peter Burden
12 middle aged women take on the Borneo Jungle: Seen on Channel 4
ISBN: 1903070058 • Price: £7.99 $14.95

Travels With My Daughter | Niema Ash
Forget convention, follow your instincts.
ISBN: 190307004X • Price: £7.99 $14.95

Grey Paes And Bacon | Bob Bibby
A hilarious romp through the bowels and vowels of the Black Country.
ISBN: 1903070066 • Price: £7.99 $14.95

What For Chop Today? | Gail Haddock
Experiences of VSO in Sierra Leone.
ISBN: 1903070074 • Price: £7.99 $14.95

Riding With Ghosts: South Of The Border | Gwen Maka
Second part of Gwen's epic cycle trip across the Americas.
ISBN: 1903070090 • Price: £7.99 $14.95

Jasmine And Arnica | Nicola Naylor
An Indian Experience by the world's first blind travel writer.
ISBN: 1903070104 • Price: £16.99

Triumph Around The World | Robbie Marshall
Biking adventure on a British legend.
ISBN: 1903070082 • Price: £7.99 $14.95

Desert Governess | Phyllis Ellis
An inside view of the Saudi Royal Family
ISBN: 1903070015 • Price: £7.99 $14,95

Fever Trees Of Borneo | Mark Eveleigh
A daring expedition through uncharted jungle
ISBN: 0953057569 • Price: £7.99 $14,95

Discovery Road | Tim Garrett & Andy Brown
Their mission was to mountain bike around the world.
ISBN: 0953057534 • Price: £7.99 $14.95

Frigid Women | Sue & Victoria Riches
The first all female expedition to The North Pole
ISBN: 0953057526 • Price: £7.99 $14.95

The Jungle Beat | Roy Follows
Fighting Terrorists in Malaya
ISBN: 1953057577 • Price: £7.99 $14.95

Slow Winter | Alex Hickman
A personal quest against the back drop of the war torn Balkans
ISBN: 0953057585 • Price: £7.99 $14.95

Riding With Ghosts | Gwen Maka
One woman's solo cycle ride from Seattle to Mexico
ISBN: 1903070007 • Price: £7.99 $14.95

Tea For Two | Polly Benge
She cycled around India to test her love.
ISBN: 0953057593 • Price: £7.99 $14.95

Touching Tibet | Niema Ash
One of the first westerners to enter Tibet
ISBN: 0953057550 • Price: £7.99 $14.95

Travellers Tales From Heaven and Hell
More Travellers Tales From Heaven and Hell
Past winners of our competition
ISBN: 0953057518/1903070023 • Price: £6.99 $14.95

A Trail Of Visions: Route 1: India Sri Lanka, Thailand, Sumatra
A Trail Of Visions: Route 2: Peru, Bolivia, Columbia, Ecuador
Vicki Couchman
Stunning photographic essays
ISBN: 1871349338/095305750X • Price: £14.99/16.99

Around The World With 1000 Birds | Russell Boyman
One mans journey around the world to tick 1000 birds
ISBN: 1903070163 • Price: £9.99

Dancing With Sabrina | Bob Bibby
A walk from source to sea of the River Severn
ISBN: 1903070244 • Price: £9.99

Cry From The Highest Mountain | Tess Burrows
Their goal was to climb to the point furthest from the centre of the earth
ISBN: 1903070120 • Price: £9.99

Travels in Outback Australia | Andrew Stevenson
A journey in search of the Aboriginal People
ISBN: 1903070147 • Price: £9.99
